Hedge Fund
Course

Founded in 1807, John Wiley & Sons is the oldest independent publishing company in the United States. With offices in North America, Europe, Australia, and Asia, Wiley is globally committed to developing and marketing print and electronic products and services for our customers' professional and personal knowledge and understanding.

The Wiley Finance series contains books written specifically for finance and investment professionals as well as sophisticated individual investors and their financial advisors. Book topics range from portfolio management to e-commerce, risk management, financial engineering, valuation, and financial instrument analysis, as well as much more.

For a list of available titles, visit our Web site at www.WileyFinance.com.

Hedge Fund
Course

STUART A. McCRARY

WILEY

John Wiley & Sons, Inc.

Published by John Wiley & Sons, Inc., Hoboken, New Jersey.
Published simultaneously in Canada.

For general information on our other products and services, or technical support, please
contact our Customer Care Department within the United States at 800-762-2974, outside
the United States at 317-572-3993 or fax 317-572-4002.

Wiley also publishes its books in a variety of electronic formats. Some content that appears
in print may not be available in electronic books.

For more information about Wiley products, visit our web site at www.wiley.com.

Library of Congress Cataloging-in-Publication Data:
McCrary, Stuart A.
    Hedge fund course / Stuart A. McCrary
        p.   cm. — (Wiley finance series)
    Includes bibliographical references and index.
    ISBN 0-471-67158-4 (pbk.)
1. Hedge funds. I. Title. II. Series.
  HG4530.M379   2005
  332.64'524—dc22
2004015547

Printed in the United States of America.

10 9 8 7 6 5 4 3 2 1

To my loving wife, Nancy

Contents

Preface

Business bookstores contain many different books on the general topic of hedge funds. Most of these books are written for potential investors. These books focus primarily on the investment characteristics of hedge funds, admittedly the most important topic related to this investment alternative. Some of these texts are little more than marketing devices designed to encourage greater use of hedge funds in investor portfolios. An investor considering an investment in a hedge fund for the first time should read one or two of these books before making an investment.

To reach a large market, these investment books are mostly written at a very simple level. They generally do not presume any prior knowledge of investments, finance, mathematical methods, accounting, or the law. The authors develop a survey that usually leaves the reader less than an expert after reading the text. After getting a general background, the investor will likely need to hire some combination of investment professionals, tax advisers, accountants, and lawyers before making an investment.

A small number of books have been written for professionals. Usually, these books are not sold commercially. Instead, they are distributed by law firms and accountants to their customers, and most readers cannot get copies of them. Even if available, these books, while they are extremely valuable to professionals, should provide little value to most readers because of the highly technical treatment of narrow topics.

The academic research on hedge funds is accumulating. The ambitious student can read a survey of the important papers concerning hedge funds and develop a good understanding of this important investment product. But few people have the time or background to learn about hedge funds from academic papers.

Some books have been written for the entrepreneur who wants to start a hedge fund. I wrote one of these for John Wiley & Sons a couple of years ago and have discovered that there is considerable demand for a book that bridges the gap between the nontechnical texts written for mass appeal and the technical books and academic papers. Although the previous book was a bit more technical than most others on the market, it also included information needed by hedge fund venture capitalists.

This book serves to bridge another gap. It provides an extensive survey of the hedge fund management business. The course book format is written at a more technical level than most books. Although no specific prior knowledge of statistics, accounting, or finance is required, the reader will find that a background in these fields will be helpful.

This book is written for students in a classroom or students in their own self-study program. It could be the basis for a class in a graduate business school or the curriculum of training programs created for new employees in banks and brokerage firms. This book is also perfect for someone who works for a hedge fund or hopes to get a job with a hedge fund and needs to learn the essential facts about this important industry. Finally, lawyers and accountants who serve the hedge fund industry can learn about the business of their hedge fund customers.

The course book format is designed to let readers quickly learn as much or as little as they require. Readers can read chapters in any order and may skip chapters or parts of chapters. Short chapters describe the essential facts on a particular topic. Questions follow each chapter, and answers are at the back of the book. The questions are not designed to test the reader's understanding of the reading. Instead, the questions and answers delve more deeply into the topics reviewed in the text. The question sections contain most of the quantitative material of the book, so readers comfortable with the mathematics should be careful not to skip this valuable bonus material.

TOPICS INCLUDED

Chapter 1—Introduction

The first chapter provides a primer on the hedge fund industry. It explains how a hedge fund differs from other investment products, the growth of the industry, and basic vocabulary and operation of hedge funds.

Chapter 2—Types of Hedge Funds

Most of the thousands of hedge funds resemble one of a handful of strategies. This chapter describes the most popular strategies that comprise most of the hedge fund assets under management.

Chapter 3—Types of Hedge Fund Investors

Although individuals began investing in hedge funds before most types of institutional investors, today nearly all types of investors invest in hedge funds. The needs and wants of individual investors differ greatly from those of pension funds and endowments. This chapter describes the most important groups of hedge fund investors.

Chapter 4—Hedge Fund Investment Techniques

Certain investment techniques have been developed in broker-dealers or private equity funds and fit well into hedge funds. This chapter describes investment techniques outside the domain of the traditional portfolio manager.

Chapter 5—Hedge Fund Business Models

Hedge funds and hedge fund managers are organized as corporations, partnerships, and limited liability corporations to get maximum tax advantages and limited liability for investors. Offshore funds combine several structures to comply with U.S. and offshore regulations.

Chapter 6—Hedge Fund Leverage

This chapter describes the many techniques used by hedge funds that allow a hedge fund to carry positions larger than the hedge fund capital. The chapter also describes how hedge funds can create short positions to implement trading strategies and control risk.

Chapter 7—Performance Measurement

Hedge fund investors closely monitor hedge fund performance. Investors have developed a collection of tools to measure performance and risk. Hedge funds share some of these tools with traditional asset managers, but they also have methods designed for leveraged portfolios.

Chapter 8—Hedge Fund Legislation and Regulation

Anyone who thinks a hedge fund is not affected by rules and regulations hasn't read a risk disclosure document. Although most securities laws contain exemptions that allow hedge funds to escape some of the burdens of regulation, the exemptions create complications as well.

Chapter 9—Accounting

This chapter describes the accounting requirements unique to hedge funds. Hedge funds pose all the challenges typical of portfolio accounting. Hedge funds create additional challenges because they carry short positions, may finance their long positions, and may turn over their positions rapidly.

Chapter 10—Hedge Fund Taxation

Tax reporting is one of the most complicated topics affecting hedge fund investors. Taxes have a powerful impact on the after-tax return of investors yet tax reporting is one of the least-discussed topics affecting hedge fund investors.

Chapter 11—Risk Management and Hedge Funds

Risk management is more than risk measurement, but measurement is the first step. Some hedge funds take more risks than traditional portfolio managers and hedge funds almost always take different risks than traditional portfolio managers. Risk measurements provide managers, investors, and creditors with valuable insights into the nature of hedge fund positions.

Chapter 12—Marketing Hedge Funds

Regulations define how hedge fund managers can market their funds. A specialized industry has evolved to help managers raise money.

Chapter 13—Derivatives and Hedge Funds

One of the latest developments in hedge fund investing involves investing indirectly into hedge funds through derivative products. These new structures offer several potential advantages over direct hedge fund investing.

Chapter 14—Conclusions

This chapter provides a review of the state of the hedge fund industry and provides insight into the future of the hedge fund marketplace.

Acknowledgments

I want to thank everyone who assisted me in writing this text. I received invaluable comments from Ricardo Cossa and John Szobocsan, who spent many hours reviewing drafts and offering suggestions.

I must also thank my wife Nancy and children Kate, Lauren, and Douglas, who endured my absence while writing and revising this text.

—SMc

About the Author

Stuart A. McCrary is a principal with Chicago Partners L.L.C. and specializes in options, mortgage-backed securities, derivatives, and hedge funds. As president of Frontier Asset Management, McCrary managed and ran his own hedge fund before joining Chicago Partners. He has also worked as a senior options trader at Fenchurch Capital Management, as vice president in the mortgage department and in proprietary trading at First Boston Corporation, and as a portfolio manager with Comerica Bank. He has taught graduate-level courses in creating and managing a hedge fund at the Kellstadt Graduate School of Business at DePaul University and courses in accounting in Northwestern University's Masters in Product Development program and options and financial engineering classes at the Stuart School of Business at the Illinois Institute of Technology. He received his BA and MBA from Northwestern University.

Hedge Fund
Course

CHAPTER 1

Introduction

The first known hedge fund was created by Alfred Winslow Jones in 1949. His fund should look familiar to today's hedge fund participants. The fund was organized as a limited partnership and used private placement rules to avoid registration. It invested primarily in common stocks and used moderate leverage to carry long and short positions modestly larger than the fund capital.

The number of hedge funds has grown significantly, and there are many different types of hedge funds. But this first hedge fund bears a close resemblance to the most common hedge fund strategy today, called long/short equity.

DEFINITION OF HEDGE FUND

Definitions of hedge funds run into problems because it is exceedingly difficult to describe what a hedge fund is without running into trouble with funds that don't fit into the rules. There are investment pools that closely resemble hedge funds but are generally regarded as a different type of investment. Still other types of investments may contain characteristics that are generally associated with hedge funds.

As a starting point, begin with a rather typical definition of a hedge fund:

> *A hedge fund is a loosely regulated investment company that charges incentive fees and usually seeks to generate returns that are not highly correlated to returns on stocks and bonds.*

Many traits of hedge funds aren't useful in defining what is and what is not a hedge fund.

1

Regulation and Hedge Funds

Chapter 8 describes the laws and regulations that control hedge funds. While hedge funds are not unregulated, as is sometimes asserted, they are more loosely regulated than mutual funds and common trusts run by bank trust departments. Other types of investments are also loosely regulated, though, including private equity partnerships, venture capital funds, and many real estate partnerships.

Investors may feel they will "know it (a hedge fund) when they see it," but there are no firm lines separating hedge funds from these other types of investments. Hedge funds may invest part of their assets in private equity, venture capital, or real estate.

To further blur the distinction between hedge funds and regulated investment companies, there is increasing pressure from the Securities and Exchange Commission (SEC), bank regulators, auditors, and exchanges for hedge funds to disclose more information and to control permitted activities. Hedge funds may soon be required to disclose much of the information that mutual fund companies must report. The SEC has proposed to require all hedge fund management companies to register as investment advisers.

Limited Liability

Sometimes, the definition of hedge funds mentions that hedge funds are a vehicle where investors have no liability for losses beyond their initial investment. It certainly is true that most hedge funds in the United States are organized as limited partnerships or limited liability corporations (see Chapter 5) that protect the investor from liability. However, offshore funds are usually organized as corporations and, despite this difference, also create a limited liability investment.

Most other investments are also limited liability investments. Investors can lose no more than 100 percent of the value of long positions in stocks and bonds. Mutual funds also protect the investor from losses in excess of the amount of money invested. While accurate for hedge funds, the characteristic of limited liability does little to define hedge funds.

Flow-Through Tax Treatment

Hedge funds are not taxed like corporations. Instead, all the income, expenses, gains, and losses are passed through to investors. This feature does not define hedge funds because many other investment types are flow-through tax entities. Real estate investment trusts (REITs), mutual funds, venture capital funds, and other private equity funds are regularly constructed to receive flow-through tax treatment.

Hedge funds organized outside the United States are frequently organized in locations that have little or no business tax. In these locations, hedge funds are not organized to get flow-through tax treatment. Instead, these funds are organized as corporations that do not require investors to include the annual hedge fund income and expenses on investor tax returns.

Hedge Funds and Their Use of Leverage

Many hedge funds use leverage to carry long and short positions in excess of their capital. Not all hedge funds use leverage, and many hedge funds use leverage of two times or less (see Chapter 6).

Other types of investments also use leverage to carry assets in excess of capital. Some mutual funds use leverage. Leverage is common in real estate investments. Private equity funds may borrow money to limit the equity needed to carry investments.

Hedge Funds Charge Incentive Fees

Hedge funds charge a variety of fees, including a substantial management fee and an incentive fee. The management fees are similar to management fees at mutual funds, private equity funds, and real estate funds. Incentive fees are also typical in private equity funds, real estate funds, and (to a limited extent) mutual funds.

Hedge Funds and Lockup Commitments

Many hedge funds require investors to leave funds invested for a year or more. This lockup provision is not typical of mutual funds, but the load fees strongly encourage investors in mutual funds to hold their investments for several years. Private equity funds frequently have lockup provisions. Venture capital funds in particular may grant the investor no opportunity to exit before assets are liquidated. Real estate funds may have similar restrictions.

CONTRASTING MUTUAL FUNDS WITH HEDGE FUNDS

One definition of a hedge fund is that it is a mutual fund that doesn't have to follow any rules. This overly simple distinction may help the uninitiated get a rough idea of what a hedge fund can do. Of course, there are lots of rules that a hedge fund must observe, and hedge funds are organized differently from mutual funds. The distinction loses meaning as mutual funds have been given broader investment rules over time. Recently, U.S. regulators have been pressing to tighten the regulation of hedge funds. Nevertheless, there are some consistent differences between mutual funds and hedge funds.

Fees

Most mutual funds charge a management fee but not incentive fees. Mutual funds may charge management fees from less than 0.25 percent up to several percent of assets under management. Hedge funds also charge management fees, usually between 1 percent and 2 percent of assets. Mutual funds usually charge no incentive fee, but hedge funds charge incentive fees of 20 percent of profit or more. While mutual funds may be sold with no sales charge (called no-load mutual funds), many are sold with commissions of 5 percent of assets or more. Mutual funds may also assess other sales charges called 12b-1 fees. In contrast, hedge funds generally don't charge sales commissions.

Leverage

A small number of mutual funds borrow to carry long positions in excess of capital or to carry short positions. One mutual fund, Northeast Investors Trust, bought corporate bonds as long as 30 years ago using borrowed funds to increase the return on the fund. Most mutual funds use debt only to provide short-term liquidity to accommodate withdrawals. Mutual funds also use derivative instruments in lieu of investing in cash securities, not to create leverage.

In contrast, a survey conducted by Van Hedge Fund Advisors International, LLC in 1997 reported that 70 percent of hedge funds used leverage.[1] During the time of the study, some fixed income hedge funds ran positions 70 times their capital or higher.

Transparency

Mutual funds publish quarterly income statements and balance sheets at least quarterly. The balance sheets aggregate assets so that investors cannot see details of individual positions. Nevertheless, mutual funds publish detailed portfolios annually, albeit with substantial delays.

Hedge funds have typically refused to disclose positions or trade details to the public. Some funds would disclose this information to a small number of important investors. More recently, funds of funds investors have often demanded to know position details. A survey by Deutsche Bank found that one-third of investors demanded transparency and information about risk.[2] Only 3 percent of investors would invest in funds that refused to provide any position information to investors.

Liquidity

Mutual fund investors generally may redeem shares at any time, not subject to restrictions on exit under normal market conditions. In some cases, fees encourage investors to remain invested for several years, but investors may otherwise exit without restrictions. Mutual funds generally accept or redeem investments on the same day or next day. In contrast, hedge funds allow entry or exit only at certain times of the year, monthly, quarterly, or annually. In addition, hedge funds may restrict redemptions for a year or more.

CONTRASTING PRIVATE EQUITY FUNDS WITH HEDGE FUNDS

Private equity funds include leveraged buyout funds, venture capital funds, mezzanine financing funds, and other portfolios of direct investment in private corporations.

Legal Structures

Private equity funds entities are organized as limited partnerships or limited liability corporations if located in the United States or as corporations in tax-favored offshore locations. Private equity funds use the same exemptions that hedge funds use to escape many of the regulations that affect regulated investment companies.

Fee Structures

Private equity funds generally charge both an incentive and a management fee much like the fees charged by hedge funds. Unlike hedge funds, though, many private equity funds charge no incentive fees until individual investments are liquidated because there is no verifiable way to mark the assets to market prior to sale. Upon sale, the investment and gain are returned to investors less an incentive fee on profits. Occasionally, hedge funds will carve out portions of their assets and treat them similarly to private equity investments. These assets are called side-pocket allocations.

Leverage and Private Equity Investments

Like hedge funds, private equity funds can borrow money to buy assets in excess of their capital. Leveraged buyout funds and venture capital funds may carry the debt on the balance sheet of the companies they own. Leverage in private equity is lower than the leverage in the most leveraged hedge funds.

Private Equity and Absolute Returns

Many hedge funds seek returns that are relatively uncorrelated to stock and bond returns. They don't try to keep up with the stock market when returns are very high on stocks. Likewise, they seek to avoid losing money in periods when stock returns are negative. These hedge funds are seeking absolute returns, to contrast the traditional portfolio manager that benchmarks return relative to a market index.

Most private equity strategies are not absolute return strategies. Venture capital returns, for example, are highly correlated with Nasdaq returns because the venture capital funds and the Nasdaq share a concentration of investment in technology companies.

Private Equity and Liquidity

Private equity funds generally offer little or no liquidity to investors. As mentioned earlier, venture capital funds generally don't charge incentive fees until assets are liquidated because it is difficult to defend mark-to-market valuations of their assets. For the same reason, venture capital funds generally don't redeem their investments until assets are liquidated to avoid having to defend a mark-to-market net asset value. As a practical matter, the venture capital fund may not have cash available to redeem investments and no means to readily generate cash because it carries assets with limited marketability.

CONTRASTING COMMODITY POOLS WITH HEDGE FUNDS

It is particularly vexing to distinguish commodity pools from hedge funds. In fact, any hedge fund that trades futures or commodities only minimally must also register as a commodity pool (see Chapter 8). Nevertheless, as long as a fund invests significantly in cash instruments (that is, not commodities or futures), it is generally described as a hedge fund, not a commodity pool. A fund is called a commodity pool if substantially all its holdings are in commodities, futures, and options on futures.

Unfortunately, hedge funds and commodity pools are similar in other ways. These similarities make it difficult to draw a distinction between hedge funds and commodity pools.

Legal Structures

Commodity pools are structured using the same types of businesses used to create hedge funds. Pools organized in the United States are structured as limited partnerships or limited liability corporations. Pools organized offshore are generally located in tax-favored locations and are structured as corporations.

Commodity pools use the same exemptions from registration that are used by hedge funds to avoid registration. Commodity pools can be sold to individuals who pass certain income and wealth tests (see Chapter 8). The tests are similar to income and wealth tests used by hedge funds to qualify for exemptions from regulation.

Liquidity and Commodity Pools

Typically, a commodity pool restricts entry to and exit from the pool to month-end or quarter-end. Commodity pools have somewhat simpler tax reporting than hedge funds but don't allow daily entry or exit in order to simplify tax computations.

Some commodity pools may impose a lockup on funds invested. The commodity pool has less need to lock up investment funds because the pool's assets are generally liquid and reasonably easy to liquidate. However, a commodity pool will impose a lockup if investors will tolerate a lockup to try to hold on to investment funds longer.

SIZE AND GROWTH OF HEDGE FUNDS

Because hedge funds avoid most of the registration requirements of traditional money managers, no business or governmental agency has precise knowledge of the number of hedge funds in existence. Businesses that collect performance data on large numbers of hedge funds maintain estimates of the number of hedge funds. Fortunately, the estimates are fairly close.

For example, in Figure 1.1, Van Hedge Fund Advisors International has estimated the number of hedge funds worldwide at 8,100. Other estimates are generally within about 10 percent of this estimate.

The number of hedge funds has risen by about 12.6 percent annually since 1988.[3] This total represents the new funds created and the funds that shut down. Hedge fund professionals believe that the average hedge fund has been in existence for about eight years. The lack of hard data on hedge fund assets means that this average life is uncertain; but if it is true, each year many more hedge funds are created and a large number of funds exit.

The same sources that estimate the number of hedge funds also estimate the assets under management (AUM). Figure 1.2 shows the hedge fund assets estimated by Van Hedge Fund Advisors International each year-end from 1988 through 2003. The hedge assets are also subject to uncertainty. However, Tass Research separately estimated the global hedge fund assets at $750 billion on December 31, 2003.

The assets invested in hedge funds have risen by 21.9 percent annually since 1988.[4] Figure 1.2 shows that although the growth has been irregular, the industry has grown every year.

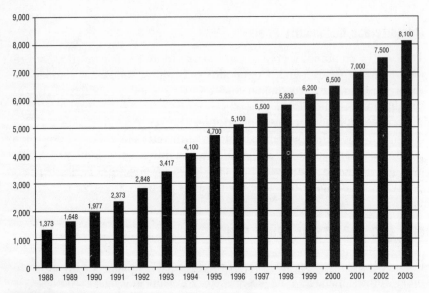

FIGURE 1.1 Estimated Number of Hedge Funds
Source: ©2004 by Van Hedge Fund Advisors International, LLC, and/or its licensors, Nashville, TN, USA.

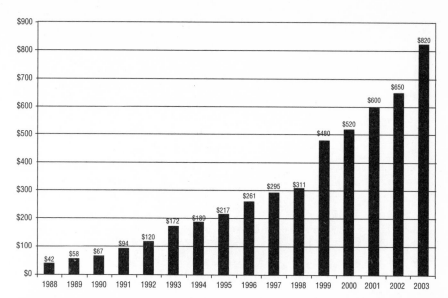

FIGURE 1.2 Estimated Hedge Fund Assets under Management ($Billions)
Source: ©2004 by Van Hedge Fund Advisors International, LLC, and/or its licensors, Nashville, TN, USA.

Because the assets under management have been growing faster than the number of hedge funds, it is clear that the size of the average hedge fund is rising. Figure 1.3 shows the average size calculated from the data in Figure 1.1 and Figure 1.2.

The size of the average hedge fund grew irregularly over the past 15 years. Although the assets grew by an average rate of 8.3 percent annually,[5] the average size remained about the same or declined in about a third of the years.

Funds of hedge funds have been growing somewhat faster than single-manager hedge funds. Figure 1.4 shows the assets under management including both direct investments and investments through a fund of funds intermediary. Single-manager funds (funds that implement hedge fund strategies other than fund of funds strategies) have grown at 21.5 percent annually.[6] Fund of funds investments in hedge funds have grown at 26.0 percent annually.[7] For this time period, the combined hedge fund assets have grown at 22.6 percent annually.[8]

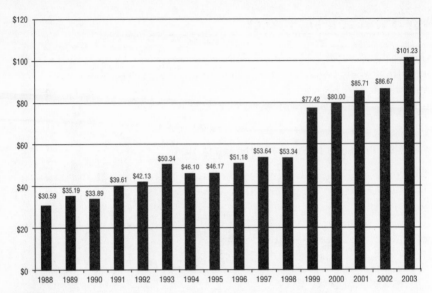

FIGURE 1.3   Estimated Hedge Fund Average Size (AUM $Millions)
Source: ©2004 by Van Hedge Fund Advisors International, LLC, and/or its licensors, Nashville, TN, USA.

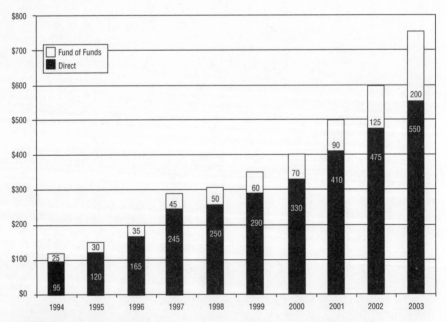

FIGURE 1.4   Estimated Hedge Fund Assets under Management ($Billions)
Source: Tass Research.

WHY INVEST IN HEDGE FUNDS?

Marketing literature describes a number of reasons why investors should put part of their portfolios into hedge funds. Generally, those reasons fall into one of three somewhat overlapping motivations: (1) to increase return, (2) to reduce risk, and (3) to increase diversification.

Investing in Hedge Funds to Increase Return

With thousands of hedge funds in existence, it is difficult to generalize much about the expected return. Funds can experience higher returns or lower returns than traditional assets, including stocks and bonds. Nevertheless, some hedge fund managers seek to make very high returns and are willing to accept substantially more risk in their portfolios to achieve that return.

Adding high returns to a portfolio increases the return in a predictable way. The return on a portfolio is equal to the weighted average of the individual returns; see equation (1.1):

$$r_{\text{Portfolio}} = \sum_{i=1}^{N} w_i \times r_i \qquad (1.1)$$

where r_i represents the return of individual assets in the portfolio and w_i represents the weight of each asset in the portfolio.

In the late 1980s and early 1990s, a number of global macro hedge funds (see Chapter 2 for a description of this and other hedge fund styles) caught the public's attention. This group of funds made levered investments in U.S. and international stocks, bonds and foreign currencies. Despite the name, they were generally not hedged, although the variety of their positions may have provided some risk control in the form of diversification.

Chapter 11 demonstrates that the typical hedge fund is not as risky as a buy-and-hold investment in the Standard & Poor's 500 stock index. For some investors, hedge funds serve a valuable role in increasing the expected return on a portfolio. These investors may not be happy about accepting additional risk but are nevertheless willing to take on more investment risk to achieve a higher portfolio return.

Over the past decade, the stock market has enjoyed high returns and violent losses. Bonds have also enjoyed good performance over the past two decades. During the periods of high stock and bond returns, investors have not needed to move into hedge funds to get excellent returns. During the downturn in 2001–2002, most hedge fund performance was higher than stock returns. During this period, although some investors have been motivated by the higher performance, an increasing number of investors looked for a nondirectional return.

Investing in Hedge Funds to Reduce Risk

Hedge fund investors face many risks. These risks include the risks introduced by the securities and currencies held by the fund; the use of leverage, which may concentrate risks present in the positions; the risk of financing positions; and other risks (see Chapter 11). However, many hedge funds are considerably less risky (by several risk measures) than the S&P 500, and many funds are less risky than the more conservative Lehman Brothers Aggregate Bond Index.

Investors who add assets that are less risky than assets held in the portfolio can lower the risk of the portfolio. If the investor can pick less risky assets that are expected to earn as high a return as the other assets in the portfolio, the investor can lower the risk of the portfolio without lowering expected return.

Investing in Hedge Funds to Increase Diversification

Diversification can significantly lower portfolio risk, compared to the risk of individual assets. Many hedge funds do not track stock or bond returns closely so they are more effective in reducing risk through diversification than simply splitting the debt and equity investments over more securities in a portfolio.

One of the most popular measures of risk is the standard deviation of returns. This measure is used by academic writers, traditional investors, and hedge fund investors. The standard deviation of return is shown in equation (1.2) and can be found in almost any introductory statistics textbook:

$$\text{Standard Deviation} = \sigma = \frac{\sum_{t=1}^{N} r_t - \bar{r}}{N-1} \tag{1.2}$$

where r_t represents a series of returns over N time periods. Usually, the standard deviation is annualized by multiplying the results of equation

(1.2) by the square root of the number of observations per year. Equation (1.3) shows the standard deviation for monthly data:

$$\sigma = \frac{\sum_{t=1}^{N} r_t - \bar{r}}{N-1} \times \sqrt{12} \tag{1.3}$$

Assuming the returns of two assets are normally distributed, the sum of risk of owning two assets is determined by the risk of the two assets and the covariance between the two assets. The standard deviation of a two-asset portfolio is shown in equation (1.4):

$$\sigma_{A,B} = \sqrt{w_A^2 \sigma_A^2 + w_B^2 \sigma_B^2 + 2 w_A w_A \sigma_{A,B}} \tag{1.4}$$

Suppose an investor can invest in asset A, which has an expected return of 10 percent, or asset B, which has an expected return of 9 percent. However, both assets are equally risky, having a standard deviation of return equal to 15 percent. The correlation between the returns of the two assets is 50 percent. The covariance is calculated from the correlation in equation (1.5):

$$\sigma_{A,B} = \sigma_A \sigma_B \rho_{A,B} = 15\% \times 15\% \times 50\% = 1.125\% \tag{1.5}$$

Table 1.1 is created by applying equation (1.4). The risk reduction is clear on a graphical view of Table 1.1, as shown in Figure 1.5.

TABLE 1.1 Portfolio Return and Risk for Various Weights

w_A	w_B	$r_{A,B}$	$\sigma_{Portfolio}$
100%	0%	10.00%	15.00%
90%	10%	9.90%	14.31%
80%	20%	9.80%	13.75%
70%	30%	9.70%	13.33%
60%	40%	9.60%	13.08%
50%	50%	9.50%	12.99%
40%	60%	9.40%	13.08%
30%	70%	9.30%	13.33%
20%	80%	9.20%	13.75%
10%	90%	9.10%	14.31%
0%	100%	9.00%	15.00%

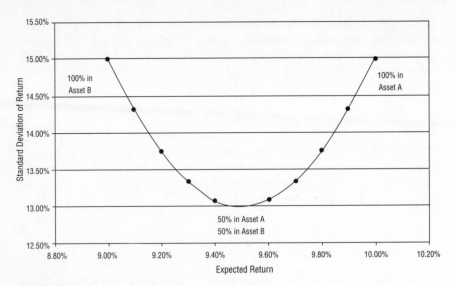

FIGURE 1.5   Risk and Reward

HEDGE FUND BASICS

Many investors are unfamiliar with the way a hedge fund investment be-
haves. In addition to having more investment latitude than traditional investment managers, a hedge fund manager may charge a variety of fees and
place restrictions on exit from a hedge fund.

Fees

Hedge funds charge a variety of fees. Other types of investment pools, including mutual funds, private equity funds, and real estate investment
trusts, charge the same types of fees, but the structures of the fees may differ slightly in the hedge fund industry.

A management fee is charged as a flat percentage of assets under management. Hedge funds generally charge an annual management fee between 1 and 2 percent. For example, if a fund charges 1.5 percent, it might
assess a monthly fee equal to .125 percent (1.5%/12) based on the value of
the fund's capital at month-end. This fee is charged regardless of whether
the fund has been profitable. Some funds calculate the management fee
quarterly or less frequently.

An incentive fee is based on the profits made by the hedge fund.

Hedge funds generally charge 15 percent to 25 percent of profit as an incentive fee. Suppose a fund makes 2 percent or $2 million on assets of $100 million in a particular month before incentive fees but after the management fee has been deducted. If the fund collects a 20 percent incentive fee, the fund will pay $400,000 ($2 million × 20%) to the management company.

Funds usually charge no incentive fee on profits that offset prior losses. This is called a high-water mark provision. For example, suppose a hedge fund started with a net asset value (NAV) of $1,000. Over several months, the NAV rose to $1,500 and the management company charged incentive fees based on this return. If the NAV declined to $1,400, the manager would refund no incentive fees, but the fund would pay no incentive fees on any returns until the value to investors rose above the previous high-water mark of $1,500.

Sometimes a fund pays incentive fees on returns above a certain minimum return. Suppose a $100 million hedge fund pays a 20 percent incentive fee on returns above the London Interbank Offered Rate (LIBOR). If LIBOR was 3 percent (annualized to 3%/12 or .25% for a month) and the fund return was 3.5 percent in one month, the fund would collect an incentive fee on 3.25 percent; thus, $100 million × (3.5% − .25%) × 20% = $650,000.

A fund may subject previously paid incentive fees to a look-back provision. In this case, a manager may be required to refund incentive fees back to the fund if the fund experiences a loss shortly after an incentive fee is paid. Look-back provisions are not common, and the specific provisions can vary from fund to fund. For example, one fund limits the look-back to three months. Another fund limits the incentive fee look-back to a calendar quarter.

Hedge fund managers may charge other fees, such as commissions, financing charges, and ticket charges. The management company may keep some or all of these fees or may pay out part of these fees as sales incentives to individuals who market the hedge fund to investors. The existence and the magnitude of these fees vary from fund to fund. The fund should disclose these fees to investors, but investors may nevertheless have trouble determining how much these fees affect the return of the fund.

Other Hedge Fund Provisions

Funds may impose a lockup, meaning that investors may not withdraw their investments for a period of time, usually between one and three years. Often, the fund will let an investor withdraw gains but require the investor to keep the initial capital in place during the lockup period.

Funds allow entry into or exit out of the hedge fund at a limited number of times per year. Restricting flows to month-end, quarter-end, or year-end greatly simplifies the tax-reporting burden on the hedge fund administrator. Funds sometimes require investors to advise the manager in advance of withdrawing funds. Some managers require 10 to 90 days' notice to redeem hedge fund interests. These provisions, along with lockup provisions, seek to make hedge fund investments more sticky (investors remain in a hedge fund for a longer period of time).

HEDGE FUND MYTHS

As mentioned earlier, the public perceives hedge funds as risky investments appropriate for thrill-seeking investors. This myth and others persist despite evidence to the contrary.

Hedge funds are sometimes called absolute return strategies. The idea of absolute return is in contrast to traditional money management, where returns are compared to a benchmark of returns on similar assets. The return on a portfolio of stocks is compared to the S&P 500 or other index, and a manager is judged not on whether the portfolio was profitable but rather on how the portfolio return compared to the market return. In contrast, absolute return strategies can be expected to be profitable regardless of what happens to any identifiable index. In theory, the absolute return manager would be judged only on the size and consistency of returns.

However, most hedge funds retain at least some correlation to stock and bond returns. Academic studies have shown that the returns on hedge funds can at least in part be explained by market returns and other economic factors (credit spreads, volatility, and others). Further, for hedge funds that follow a popular strategy, it is possible to benchmark an individual fund's return against peer fund returns. Finally, hedge fund indexes now exist that provide reasonable benchmarks for many hedge funds.

Another hedge fund myth involves assumptions about the life cycle of hedge funds. Many investors refuse to invest in hedge funds that have less than, for example, two years of performance in the belief that young funds are more likely to fail. Other investors seek to invest in young funds because they believe that smaller, newer hedge funds provide higher returns than large funds that have been in existence for many years. In addition, there is a belief that hedge funds don't tend to survive longer than about eight years.

In fact, many factors affect the riskiness of hedge funds, the return to particular funds, and the popularity of an investment style. Certain strategies such as convertible bond arbitrage remain attractive, despite existing for decades. The early demise of many new hedge funds can be explained by weaknesses in investment strategy, failure to establish systems and operating procedures, or simply bad timing for a fund of a particular style or strategy.

QUESTIONS AND PROBLEMS

1.1 List three reasons to invest in hedge funds.

1.2 Why are press reports describing disasters with hedge fund investments not a valid reason to avoid investing in the products?

1.3 What is the difference between absolute return strategies and relative return strategies?

1.4 Is it generally true that low correlation is better than high correlation?

1.5 The growth in hedge fund assets under management has been much more rapid than the growth in the number of hedge funds. How is this possible?

1.6 Are any of these fees and/or design structures incompatible and never be used together in the same fund: management fee, incentive fee, hurdle rate, surrender fee, high-water mark, look-back, commission, and ticket charge?

1.7 It is typical in a private equity fund to levy no incentive fee until an investment is liquidated. Explain why this practice differs from the pattern in hedge funds, where an incentive fee is levied on mark-to-market gains in the fund.

1.8 Distinguish a commodity pool or futures fund from a hedge fund.

1.9 You run a hedge fund with $100 million under management. You charge a management fee of 2.25 percent. What is the management fee assessed on the entire fund for the month of February 2004?

1.10 Assume the hedge fund in question 1.9 earned 4.5 percent (gross return before fees). What incentive fee would the management company earn if the fund paid an incentive fee of 15 percent?

1.11 What is the incentive fee, assuming the same facts from question 1.9 but incorporating a hurdle rate of 5 percent?

1.12 Assume the same facts from question 1.9 but a high-water mark provision. In addition, the hedge fund lost 7 percent in January 2004. What is the incentive fee for February 2004?

NOTES

1. Quoted by Steven Lonsdorf in a message to Congress. Data as of December 31, 1997.
2. Allison Bisbey Colter, "Hedge Fund Investors Seek Detailed Data, Survey Finds," *Wall Street Journal*, April 1, 2003.
3. The estimated number of hedge funds in 1988 (1,373) grows to 8,100 at 12.6 percent annually in 15 years.
4. The estimated hedge fund assets under management in 1988 ($42 billion) grows to $820 billion at 21.9 percent annually in 15 years.
5. The size of the average hedge fund based on the data in Figure 1.1 and Figure 1.2 in 1988 ($30.59 million) grows to $101.23 million at 8.3 percent annually in 15 years.
6. The estimated hedge fund assets under direct investment in 1994 ($95 billion) grows to $550 billion at 21.5 percent annually in nine years.
7. The estimated hedge fund assets under fund of funds investment in 1994 ($25 billion) grows to $200 billion at 26.0 percent annually in nine years.
8. The estimated hedge fund assets under either direct investment or through funds of hedge funds in 1994 ($120 billion) grows to $750 billion at 22.6 percent annually in nine years.

CHAPTER 2

Types of Hedge Funds

CLASSIFYING HEDGE FUNDS

With thousands of hedge funds in existence, classifying individual funds into 10 or 20 groups in a challenge. Some funds might fit in more than one category or none of the categories used to classify hedge funds. Nevertheless, fund managers and investors rely on hedge fund classifications.

Importance of Classifications

There are many reasons to categorize hedge funds and group them into subsets. Investors often study a hedge fund style by reviewing aggregate performance data, selecting a sector, then reviewing funds within the sector. The classification makes the average return a meaningful benchmark and permits the investor to match up with the right fund manager.

To make the classifications meaningful, many investors prefer hedge funds that fit neatly into a single strategy. Style purity measures how much a hedge fund keeps to a single, identifiable strategy. The investor preference for style purity is easy to understand. Suppose an investor researches several hedge fund styles and decides that a particular style would be an attractive addition to the investor's existing portfolio of assets. That investor would be sorely disappointed if the individual fund selected failed to track the composite.

For a variety of reasons, funds may choose to pursue multiple strategies in a single hedge fund. In some ways, the aggregate performance resembles a fund of funds that gains some benefits from diversification. Academic writers are often quick to point out that well-healed investors can accomplish the same diversification (perhaps more efficiently). However, some investors nevertheless prefer the multistrategy funds, either because they lack the financial resources to get the maximum benefit from diversification or because the multistrategy fund avoids a layer of fees present in the fund of funds.

Who Categorizes Hedge Funds?

Many types of organizations label hedge funds according to the style or investment philosophy they follow. Hedge funds frequently categorize themselves in their disclosure documents and marketing literature. Hedge fund data providers such as Evaluation Associates Capital Markets (EACM), CSFB Tremont, Hennessee, Hedge Fund Research (HFR), and the Center for International Securities and Derivatives Markets (CISDM) track thousands of hedge funds and assign most of them to 10 or 15 styles. (Data from these providers can be used to study the characteristics of the types of hedge funds discussed here.) A growing industry of hedge fund indexers begins by creating a benchmark that can be replicated; then the indexers invest in individual funds to create a portfolio that tracks their benchmarks. The media often classifies hedge funds, sometimes without regard to the facts. Finally, analysts and academic researchers may categorize hedge funds based on their actual performance, explaining returns based on broad economic factors like interest rates, stock returns, default risk, volatility, and other factors.

Inconsistency of Hedge Fund Categorizations

Regardless of how and why hedge funds are classified, the results are occasionally inconsistent. Sometimes categories overlap, so the choice of strategy is a bit arbitrary. Sometimes a fund will shift strategies gradually (called style drift); one data provider might classify the fund by the current strategy and another might include it in the style previously followed. Some funds may be tough to categorize because the manager deviates from the announced strategy. Other funds may follow multiple strategies so can't fit into a single category. Finally, some funds may be erroneously classified either because of human error or because there aren't enough categories to match all hedge funds.

SHARE OF THE MARKET BY STRATEGIES

The changing popularity of individual hedge fund strategies has led to changes in the composition of the hedge fund universe. Popular strategies become a large part of the mix of hedge fund assets. Out-of-favor strategies may shrink in size.

Size Shifts

The largest category of hedge funds contains mostly common stocks, although they may pursue several different strategies. Although the first hedge funds were also predominately equity funds, different styles have come in and out of favor over the years.

For example, global macro hedge funds (see descriptions of this and other styles later in this chapter) were very popular in the early 1990s, offering high returns and high risk. Later in the same decade, various fixed income arbitrage funds provided low risk and low returns; however, this latter style went out of favor after several high-profile fixed income funds suffered large losses. Investors are returning to equity strategies seeking an attractive combination of moderately high returns and moderately low risk.

Prevailing Trends

By 1990, the public had become aware of hedge funds, primarily because of the trading activity of the global macro hedge funds. These funds were large, traded large positions, and frequently influenced market prices. Figure 2.1 suggests part of the reason for this notoriety: This

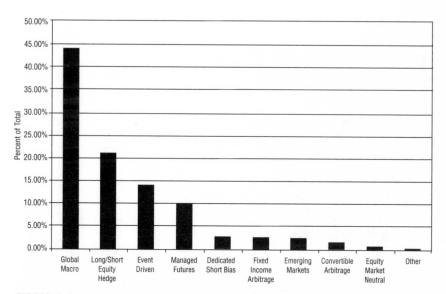

FIGURE 2.1   Hedge Fund Allocations by Style, December 31, 1990
Source: Tass Research.

group controlled 43.99 percent of all hedge fund assets. Other sources put the global macro portion as high as 70 percent of all hedge fund assets in 1990.[1]

Figure 2.2 shows the same hedge fund groups in 2003. Global macro hedge funds constitute the sixth largest group, comprising only 5.57 percent of the total. Most other groups have grown at the expense of global macro hedge funds.

The same styles are listed in Figure 2.1 and Figure 2.2, both ranked in order of assets in 1990. Long/short equity hedge funds have risen from 20.99 percent of the total in 1990 to 45.19 percent in 2003.

HEDGE FUND CATEGORIES

Although individual funds vary within the following categories, a description of a strategy typical for the group provides a definition for each category. Note that his list includes subcategories not broken out in Figure 2.1 and 2.2.

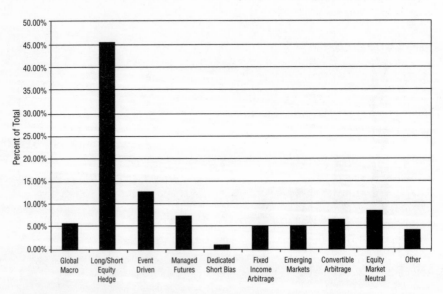

FIGURE 2.2   Hedge Fund Allocations by Style, December 31, 2003
Source: Tass Research.

Equity Hedge Funds

Equity hedge funds include those categories that invest primarily in common stocks.

Equity Long Biased   This group of hedge funds is the most familiar style to many people. The group may carry short positions, but the size of the long positions is usually larger than the size of the short positions. This group is one of several styles that are included in the broader category in Figure 2.2 and 2.2. The managers usually seek to generate returns by selecting a narrow portfolio of common stocks. Individual managers may seek to supplement the returns from stock selection by overlying a market-timing strategy. The stock selection may be based on fundamental analysis or, less commonly, on technical analysis. Often, hedge funds employ proprietary strategies to construct the portfolio. The portfolios in this group generally have low leverage (2 to 1 or less).

The equity long biased hedge funds have produced returns somewhat higher than broad equity returns, with risk (volatility of returns) about equal to index returns. Not surprisingly, the performance of long biased hedge funds correlates highly with stock returns (70 percent) but not particularly with interest rates. The VIX index measures implied volatility on equity options. Correlation between the long biased funds and this measure is high but somewhat less than stock index returns.

Equity Market Neutral   Equity market neutral hedge funds may use a variety of strategies. Arbitrage trading includes trading between futures and underlying common stocks (basis or basket trading), buying and selling related classes of common stock (pairs trading) or certain options strategies. The category also includes hedge funds that balance long and short positions (matched issue by issue or as a portfolio) to hedge market impact.

Equity market neutral hedge funds have provided returns about equal to those of broad indexes while assuming much less risk than a portfolio of common stocks (perhaps half the volatility of returns of the S&P 500 index). Despite the name given to this category, the group remains somewhat linked to market stock returns (30 to 40 percent). The equity market neutral hedge funds are much less linked to uncertainty in the financial markets than a traditional pool of common stocks. The correlation of the S&P 500 index to the VIX index of volatility is above 65 percent versus the equity hedge funds, which have a correlation about 20 percent to the VIX index.

Equity Arbitrage   This strategy is sometimes incorporated in the equity market neutral category. While the equity market neutral group is broad and a bit too inclusive, the equity arbitrage group includes funds that trade definable, tradable relationships between securities.

When data vendors provide a separate breakdown of equity arbitrage from other equity market neutral strategies, the arbitrage group provides higher returns and somewhat higher risk (as measured by the standard deviation of returns). The high risk and return is probably attributable to the higher leverage in the arbitrage funds compared to other equity market neutral strategies. As a portfolio investment, this higher risk may be forgivable because the volatility remains well below traditional stock returns. In addition, the performance of the equity arbitrage funds is less correlated to stock returns (about 25 percent) than any other equity hedge fund strategy.

Long/Short Equity   Generally, this category includes hedge funds that may be either long *or* short.[2] In particular, the funds can be levered long (probably no more than 2 to 1), market neutral, or modestly short. Performance depends both on stock selection and market timing.

The performance of this group depends on the data source. The group of long/short hedge funds tracked by both CSFB Tremont and CISDM between January 1, 1990, and December 31, 2003, had higher returns than the S&P 500 index while the data from EACM reported returns only half the level of the S&P 500 return. Although differences are common between data providers, this discrepancy is untypically large. The hedge fund group was a bit more consistent over time than the S&P (as might be expected from a group of nondirectional investors) so the differences depend more on the return of the index than the returns in the group. The returns for long/short hedge funds can be rather volatile, although usually less than an investment in a market portfolio of common stocks such as the S&P 500 index. The correlation of the long/short group to stock returns ranges from very high to very low across different data vendors, although the correlation has been low recently.

Event Driven   The event driven category includes several strategies often tracked separately. This group includes hedge funds involved with risk arbitrage (also called merger arbitrage), bankruptcy and reorganization (and other high-yield variations), spin-offs, and Regulation D funds. The category includes funds that invest purely in one of these strategies and multistrategy funds that may pursue several of the strategies.

The individual event driven strategies (risk arbitrage and Regulation D funds) are described separately. As a group, the strategies provide returns and risk typical of hedge funds. That is, they provide returns about equal to stock returns (more or less depending on the particular strategy) and substantially less risk than stock returns (about median among hedge fund returns). The performance is fairly correlated to stock returns (50 percent) and has a fairly high correlation to market uncertainty (correlation to VIX around 40 percent).

Risk Arbitrage   Risk or merger arbitrage generally involves buying the target company of a takeover after an attempt is announced and selling short the acquiring company. Although complicated terms may require more complicated positions, the typical position includes a long position that can be delivered to close out the short position if the deal is completed.[3]

Risk arbitrage provides relatively low returns (somewhat less than stock returns), compared to other hedge fund strategies but involves rather low risk. Early returns were higher than recent and a wave of deals may raise the return in the future. Returns remain highly correlated to stock returns (45 to 50 percent) and are sensitive to market uncertainty (correlation to VIX around 50 percent).

Regulation D   This group of hedge funds buys private equity positions in young, often very small companies. Frequently, these investments may be structured as convertible bonds with features designed to provide downside protection.

Performance on this section ranks among the highest of hedge fund strategies, up to twice the return on the S&P 500 index. Return volatility is very low when based on monthly net asset value (NAV) data, but the NAV is probably not as stable as the data suggest. The returns on private equity positions are frequently more volatile than the reported performance would indicate because hedge funds often don't mark private equity positions to market. Likewise, a low correlation to the VIX index probably understates the sensitivity of these positions to market sentiment.

Convertible Arbitrage   Convertible bonds and convertible preferred stock are fixed income instruments that may be exchanged for common stock. The typical issuers of convertible securities are young and fast growing and have a low debt rating. The debt structure might appear to offer some downside protection if the investor expects to get back the full principal value of the investment as a worst case. In practice, the market value of the debt is usually closely tied to the market value of the common stock because the company can reliably repay the bonds if the company does well, and if the company does well the common stock does well.

The option to convert is an option to exchange the bonds for stock. This type of option is more difficult to value than a simple call option. To further complicate matters, convertible securities may include call options, put options, and features to force the holder to convert to stock.

In its purest form, the convertible arbitrage fund buys the convertible instrument, sells short the common stock, buys or sells options on the common stock, and perhaps hedges the interest rate risk(s). In practice, the fund may not be able to hedge all the risks or may choose to hedge only some of the risks.

The performance of convertible arbitrage funds approximates the return of a basket of unlevered common stock, although the volatility of return is considerably lower for the convertible strategy than for the stock portfolio. The strategy has fairly low correlation to stock and bond returns and market uncertainty. It is somewhat sensitive to changes in credit spreads.

Sector Funds Sector funds include a collection of long-only or long biased hedge funds invested in a narrow sector of the stock market. Sector funds pursue a wide range of sectors, but the most common sector funds involve health care companies, biotechnology, the technology sector, real estate, and energy. Because these sectors tend to be volatile anyway, these hedge funds use little or no leverage. The returns on the individual funds depend on stock selection, but a major part of the return is determined by the performance of the sector.

These sectors have substantially outperformed broad stock indexes like the S&P 500 (except for real estate, whose returns have roughly matched the S&P). The returns published by the major hedge fund data providers for most sector funds have been more or less as volatile as stock returns, which means they are much more volatile than most other hedge funds. Because of their narrow concentration, their performance is relatively uncorrelated with broad market returns (30 to 50 percent correlation to the S&P 500 index) so they might be a good choice for an investor seeking to diversify a traditional stock portfolio. Many sector funds are concentrated in technology stocks, so they would not be as effective in diversifying a technology-heavy portfolio.

Fixed Income Hedge Funds

Fixed income strategies include the hedged strategies that invest in bonds and other fixed income instruments. Fixed income strategies include fixed income arbitrage, mortgage funds, various default-risk funds, and emerging markets debt funds.

Fixed Income Arbitrage Fixed income arbitrage funds rely primarily on debt instruments. Sometimes the group is called just "fixed income fund" to recognize that some of these funds retain substantial risks, albeit typically not the risk of rising or declining rates. The funds combine long and short positions with derivative instruments to hedge the level of interest rates, the rates of one maturity sector versus other maturity sectors (the "yield curve"), credit risks, and other factors.

Fixed income arbitrage funds have very effective hedges because interest rates tend to move up and down together (to a lesser extent when hedges span international borders or involve significantly different default risks). Because these hedges remove much of the day-to-day portfolio risks, arbitrage funds or "arb" funds usually have the highest leverage of all hedge fund strategies.

Fixed income arb funds may have sizable positions in foreign currencies but the currency exposure is usually hedged away. Similarly, the funds frequently buy individual issues that have considerable interest rate risk. However, this category of hedge fund would hedge away most of this risk.

As a group, fixed income funds have produced the lowest returns over time. However, the returns are rather consistent over time and the funds have low volatility of returns. The performance is nearly independent of stock and bond returns. Fixed income funds are viewed as more risky than the historical data would suggest because several fixed income funds have failed and created a major impact on the markets. For example, both the Granite Fund and Long-Term Capital Management lost nearly 100 percent of their capital while investing primarily in fixed income assets. Each of these highly publicized failures was accompanied with dislocations in the fixed income markets.

Mortgage-Backed and Collateralized Debt Obligations   Mortgage-backed securities (MBSs) include a variety of bonds backed by mortgage loans. Most mortgage loans (especially residential loans) can be repaid with little or no penalty at any time. This right closely resembles an option because the homeowner can refinance if rates decline but force a lender to hold to a fixed rate if rates rise.

When borrowers repay these mortgage loans, investors must reinvest, often at a lower rate. A variety of engineered securities—collateralized mortgage obligations (CMOs), real estate mortgage investment conduits (REMICs), and interest-only (IO) and principal-only (PO) notes—divide the many risks of the underlying loans in ways that may be more attractive to most investors. As it works out, much of the option risk gets distilled into a couple of high-yield, high-risk assets. Usually MBS strategies concentrate on buying this tricky category and hedging the many risks present in the investment.

Collateralized debt obligations (CDOs) resemble the engineered mortgage securities except that they involved other debt instruments, usually moderately low to low grade corporate bonds. Hedge funds use these instruments—including collateralized loan obligations (CLOs) and collateralized bond obligations (CBOs)—to earn credit spread without taking substantial interest rate risk, to arbitrage against other credit default instruments, or as a way of financing positions.

The MBS and CDO funds are often included in the fixed income category of hedge funds. Like the other fixed income funds, these funds have had lower average returns and lower volatility of returns than most hedge fund strategies. Investors have become nervous about holding MBS hedge funds after the losses at Granite fund and other mortgage funds, which probably explains why this sector remains small.

Credit, Bankruptcy, and Distress   This category of hedge fund is listed with other fixed income strategies. But while these funds tend to invest in debt instruments of financially troubled companies, the category is broad enough to include equity investments.

Generally, hedge funds buy and hold debt instruments of companies in or near default. Hedge funds may sell short securities of some companies. The managers may create hedges, buying one security and selling short other issues of the same company (hedging debt by selling common, for example) or instruments of other companies. The hedge fund may also hedge a portfolio of instruments with credit derivatives.

Most of the data vendors track a distress category of hedge funds. Performance has been fairly high on distress hedge funds, with low to moderately low risk. In general, these funds tend to do best when stock returns are positive. There is a moderate tendency for these funds to do well when rates rise. These funds also do well when securities markets are calm. For example, most indexes of bankruptcy and distress strategies are negatively correlated with the VIX index of stock option volatility (when volatility declines, these funds do well).

Emerging Markets   As the name of the category suggests, emerging markets hedge funds invest in securities issued by companies or countries that don't have well-established securities markets. These investments can be either debt or equity investments. Hedge funds may acquire a widely diversified portfolio of instruments from many countries or may focus on a particular country or economic region.

Generally, these funds cannot or do not hedge the risk in these portfolios, either because there is no futures or derivatives market for hedging or because the fund manager wants to retain the market exposure. Because the securities are fairly risky and generally unhedged, these funds tend to use little or no leverage.

Emerging markets hedge funds have been among the highest-performing groups, although the category shows up as only average in the performance data published by some data providers. The strategy produces inconsistent returns, having one of the highest volatilities of returns of all hedge fund strategies (about equal to an unlevered invest-ment in the Standard & Poor's 500 index). The strategy is moderately correlated to stock returns (around 50 percent versus the S&P 500). Like most hedge fund strategies, the performance in emerging markets hedge funds is correlated to the level of uncertainty in the financial markets. For example, the strategy has a correlation of about –30 percent versus the VIX index of stock option volatility (the funds do well when volatil-ity declines).

Other Hedge Fund Strategies

With 8,000 or more hedge funds in existence, it is not surprising that they do not fit neatly into a few categories. Other categories are important not so much because of the assets committed to these strategies but rather be-cause they extend the range of investment opportunities.

Global Macro   The global macro hedge funds brought the concept of hedge fund trading to the attention of many investors for the first time. These funds generally started out as equity portfolios but the managers also traded debt and foreign currency. Despite being called hedge funds, these funds generally take speculative, directional positions in stocks, bonds, and currencies worldwide, based on macroeconomic forecasts.

Global macro hedge funds have some of the highest returns of all hedge fund strategies. Nevertheless, the volatility of returns is (at least as a group) lower than stock market volatilities but considerably higher than most hedge fund strategies. Because these funds may take either long or short positions and carry positions from a broad universe (including many emerging markets), correlation to stock and bond returns is relatively low (20 to 40 percent correlation to stock returns and 20 to 30 percent correla-tion to bond returns). This group has a higher correlation to bond returns than most hedge fund strategies.

Currency   Currency hedge funds may be seen as a particular kind of global macro hedge fund. However, this group invests in currencies strategically and invests in fixed income markets only incidentally or as part of an arbitrage strategy. The group contains arbitrage traders that produce low returns but take little risk. The group also contains funds that take strategic positions in a variety of currencies (not necessarily hedged and generally not part of arbitrage positions). This second group is an example of a "portable alpha strategy." A portable alpha strategy is an investment strategy, possibly part of a traditional, long-only portfolio strategy that has favorable performance and can be recast as a strategy that: (1) is extracted from the traditional portfolio and (2) could be added to any type of portfolio to improve the return on the portfolio. These traders have adapted trading styles from other types of investment vehicles to create a nondirectional investment strategy.

Funds of Funds

Funds of hedge funds invest in other hedge funds. On the surface, this seems redundant and the investor might hesitate to pay fees to a fund of funds manager on top of the fees paid to the managers directly managing the funds.

Funds of hedge funds have several advantages to both large institutional investors and investors with considerably less sophistication and with smaller portfolios. First, the minimum investment is often smaller for a fund of funds than for a hedge fund. Second, the fund of funds invests in many funds, so the investor gets some risk reduction from diversification, especially for investors who have limited resources to invest in hedge fund assets. Third, the fund of funds may negotiate a reduction on fees so an investor may not pay significantly higher fees investing through a fund of funds intermediary. Fourth, the fund of funds manager may have access to information about funds and may perform analysis of funds that improves return or reduces risk. Fifth, the fund of funds manager may be able to invest in funds otherwise closed to new investment because of agreements made to get preferential access to hedge fund capacity.

SUMMARY AND CONCLUSION

It is impossible to classify 8,100 hedge funds into a dozen categories. The strategies or styles described in this chapter include the largest categories.

Each of these styles is tracked by one or more data provider. While these categorizes may be defined somewhat inconsistently, they nevertheless serve as a helpful resource to the fund investor.

The performance of the many styles of hedge funds derives from the inherent characteristics of the assets in the hedge fund portfolios. The performance is also affected by the way the instruments are combined. The resulting returns can be predicted in an important way. It is difficult to forecast the performance of a particular fund or sector next month. It is possible, though, to predict which hedge funds will do well (or poorly) if certain things happen (rising interest rates, changes in corporate borrowing spreads, rising volatility, etc.). Because of this predictability, investors can combine these hedge fund assets with traditional portfolios to improve the risk and return characteristics of their portfolios.

QUESTIONS AND PROBLEMS

2.1   Why do so many organizations provide hedge fund indexes?

2.2   What is a long/short equity hedge fund?

2.3   What is an equity arbitrage hedge fund?

2.4   What is an equity pairs strategy?

2.5   What is an equity market neutral hedge fund?

2.6   What are some of the types of strategies an event driven hedge fund would pursue?

2.7   Describe the nature of a convertible bond investment.

2.8   What kinds of trades would you expect to find in a fixed income arbitrage hedge fund?

2.9   What kinds of securities would you expect to find in an emerging markets hedge fund?

2.10 What is the biggest risk to an investment in a distressed securities hedge fund?

2.11 What kind of fund would call itself a global macro hedge fund?

2.12 What is a fund of funds?

You own a portfolio of common stocks that more or less tracks the stock index in the preceding table. The statistics are historical but you believe they are reasonable forecasts of future returns. Rely on the following table to answer questions 2.13 to 2.17.

Performance of Hedge Fund Styles (Hypothetical)

Fund Style	Return	Standard Deviation	Correlation to Stocks
Convertible arbitrage	8.00%	4.33%	10.00%
Global macro	12.00%	12.99%	25.00%
Long/short equity	10.00%	8.66%	50.00%
Stock index	10.00%	17.32%	100.00%

2.13 What is the expected return on the portfolio if you reallocate 10 percent of the stock portfolio into a convertible arbitrage hedge fund? What is the standard deviation of the portfolio comprising 90 percent stocks and 10 percent convertible bond hedge fund?

2.14 What is the expected return on the portfolio if you reallocate 10 percent of the stock portfolio into a global macro hedge fund? What is the standard deviation of the portfolio comprising 90 percent stocks and 10 percent global macro hedge fund?

2.15 What is the expected return on the portfolio if you reallocate 10 percent of the stock portfolio into a long/short equity hedge fund? What is the standard deviation of the portfolio comprising 90 percent stocks and 10 percent long/short equity hedge fund?

2.16 Based on your results in questions 2.13 to 2.15, which hedge fund should you invest in?

2.17 Suppose you could invest in a hedge fund that would provide an expected return of 8 percent and have volatility of 20 percent with a correlation of 50 percent to stock returns. Should you move some of the stock money into this fund?

2.18 An individual has half of the family net worth tied up in a closely held public business and the balance in a broadly diversified portfolio of common stocks. What special concerns would this investor have in selecting a hedge fund style?

2.19 What advantages does an investor get from investing directly in a portfolio of individual hedge funds rather than investing in a fund of funds?

2.20 Why do so many different hedge fund styles exist?

2.21 Why would an investor put money in a hedge fund that followed a short-only strategy?

2.22 How is it possible to reconcile the low measured risk (at least in terms of the standard deviation of return) of the fixed income arbitrage strategy and the investor perception that this is a risky strategy?

NOTES

1. Data collected by Hedge Fund Research, Grosvnor Capital Management, and Undiscovered Managers, LLC, as presented on the Undiscovered Managers web site in *Alternative Investments and the Semi-affluent Investor*; Chapter 2: "Absolute Return Strategies—Part 1," 2001, page 16.
2. The indexes published by the Center for International Securities and Derivatives Markets (CISDM) include an equity market neutral long/short category.
3. The obvious complication is a bid to buy in cash. If the deal is completed, the fund becomes outright short the acquirer. At least part of the profit in the deal would depend on where the short hedge could be covered. Other combinations include a combination of cash and securities (including common, preferred, and debt) and multistep bids (where a bid is made for a controlling amount of stock with the hope of buying back the minority positions more cheaply).

CHAPTER 3

Types of Hedge Fund Investors

The individuals and institutions that invest in hedge funds are surprisingly different in terms of risk tolerance, investment horizon, investment objectives, and investment restrictions. (See Figure 3.1.) Many of the differences between investors involve the way they are taxed (if they are taxed at all). This chapter includes a discussion of the tax treatment of these investor types. (Hedge funds usually pay little or no tax but must flow through the taxable amounts to investors in many countries, including the United States. For a description of how a partnership calculates the tax consequences of the hedge fund investments, see Chapter 10.)

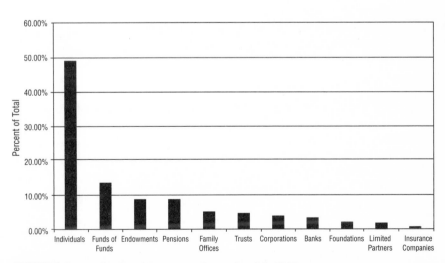

FIGURE 3.1   Hedge Fund Investors, December 31, 1999
Source: Tass Research.

INDIVIDUAL INVESTORS

In the United States, individuals provide more money to hedge funds than does any other group. They were prominent among early hedge fund investors. They have always been an important group to understand for marketing, investment policy, tax reporting, and public policy.

On first impression, one would think that the motives of individual investors should be easy to understand because they should have the same concerns about returns, risk, and taxes. In fact, investors' interests may differ markedly.

Individuals are likely to invest directly in single-manager hedge funds. Other types of investors are much more likely to invest in funds of hedge funds (see Chapter 2 for a description of funds of funds). Recently, however, individuals have begun placing much of their new money into funds of hedge funds.

High-Net-Worth Individuals

Most individuals who invest in hedge funds are affluent and are taxed at high marginal rates. High-net-worth individuals have a disproportionate portion of the investment assets simply because of their high net worth. Federal securities laws also severely restrict middle-income and low-income investors from investing in hedge funds (see Chapter 8), so high-net-worth individuals contribute most of the investment dollars from individuals.

Security regulations define a high-net-worth individual in a variety of ways. An individual who is an "accredited investor" has income of at least $200,000 or assets of $1 million (see Chapter 8 for greater detail about securities regulations related to accredited investors and other topics discussed in this chapter). Other regulations draw the line at $2 million for a "qualified eligible participant" (QEP). Finally, a "qualified purchaser" is an individual investor with a net worth exceeding $5 million.[1]

Regardless of how these break points are defined, the typical investor has a high marginal tax rate. Yet the typical hedge fund produces most of its return as short-term capital gains or ordinary income, both of which are taxed at high marginal tax rates. In contrast, other investments are taxed more favorably. Municipal bonds are not taxed at the federal level and may be exempt from state and local income tax. Other investments, such as common stocks, provide a large part of their return in the form of capital gains that may be taxed at a lower rate for long-term gains. The tax may be postponed indefinitely (if the investment is held indefinitely), or may even escape income taxation if held until death.

Suppose an individual paid individual income tax at the 37 percent rate for ordinary income and short-term gains and paid 18 percent on long-term gains.[2] Suppose further that capital gains can be postponed on stock investments for five years. The after-tax return on the stock portfolio, assuming a pretax annual return of 10 percent and a short-term discount rate of 5 percent, is given by equation (3.1).

Long-term stock return in constant dollars:

$$\text{After-Tax Net Return} = 10\% - \frac{10\% \times 18\%}{[1 + 5\% \times (1 - 37\%)]^5} = 8.4586\% \quad (3.1)$$

To do as well in a hedge fund investment, the after-tax net return should be at least as high. The break-even return on a hedge fund whose results are taxed at the 37 percent ordinary rate and where there is no deferral of tax liability is shown in equation (3.2) to be 13.4263 percent.

Short-term hedge fund return:

$$8.825\% = r\% - (r\% \times 37\%) \quad (3.2)$$

(Ignoring any possible delay in paying current tax liability)

$$r\% = 13.4263\%$$

In other words, in this scenario, a high-net-worth individual must earn 34 percent higher pretax return than stocks to do as well after taxes.

High-net-worth individuals may invest in hedge funds because they expect a sufficiently higher return to accept the tax disadvantage of the investment vehicle. These individuals may believe that hedge fund returns are less volatile than stock returns to justify the tax-disadvantaged investment. Finally, the hedge fund may provide a low correlation of return to other assets in the portfolio so a small investment in hedge funds (say 10 percent to 20 percent) may lower the volatility of the portfolio enough to justify making a hedge fund investment.

The answer to question 2.13 in Chapter 2 presents a formula for the average return on a portfolio. That formula with an extension account for taxes is shown in equation (3.3). Assume that the pretax expected return is 10 percent for both a traditional stock position and a hedge fund. Assume also that the investor pays ordinary income tax at 37 percent and long-term capital gains are taxed at 18 percent. Suppose that 100 percent of the stock return is taxable as long-term capital gain and 100 percent of the hedge fund return is taxed as ordinary income. For simplicity, assume that the stock strategy does not defer the taxable gain at all. Equation (3.3) shows the after-tax return for an individual with a stock portfolio comprising 90 percent of the investment assets and a hedge fund with the remaining 10 percent of the assets.

$$
\begin{aligned}
r_{\text{Portfolio}} &= w_A \times r_A \times (1 - T_A) + w_B \times r_B (1 - T_B) \\
&= 90\% \times 10\% \times (1 - 18\%) + 10\% \times 10\% \times (1 - 37\%) \\
&= 90\% \times 8.20\% + 10\% \times 6.30\% \\
&= 8.01\%
\end{aligned}
\tag{3.3}
$$

where w_A = Portfolio weight in stock assets = 90%
w_B = Portfolio weight in hedge fund assets = 10%
r_A = Expected return on stock portfolio = 8.20% after-tax
r_B = Expected return on hedge fund = 6.30% after-tax
$r_{\text{Portfolio}}$ = Expected return on portfolio of stock and hedge fund
T_A = Tax rates for long-term capital gains (applies to stock portfolio)
T_B = Tax rates for ordinary income and short-term gains (applies to hedge fund)

In this scenario, the hedge fund return lowers the aggregate after-tax return because the higher tax rate on the hedge fund's pretax return lowers the after-tax return below the stock after-tax return.

Assume that the stocks and the hedge fund in the preceding example have standard deviation of return (also called volatility) of 20 percent annualized. However, the returns have a correlation of only 25 percent. Relying on the formula for portfolio volatility presented in answer 2.13, the standard deviation of return on the portfolio is given by equation (3.4):

$$
\begin{aligned}
\sigma_{\text{Portfolio}} &= \sqrt{w_A^2 \sigma_A^2 + 2w_A w_B \sigma_{A,B} + w_B^2 \sigma_B^2} \\
&= \sqrt{w_A^2 \sigma_A^2 + 2w_A w_B \sigma_A \sigma_B \rho_{A,B} + w_B^2 \sigma_B^2} \\
&= \sqrt{90\%^2 \times 20\%^2 \times 90\% \times 10\% \times 20\% \times 20\% \times 25\% + 10\%^2 \times 20\%^2} \\
&= 18.60\%
\end{aligned}
\tag{3.4}
$$

where σ_A = Standard deviation on stock portfolio = 20%
σ_B = Standard deviation on hedge fund = 20%
$\rho_{A,B}$ = Correlation between the stock portfolio and the hedge fund

The hedge fund provides a lower after-tax return but also a lower level of volatility in the combined portfolio. Clearly, if the individual investor can locate a hedge fund with returns higher than the investment alternatives, this comparison looks more favorable still.

It is also clear that individual investors would prefer hedge funds that: (1) have higher expected return; (2) have lower volatility; and (3) have lower correlation to assets already in the portfolio. Similarly, if a hedge fund could deliver some portion of its return as long-term capital gain, it could create higher after-tax portfolio returns than hedge funds that provide a return taxed as ordinary income.

Semiaffluent Investors

There is currently much attention directed at those investors who marginally qualify to invest in private hedge funds or would not qualify to invest in a hedge fund sold as a private placement but could invest if the fund was registered (see Chapter 7). This group is sometimes called semiaffluent or nearly affluent.

Writers define this group differently. Some categorize individuals with a net worth of between $1 million and $10 million as semiaffluent.[3] Others include investors with between $500,000 and $1 million in this group.[4] J. P. Morgan also includes investors above $1 million in a group called semiaffluent.[5] Regardless of how this group is defined, it includes investors who historically have not had access to hedge funds. Due to changing attitudes, changes in the risk profile of the hedge funds, and new legal developments (notably the registered fund of fund), this group represents a large, almost untapped market.

The appeal of marketing to this group of investors is: (1) it constitutes many investors; (2) despite the more limited resources of individual investors, it constitutes a large potential pool of funds (by one account, semiaffluent investors control between $6 trillion and $8 trillion in assets[6]); and (3) this group has invested little in hedge funds to date.

The semiaffluent investors want to invest in hedge funds for the same reasons that high-net-worth investors invest in hedge funds. Because many hedge funds are less volatile than a broadly diversified portfolio of common stocks, these investors may invest in hedge funds to lower the risk of their portfolios. With similar objectives, these investors may seek to lower the volatility of their investment portfolios by diversifying into hedge funds with low correlation to stock and bond returns. Finally, some semiaffluent investors seek out hedge funds to increase the return on their investment assets.

As with any group, there are great differences between individuals who could be considered semiaffluent. At the risk of ignoring these differences, it is still possible to distinguish this group from the high-net-worth investors in hedge funds. First, the semiaffluent investors are less likely to have ready access to professional investment and legal advice. Second, the semiaffluent investors are less likely to feel comfortable investing in high-risk/high-reward strategies. Third, the semiaffluent investors are more likely to invest in hedge funds indirectly, by investing in funds of hedge funds that permit smaller minimum investments than single-manager hedge fund minimum investments. Sometimes these funds of funds have been registered and accept investments as low as $25,000.

Considering the many benefits hedge funds offer to investors, it is reasonable to encourage the semiaffluent investors to move into hedge funds. Securities law and practices often prevent hedge funds from accepting investments from this group. The Securities and Exchange Commission and the Commodity Futures Trading Commission appear to be interested in improving access to hedge funds by the semiaffluent.

Individual Retirement Plans, Including IRA, 401(k), Keogh

Individuals may invest money held in retirement accounts in hedge funds. The owner of the retirement account must meet the same net worth and income requirements that investors who invest in hedge funds outside a retirement account must match. The retirement account does not need to be large enough to satisfy the net worth requirements for accredited investor, qualified eligible participant, or qualified purchaser (see Chapter 8) as long as the assets of the individual (both in and out of retirement accounts) are sufficient.

The mechanisms for investing in hedge funds differ slightly, depending on the type of retirement plan in question. For example, individual retirement account (IRA) money must be held in a self-directed account (basically a brokerage account designed for IRA investing) and must find an institution willing to act as trustee for the account. A corporation administering a 401(k) plan may make a hedge fund option available to plan participants. In each of these cases, the individual makes the decision to invest in a hedge fund.

Hedge funds produce a large portion of return in the form of ordinary income. Most hedge fund investors pay high marginal tax rates because private placement laws severely limit access to hedge funds unless the investor has both a high income and substantial assets (see Chapter 8 for a more complete discussion of the income and asset requirements typically imposed on hedge fund investors).

TABLE 3.1   Benefit of Postponing Tax Payments on Hedge Fund Returns

Year	Non-IRA	IRA	Tax If Withdrawn	Net Balance
1	$66.97	$110.00	$40.70	$ 69.30
2	$71.19	$121.00	$44.77	$ 76.23
3	$75.67	$133.10	$49.25	$ 83.85
4	$80.44	$146.41	$54.17	$ 92.24
5	$85.51	$161.05	$59.59	$101.46

Table 3.1 shows the benefit of postponing tax payments on hedge fund returns. If a taxpayer pays 37 percent marginal income tax, a $100 return would require a tax payment of $37 in the current tax year. In the table, the after-tax income is reinvested in the hedge fund, earning 10 percent but paying tax at 37 percent each year. The income with the reinvested return grows to $85.51 over five years after all taxes have been paid.

Alternatively, suppose that the tax on the $100 of income is postponed one or more years because it resides in a tax-deferred account, such as an IRA. The table shows the value of $100 of taxable income growing annually at 10 percent, as previously. If the money is withdrawn after one year,[7] the investor must pay $40.70 in income tax (37 percent of $110) but would have $69.30 available after paying income taxes. The value of the deferral rises each year, so that by the fifth year, the $100 of taxable income could represent $101.46 in funds to the hedge fund investor if reinvested in an IRA but only $85.51 without the benefit of deferral. The value of deferral on this $100 of hedge fund income continues to rise each year the investment is held in a tax-deferred retirement account. In addition, the hedge fund produces additional income each year that also benefits from this deferral.

Traditional IRA   The traditional or contributory IRA is the best known of a growing list of tax-deferred retirement savings accounts. Contributions to the fund are subtracted from taxable income. For example, suppose an investor made a $3,000 contribution to an IRA in 2003 (the maximum permitted for taxpayers with income of $95,000 or less—the permitted investment scales down to $0 for incomes above $110,000). If the investor pays a 28 percent tax (the marginal tax rate for a single taxpayer in 2003 for incomes between $68,800 and $143,500[8]), the tax liability is lower by $1,050 ($3,000 × 35) so the net cash flow is $1,950 to establish a $3,000 balance in the IRA. Any money (either the original principal or return on the investment) withdrawn from the IRA is taxed as ordinary income.

However, the taxpayer can defer the withdrawal for years or even decades. The deferral means that both the principal and taxes on the investment return can remain invested to earn additional return for the taxpayer.

If an investor made annual investments in a traditional IRA every year and the IRA earned a high rate of return, the IRA balance could grow to a size large enough to match a hedge fund minimum. For example, if an investor saved $1,500 in 1979, rising to $3,000 in 2003 (at the beginning of each year) and the IRA earned the same return as the Standard & Poor's 500 index, the IRA would be worth about $250,000 at the beginning of 2004. This would constitute a small hedge fund investment, but many hedge funds accept smaller IRA contributions from individuals.

Several other provisions conspire to limit the number of investors with $250,000 in an IRA. First, the investor must have had taxable income in each of the prior 25 years to be eligible to make contributions. Second, although the IRA laws changed, in most years the hedge fund investor could make no pretax contributions when taxable income exceeded a threshold ($110,000 in 2003 as noted earlier) or if the investor was eligible to participate in a company pension plan. Finally, unless the IRA was invested in a portfolio earning high returns, the IRA would remain small.

Rollover IRA   A rollover IRA is an IRA that has been funded by transfer from another kind of retirement account. Most rollover IRA accounts are created when an employee leaves a company with a 401(k) plan (discussed shortly) and rolls the assets into this type of IRA. Other retirement plans, such as the simplified employee pension (SEP-IRA), may also be rolled into a rollover IRA. Contribution limits are considerably higher for these retirement plans, so rollover IRAs may be substantially larger than traditional IRA plans.

Keogh Plan   A Keogh plan is a self-directed retirement plan for employees of small businesses. The plan closely resembles a traditional IRA. Contribution limits are higher than the allowable contributions to an IRA (up to 25 percent of income with a dollar maximum of $30,000). Due to the higher contribution limits and because Keogh plans have been permitted for many years, investors are more likely to have sizable balances in Keogh plans than in traditional IRAs.

Simplified Employee Pension (SEP-IRA)   A SEP-IRA is another self-directed retirement plan primarily for self-employed workers. Like the Keogh plan, investors can contribute up to 25 percent of income (including salary and bonus) up to $40,000. However, to be eligible to make a contribution to a

SEP-IRA in a particular year, income must be less than $200,000. Because of the higher contribution limits (more than 10 times larger than the maximum IRA contribution), SEP-IRA plans are more likely to have sizable balances than traditional IRAs even though SEP-IRAs were created more recently, in 1998.

401(k) Plans A 401(k) plan is a voluntary defined contribution plan. Workers set aside part of their salaries to invest in a tax-deferred fund. Often, employers match or partially match contributions to employee 401(k) plans. Contributions are limited to 12.5 percent of income, capped at $12,000. Because 401(k) plans have been in existence for many years and have become very common, many workers have 401(k) balances that are high enough to invest in hedge funds, especially if the participating hedge fund or funds reduces the required minimum investment.

A small number of companies have begun to offer hedge fund alternatives in their 401(k) plans. Goldman Sachs and Mesirow Financial (two broker-dealers that are actively involved in the hedge fund business) offer one or more hedge fund choices in their company plans. CS First Boston allowed employees to invest in the Campbell Fund (probably more accurately described as a commodity pool) and enjoy hedge fund type returns beginning 25 years ago.

Roth IRA The Roth IRA differs significantly from the plans described earlier. Contributions to a Roth IRA do not reduce taxable income, so the Roth IRA does not enjoy the benefit of investment return on a deferred tax liability on earned income. However, investors pay no tax on either principal or investment return withdrawn from a Roth IRA. Because hedge fund returns are mostly taxed as ordinary income, it makes sense to place hedge fund assets in a Roth IRA and to hold common stocks in an ordinary investment account, to get the benefit of reduced tax rates and deferred tax liability on long-term capital gains on the stock.

Several provisions limit the ability of hedge fund investors to accumulate significant assets in a Roth IRA. First, income tests prevent high-income individuals from funding Roth IRAs. Second, similar limits restrict investors from rolling traditional IRA assets into a Roth IRA. Finally, even when an IRA or a rollover IRA can be rolled into a Roth IRA, such a rollover requires the investor to report the rolled amount as taxable income. The acceleration of tax liability on a rollover reduces the value of the tax savings compared to a traditional or rollover IRA.

Educational Savings Plans Both the so-called 529 plans and Coverdell Educational Savings Accounts (ESAs) are tax-advantaged saving plans, offering tax deferral and, in many cases, the chance to avoid tax on investment returns. Like the Roth IRA, these plans would significantly improve the return hedge fund investors keep by deferring and hopefully avoiding the tax on ordinary income that dominates hedge fund returns. Unfortunately, phaseout provisions limit the ability of high-net-worth investors to fund these plans. Perhaps as the hedge fund marketplace becomes more efficient in investing smaller amounts from the semiaffluent population, investors will begin to invest educational savings accounts in hedge funds.

Retirement Savings Plans (RSPs) Canadian employees have a self-directed retirement plan much like the traditional IRA in the United States. Two provisions have slowed the movement into hedge funds. First, no more than 20 percent of a fund may be invested in foreign assets. Unfortunately, Canadians have access to more U.S. or offshore hedge funds than Canadian hedge funds. Second, RSPs are severely restricted in their ability to invest in private (unregistered) investments. Although this would appear to make hedge fund investing impossible in RSP accounts, hedge funds are beginning to take money from RSP accounts. First a Canadian vehicle is created (for example, a fund of funds) to make the investments in Canadian and offshore funds. Second, the fund sponsors register the fund.

Restrictions on Retirement Fund Investing

First, as mentioned earlier, the owner of the IRA must be eligible to invest in the hedge fund. Second, the owner of the retirement assets must find a way to effect the investment. For example, an IRA investor must find a trustee willing to let the owner make a hedge fund investment and must have the balance in a self-directed account. A 401(k) investor must work for a company that is willing to add one or more hedge funds to the list of eligible assets.

Third, the investor must cope with a hedge fund industry that is hesitant about taking retirement money into their funds. IRA accounts, Keogh funds, and other self-directed retirement plans are all considered benefit plan investors under the Employee Retirement Income Security Act of 1974 (ERISA; see Chapter 8). Hedge funds almost universally limit plan assets to less than 25 percent of the fund to avoid being regulated as a pension fund. Some funds of funds have recently started turning down investments from retirement accounts, including the self-directed plans described here.

Nonaccredited Investors

Hedge funds sold under the private placement rules in the United States may admit up to 35 nonaccredited investors in addition to an unlimited number of employees, although having nonaccredited investors puts additional restrictions on the fund. These investors may not have sufficient income or net worth to be accredited but should be knowledgeable investors. Because of the potential for litigation if the fund loses money, often hedge funds accept no investments from nonaccredited investors.

Nonaccredited investors can be valuable to a hedge fund start-up because the additional investors demonstrate confidence in the manager. Even small investments might be helpful to hedge funds starting with limited assets under management. However, a large fund would get little benefit from a small increase in assets under management. The administrative burdens of carrying small investors may be unprofitable. Also, if a fund is nearing the maximum number of permitted investors (either 99 or 500 for U.S. unregistered funds), it may be better to turn away potential new investors unless they can invest substantial sums.

Nonaccredited investors get the same benefits from hedge fund ownership as do other types of investors. The nonaccredited investor may be seeking higher returns, lower risk, or lower correlation to other assets. Likewise, the management company may get benefits from having employees carry an investment in the fund they manage to motivate good behaviors.

FAMILY OFFICES

A family office is a group of investors who hire investment advisers, tax and accounting advisers, estate planners, and legal advisers. Family offices have existed for over a century to handle the affairs of the children or grandchildren of very wealthy individuals. Family offices may have additional responsibilities to oversee closely held assets and provide for succession of control. Family offices typically are formed to serve related individuals, but a family office may be created for any group of individuals having certain common interests.

Although the members of this investment group may form a business unit to hire a staff and provide office space, the investment funds are generally not commingled into this business or any other. Often, however, the investors own many of the same assets, including a family business, limited partnerships, and investment positions in public company shares.

Family office investment offices may act as the gatekeeper for the investment assets that might be invested in hedge funds. The investors who make up a family office are generally high-net-worth individuals and, by virtue of the expert advice provided by the office employees, are sophisticated investors.

It would be wrong to assume that all the investors in the office are ideal candidates to make hedge fund investments. The office may assist investors of two or even three generations. Various factions have more or less wealth, differing risk tolerance, and different tax sensitivities. However, it is the responsibility of the family office employees to deal with these differences. To the hedge fund, the family office represents a particularly sophisticated high-net-worth individual. However, getting an investment from the family office may mean getting separate, sizable investments from several family members.

Although family offices may invest in any kind of hedge fund, the advisers often place less priority on very high returns and more priority in balancing the expected returns against the risks assumed by investing. Similarly, the advisers generally favor strategies with low correlation to traditional investments. Family office advisers may invest indirectly in hedge funds by investing in a fund of funds to take advantage of the specialized hedge fund knowledge that may exist in those funds. Alternatively, the family office may invest in two or more funds to diversify the hedge fund returns. Finally, the advisers may blend the hedge fund into portfolios that aren't well-diversified as when family members own large positions in closely held firms. They are more concerned with the risk and return of the portfolio including the hedge fund and less concerned with the performance of the hedge fund as a stand-alone investment.

FOUNDATIONS AND HEDGE FUNDS

Foundations are generally managed to escape income tax on investment returns. Because they aren't penalized by high tax rates on ordinary income and short-term capital gains, they have been early investors in hedge funds.

What is a Foundation?

A foundation is a pool of money and a group of employees to invest that money and to distribute part of the pool to activities and organizations consistent with a set of objectives. The money donated to the foundation is treated as a charitable donation for income tax purposes. Subject to some exceptions, the investment return of the foundation is exempt from federal income taxation.

Foundations are often established to maintain voting control of a closely held company. A foundation may play a role in corporate governance. The foundation may also control management succession, particularly when a family, together with the foundation, controls a voting block of stock in a publicly traded company.

According to federal tax law, at least 5 percent of the foundation must be distributed each year to retain the tax-free status of the foundation. Although the investment returns of a foundation are not taxed, a foundation would be taxed on the returns of a business if it operates a business. The returns on such a business are unrelated taxable income. Unfortunately, income from highly leveraged hedge funds may be classified as unrelated taxable income if the fund borrows money and distributes significant interest expenses to the foundation. See Chapter 10.

Foundations may invest in offshore hedge funds organized as corporations. As described in Chapter 5, hedge funds domiciled in low- or no-tax areas are usually organized as corporations. These offshore corporate funds are not flow-through tax entities, so a foundation would not be allocated interest expense from a hedge fund.

Why Foundations Invest in Hedge Funds

Foundations invest in hedge funds for many of the same reasons that other types of investors incorporate hedge funds into their portfolios. A foundation that earns high returns can increase the funding of projects consistent with its objectives. Because of the 5 percent distribution requirement, a foundation needs to earn a substantial real return to preserve the size of the foundation relative to inflation.

A foundation may also invest in hedge funds to get the benefit of lower risk, either by incorporating hedge funds with low volatility of returns or by investing in hedge funds with low correlation to other assets in the foundation portfolio. All investors like to lower the risk in their portfolios if this is possible with little reduction in expected return. Foundations may be particularly sensitive to the effects of a short-term loss in a portfolio because the combination of the loss and the commitments the foundation has made to make distributions may shrink the size of the foundation and limit its ability to achieve its objectives in future years.

Foundations as Hedge Fund Investors

A foundation usually seeks to pursue long-term objectives. Perhaps as a consequence, foundations take a fairly long-term perspective on investment decisions. Foundations are not greatly bothered by lockup provisions, especially if the funds can justify a reason for a lockup period, based on the underlying assets held by the funds.

Because of the threat of unrelated business income tax (UBIT), foundations tend to avoid investing in highly leveraged hedge funds. As a result, foundations are less likely to invest in convertible bond strategies and fixed income arbitrage strategies, which can have leverage of 6:1 up to 40:1, unless the hedge fund is located offshore and organized as a corporation so that the foundation is not allocated significant interest expenses.

Foundations often invest in hedge funds by hiring consultants to aid in determining a portfolio strategy, suggest individual funds within a strategy, and perform due diligence analysis of alternatives. Foundations may also invest in funds of hedge funds and rely on the fund of funds manager for asset allocation, due diligence, and so on.

ENDOWMENTS AND HEDGE FUNDS

Endowments also consist of pools of funds used to support certain projects or satisfy objectives. However, an endowment is usually affiliated with a particular philanthropic organization and the endowment is created to fund a portion of the expenses in that organization.

Why Endowments Invest in Hedge Funds

Many endowments have been long-term investors in alternative assets, including real estate, venture capital, and hedge funds. Endowments may be motivated by higher returns, lower risk, or low correlations, much like other investors. The endowments of Harvard University and Yale University along with other prominent university endowments have earned spectacular returns from these alternative assets. Other endowments may feel a degree of peer pressure to include some alternative assets in their portfolios.

Endowments as Hedge Fund Investors

Endowments behave much like foundations in the way they regard hedge fund investments. Endowments usually make longer and firmer funding commitments than foundations make so are somewhat risk-averse on their investments. Endowments have had good luck using hedge funds to diversify the returns on their portfolios, so their commitment to hedge funds remains stronger than ever.

CORPORATIONS AND HEDGE FUND INVESTMENTS

Corporations (including U.S. companies and foreign businesses) invest in hedge funds for a variety of reasons. For example, some corporations invest in hedge funds with low-volatility, nondirectional strategies to improve the return on cash balances that aren't required for the company's cash management needs. Other corporations invest in hedge funds to increase the company return on assets or to reduce the company's sensitivity to volatile operating results.

Corporations pay corporate income tax on hedge fund returns. When these returns are eventually distributed to shareholders as dividends, shareholders pay ordinary income tax on the same returns. It would seem to make more sense for such cash-rich companies to distribute cash to shareholders, who could decide to invest the cash in hedge funds or other financial assets or reinvest the dividends back in the company by buying more shares. The situation is complicated because any distribution to shareholders would likely be taxed as a dividend, so shareholders would have less money after-tax to invest in hedge funds than if the company made the investment in lieu of a dividend. In addition, not all shareholders could qualify to invest in hedge funds or come up with the minimum investment amount.

PENSION FUND AS HEDGE FUND INVESTORS

Pension funds or retirement funds include a wide variety of structures created by Congress to encourage U.S. taxpayers to save for retirement. As mentioned earlier, ERISA (see Chapter 8) governs IRAs, 401(k) plans, Keoghs, plus defined benefit plans and defined contribution plans. The individually directed plans are discussed earlier in this chapter along with other types of individual investments in hedge funds. This section discusses traditional company-sponsored pension plans.

A defined contribution plan is a pension plan where the employer or employee makes contributions to the pension accounts of eligible workers. Workers may have some input as to how the pension balance is invested. More importantly, the worker bears all of the investment risk, enjoying a growing account balance when returns are good and suffering losses when performance is bad. Importantly, the employer makes no commitment to that worker that the pension benefit will be of any particular amount.

Like the IRA and Keogh plan, it makes sense for highly taxed workers who can qualify based on their incomes, net worth, and investment knowledge to invest their defined contribution balances in hedge funds. These investments would benefit from the tax deferral on the investment returns of the hedge funds. However, individuals can elect to invest in hedge funds only if the plan sponsor (usually the employer) offers that as an option. Yet most group defined contribution plans have been replaced by individually directed 401(k) plans, so company defined contribution plans are not a source of funding for hedge funds.

In a defined benefit plan, an employer makes a commitment to fund a retirement benefit at a particular level. It is typical to guarantee some percent of salary upon retirement (often with several strings attached). The company funds the plan but also bears the risk of shortfall if the contributions and investment returns fall short of providing for the promised benefits. Similarly, if the pension returns are high, the company can reduce its own contributions to the plan. Because the corporation bears all the investment risk, it is not important that many of the plan beneficiaries would not qualify to invest in hedge funds.

Pension funds have been slow to invest in hedge funds. Lately, their allocation to hedge funds has accelerated. Pension assets allocated to hedge funds have more than doubled in two years, from $30 billion in 2001 to $70 billion in 2003.[9] With trillions of dollars under management, pension funds have the potential to be sizable hedge fund investors. As discussed in Chapter 8, hedge funds are not prepared to accept large increases in funds from pensions for fear of falling under the regulations of ERISA.

Pension funds have traditionally been cost-conscious investors. The size of fees often determines the relative performance of traditional fund managers. That is, the managers that charge the lowest fees often generate the highest net return. Not surprisingly, pension funds, which have been able to negotiate low management fees for traditional portfolio management, were initially reluctant to pay the higher management and incentive fees charged by hedge funds.

Pension fund investors have also been risk-averse investors. In moving assets into hedge funds, pension fund trustees have relied on consultants to aid in selecting and monitoring hedge fund investments. Pension funds are also likely to invest in funds of hedge funds, to get the benefits of both the diversification in a fund of funds and the expertise in reviewing and monitoring hedge fund investments. Pension funds have discovered that in the world of hedge funds, the managers that produce the best returns often charge higher fees, but the net performance on these funds is still higher than hedge funds with lower gross returns.

Like other tax-exempt hedge fund investors, pension funds may be charged UBIT on hedge fund returns if interest expenses are high. As a result, pension funds generally avoid investing in hedge funds that have high leverage. They also are reluctant to invest in most arbitrage strategies, even though the risk/reward characteristics of these strategies would appeal to the trustees.

INSURANCE COMPANIES AS HEDGE FUND INVESTORS

Insurance companies in the major financial centers of the world control large amounts of financial assets but they are not large investors in hedge funds. Insurance companies themselves have two sources of funds that might be invested in hedge funds. First, insurance companies have capital, much like any other kind of business. This capital is generally called surplus. The second source of investment dollars is the deferred amounts set aside to pay future claims, called reserves. The payments are delayed for a variety of reasons. In many cases, the amount payable will be determined by a lawsuit that has not yet worked through the judicial system. Insurance companies invest the money set aside to pay claims and use the investment returns to help pay the settlement amount.

All of these balances could arguably be invested in hedge funds. Insurance companies can invest a limited amount of their funds in common stocks, real estate, and other potentially risky assets. With the average hedge fund less risky than the S&P 500, an insurance company could find hedge funds that would fit well into an insurance company portfolio. In practice, these portfolios are invested almost entirely in bonds, with small allocations to stocks and very little in alternative assets. Insurance regulations reinforce this bias toward traditional assets.

Insurance products offer significant tax advantages that could be combined with hedge funds, whose returns are generally taxed immediately at the maximum individual income tax rate. Whole-life insurance policies allow the cash value to grow free from income tax and can be structured to avoid estate tax. Deferred annuities can also allow investment balances to grow without being taxed until the return is distributed years later. These insurance products are expanding the range of allowable investments to include hedge funds, extending their favorable tax treatment to hedge fund returns.

One new development that is being used to fund tax-favored hedge fund investments involves reinsurance.[10] Investors buy shares in a reinsurance company in a location with low corporate income taxes. Most reinsurance companies involved in hedge funds have been located in Bermuda, which has no corporate income tax.

It is important that the reinsurance company is located outside the United States and other locations with corporate income taxes to avoid the double taxation of the investment returns. It is important, also, that the business is an insurance company, because they alone are exempted from special provisions designed to prevent U.S. taxpayers from placing investments in an offshore company to avoid or postpone recognizing income. It is, therefore, important that the reinsurance company actually operates as an insurance company to receive this special treatment.

The business is diagrammed in Figure 3.2. Investors deposit cash as equity investments in the company. The company receives insurance premiums in return for sharing liability on insurance contracts. The reinsurance company holds the premiums until a claim or claims are made. Typically, the reinsurance company pays out all of the premium income or more but keeps the investment returns on the money while it held the reserves.

The reserves plus much of the reinsurance company surplus are invested in hedge funds. The returns on the hedge funds accumulate tax-free. The underwriting profits (premiums minus payouts) or losses (payouts minus premiums) accumulate along with the hedge fund returns. The reinsurance investors expect that when they sell their shares, the investment returns and the underwriting gains or losses will be taxed as long-term capital gains.

The reinsurance companies that invest in hedge funds have generally been closely associated with particular hedge fund managers. MaxRe recently held 40 percent of its investment portfolio in Louis Bacon's Moore Holdings. Stockton Reinsurance invests in affiliated Commodity Corporation (owned by Goldman Sachs). Hampton Re (organized by J. P. Morgan) invests in J. P. Morgan products. Hirch Re invests in the Hirch funds. Asset Alliance Re invests in Asset Alliance hedge funds. These hedge fund

1. Invest in Reinsurance Company

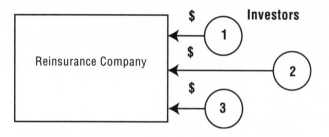

2. Take in Premiums and Invest in Hedge Funds

3. Pay Out Insurance Losses

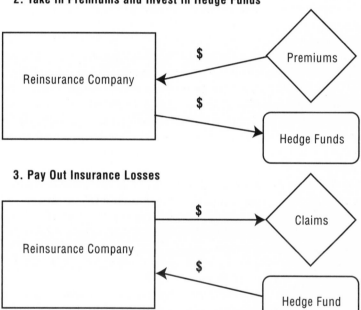

4. Redeem Leveraged Return as Capital Gains

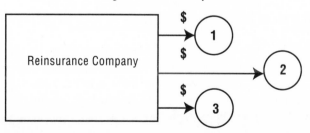

FIGURE 3.2   Investing in Hedge Fund via Reinsurance Company

managers see reinsurance as a way of gathering assets and holding on to them longer.

FUNDS OF HEDGE FUNDS

Funds of funds take money from investors, invest the funds, and charge a management and incentive fee on the gross returns. What distinguishes a fund of funds from other hedge funds is the fact that the assets held by the manager are primarily other hedge funds (which also charge a management and incentive fee).

Investors may invest in funds of funds for a variety of reasons. Fund of funds managers have considerable knowledge about hedge fund strategies and may be able to identify attractive trends. Most fund of funds managers conduct extensive due diligence research before investing in any hedge fund and may be able to reduce the chance of losing money to fraud. Funds of funds may have lower minimums and shorter lockup periods than the funds they own. Funds of funds usually invest in many hedge funds to get the risk-reducing benefit of diversification. Finally, funds of funds may have investments in hedge fund managers that are closed to new investment.

Fund of funds investors generally don't invest in new hedge funds, but many fund of funds managers seek out funds with two to five years of performance. Many larger funds of funds will not invest in small funds because they want to limit the number of funds they retain in their portfolio.

Although funds of funds create portfolios reflecting the biases and preferences of the managers, funds of funds as a group tend to follow investment trends. They tend to invest in strategies that are in favor with investors (which changes over time). They tend to underweight strategies that have recently done poorly relative to other hedge fund strategies.

CONSULTANTS AND HEDGE FUND INVESTING

Many new hedge fund investors hire consultants to assist in the decision-making processes. Although the consultants do not invest their own money in hedge funds, they can influence on how moneys are invested.

Large institutional investors are more likely to hire consultants to review their hedge fund investments. Pension funds, endowments, and foundations are more likely to employ consultants than other types of hedge fund investors.

Consultants are more sophisticated than the typical hedge fund investor. Consultants are generally not impressed with high-risk/high-reward strategies. In general, they focus on funds that deliver consistent, high returns relative to the amount of risk involved with the strategy.

CONCLUSIONS

There are many different types of hedge fund investors with different motives and risk preferences. These investors have portfolios that respond differently to market forces. Fortunately, there are many different kinds of hedge funds. Both the investors and the hedge fund managers are best served when the investors find the hedge fund that best suits their investing needs.

QUESTIONS AND PROBLEMS

3.1 Why do individual investors put money in hedge funds, which expose the returns to ordinary income tax rates (up to 35 percent), much higher than the long-term capital gain rate of 15 percent?

3.2 Explain why a non-U.S. investor in an offshore hedge fund (perhaps run by a U.S. manager) should not be liable for U.S. taxes.

3.3 If an offshore fund is located in a country that has little or no tax on the return of a hedge fund, does the investor enjoy tax-free returns?

3.4 Why would an offshore investor put money in a fund managed by a U.S. manager?

3.5 Why would endowments and foundations invest in hedge funds that are viewed as speculative by many?

3.6 Would it be more prudent for a defined benefit pension plan or a defined contribution pension plan to invest in hedge funds?

3.7 What are some reasons why it might be undesirable for corporations to invest in hedge funds?

3.8 Why do funds of hedge funds exist, considering the additional fees that this nested structure creates?

3.9 Suppose a fund of funds invests equally in four hedge funds. The returns for three months are listed for the individual funds. Each return is before management fees and incentive fees. Assume for simplicity that each hedge fund charges an annual management fee of 2 percent and an incentive fee equal to 20 percent of returns (after management fees have been deducted). Also, assume that the fund of funds charges a management fee of 0.5 percent annually and an incentive fee of 10 percent of return (after individual fund fees and fund of funds management fee).

Fund A	Fund B	Fund C	Fund D
1.00%	6.25%	−2.25%	3.12%
2.50%	−4.24%	6.15%	2.40%
3.45%	2.25%	−3.22%	1.65%

What is the average return on the fund of funds?

3.10 If an institutional investor replicated the four strategies, but implemented the strategies in-house and paid no management or incentive fees, from question 3.9, what would be the net return on the assets committed to the four hedge funds?

3.11 Assume that a single hedge fund manager created and ran the four strategies in questions 3.9 and 3.10 and charged a management fee of 2 percent and incentive fee of 20 percent. If the manager had decided to combine the strategies into a single hedge fund, what would be the performance on that fund?

3.12 Explain the differences in the average return between the three scenarios.

NOTES

1. These securities regulations also include definitions thresholds for institutional investors not described here.
2. For simplicity, ignore the additional rate reduction for gains on assets held longer than five years that recently complicated the tax code.
3. For example, Mark Hurley at Undiscovered Managers, quoted in "1999 CFP Master's Retreat in Squaw Valley, California," *Journal of Financial Planning*, January 2000 (www.fpanet.org/journal/articles/2000_Issues/jfp 0100-art3.cfm).
4. Rob Hegarty, from the TowerGroup, quoted by Jim Middlemiss, "Number of Wealthy on Rise," *Registered Representative* (online magazine), May 29, 2001 (http://registeredrep.com/ar/finance_number_wealthy_rise/index.htm).

5. Evan Simonoff, "Future Now," *Financial Advisor*, July–August 2000 (www.fa-mag.com/articles/jul_aug_2000_futurenow.html).
6. The Gallagher Group (www.thegallaghergroup.net/html/wealth-facts.html).
7. Penalties may apply for certain investors who withdraw the income after one year or any time before the hedge fund investor is 59.5 years old. Several other complications also can arise. This table represents a progress report for the investor who wants to defer the income as long as possible.
8. 2003 Tax Rate Schedules—Schedule X (www.irs.gov/pub/irs-pdf/i1040tt.pdf).
9. Based on a survey of pension assets conducted by Greenwich Associates. See Jeremy Smerd, "Survey: Pensions Increase Allocations to HF, But for How Long?," *Hedgefund.net*, March 23, 2004 (www.hedgefund.net).
10. Hal Lux, "The Great Reinsurance Hedge Fund Tax Game," *Euromoney*, April 1, 2001 (www.iimagazine.com/channel/insurance/20010412000967.htm).

CHAPTER 4

Hedge Fund
Investment Techniques

Despite the mystery surrounding hedge funds, they employ investment techniques that are also used in traditional portfolio management, in broker-dealers, or in commodity pools. In fact, many hedge fund managers gained their expertise working in broker-dealers, mutual funds, or futures funds. Therefore, the description of hedge fund techniques that follows includes discussion of methods that are not unique to hedge funds.

Hedge funds differ from other types of trading entities in many ways, though, and, not surprisingly, have adapted techniques to their unique needs. For example, a hedge fund can use leverage and has very few restrictions on applying risk management techniques. Hedge funds are able to take either long or short positions in securities. Hedge funds face few restraints on the size of positions, characteristics of those positions, or issues of investment style or strategy. Finally, hedge funds are free to apply a wide range of techniques to create investment portfolios.

COMMON HEDGE FUND TECHNIQUES

Chapter 2 describes the most popular hedge fund strategies. This chapter reviews some of the most popular hedge fund investment techniques, organized according to the type of hedge fund strategy mostly closely associated with the technique. Hedge funds are free to adopt more than one of the methods listed. Hedge funds of a particular style may also develop techniques that differ from the following methods to improve return or to modify the types of risks to the investor.

Hedge funds use the investment techniques found in traditional investment textbooks and portfolio management textbooks. These traditional methods are often divided into fundamental and technical techniques. Fundamental techniques focus on objective financial results, valuation, and comparisons between assets. In contrast, technical analysis relies mostly on the pattern of prices, interest rates, or exchange rates over time. The descriptions that follow describe neither fundamental nor technical analysis.

Like traditional asset managers, hedge funds may be organized as top-down or bottom-up investors. A top-down investment organization begins by making macroeconomic forecasts, then makes forecasts for returns on broad classes of assets. Next, the firm makes asset allocation decisions among stocks, bonds, currencies, commodities, and other assets. Next, the firm develops valuation opinions for individual assets within the asset groups consistent with the macroeconomic assumptions and broad asset expectations. Finally, the firm makes allocations to individual assets, consistent with portfolio considerations. Bottom-up investment organizations begin by valuing individual assets. Opinions on sectors and asset groups reflect these valuations. Assets are then allocated to asset groups and then into individual positions.

Long/Short Equity

As mentioned in Chapter 2, a long/short equity hedge fund may be long or short. Typically, this type of fund will carry both long and short positions, but the sizes of the positions can vary to profit from either rising or declining prices of stock.

A long/short equity hedge fund may commit to net long or net short equity exposure based on either fundamental or technical analysis. A firm may develop a fundamental valuation opinion from either top-down or bottom-up methods. The fund will carry an overweighting in long or short positions but maintain offsetting positions in individual stocks, often concentrated in a few narrow sectors. Frequently, the long/short hedge fund will carry net equity exposure based on technical models. Finally, a fund may make the long/short decision based on a combination of factors and trader discretion.

The hedge fund will also pick sectors and individual stocks based on either fundamental or technical valuation. For example, a fund may value a large number of stocks and carry long positions in a subset of stocks that are undervalued and short positions in a subset of stocks that are overvalued.

Event Driven—Merger Arbitrage

Hedge funds that invest based on a variety of events that can affect corporate control of a firm are called event driven hedge funds. Event driven hedge funds may combine trading in shares of companies involved in mergers, bankruptcies, and/or divestitures. The largest subgroup of event driven hedge funds invests in merger arbitrage.

The merger arbitrage strategy developed first at broker-dealers. Many traders have left the dealer community to form hedge funds, and other traders have copied the strategy. These traders typically buy the target of a rumored or announced merger and sell short the shares of the acquirer company.

One a company announces a bid to acquire a target, share prices quickly reflect the terms of the proposed acquisition, adjusted for the chance that the deal with close, financing costs, and other factors. The target company is usually purchased at a premium to the level the company's shares traded at prior to the bid effort. For this reason, merger arbitrage traders may try to anticipate a takeover attempt. Although share prices quickly reflect takeover news, traders may try to acquire positions quickly, before prices fully reflect the takeover proposal.

To understand the nature of merger arbitrage, consider a hypothetical example. Shares of Company A are trading at $20. Shares of Company B are trading at $70. You estimate that Company A will pay a quarterly dividend of $.25 per share on January 15, April 15, July 15, and October 15. You estimate that Company B will pay a quarterly dividend of $.50 per share on February 15, May 15, August 15, and November 15.

On March 15, Company A announces a bid to buy Company B, exchanging five shares of A for each share of B. Trading in Company B shares is immediately suspended and trading resumes the next day at $90. You buy 10,000 shares of Company B and sell short 50,000 shares of Company A.

The shares of Company B cost $900,000 ($90 × 10,000). Suppose for simplicity that you are able to borrow the entire amount at an annual interest rate of 5 percent. (For a more complete discussion of the stock loan market and leverage, see Chapter 6). The sale of Company A shares generates cash of $1 million. However, to be paid this amount, the hedge fund must simultaneously deliver the shares. The fund borrows the shares but must collateralize the loan with $1 million in cash. On that cash, the securities lender pays an annualized rate of 3 percent.

The hedge fund expects the deal to be completed in six months. Therefore, it must make a substitute payment of $12,500 ($.25 per share on 50,000 shares) on April 15 and July 15. The hedge fund receives a dividend of $5,000 ($.50 per share on 10,000 shares) on May 15 and August 15. Finally, on September 15, when the deal is completed, the hedge fund receives 50,000 shares of Company A in exchange for the 10,000 shares of Company B. To complete the transaction, the hedge fund repays the securities loan of $900,000 plus $23,000 in interest.[1] The fund also returns the shares in Company A to the securities lender, who repays the $1 million collateral deposit along with $15,333 in interest.[2] The gross profit of $100,000 is reduced to $77,333 after financing expenses and dividends. See Table 4.1.

As described, the trade would require no initial investment of capital because the full value of the long and short positions is financed. In reality, however, the hedge fund would need to put up excess collateral on both sides of the financing trades. Also, the net outflow of cash for dividend payments would be funded out of hedge fund capital. It is also important to point out that, if the deal collapses and the shares of Company B revert to the previous trading level, the hedge fund could face a loss of $200,000 before financing expenses (adjustment in price from $90 to $70 per share on 50,000 shares).

This example is considerably simpler than many merger deals. In some deals, the acquiring company offers a mixture of stock, cash, and bonds in the merged entity. Also, even if the purchase is completed, the buyer may not buy all the shares offered for sale.

The merger arbitrage strategy removes much of the risk from general equity market price movement because the hedge fund buys one security and sells short another. As long as the deal is completed, the positions are hedges. However, the hedge fund is completely exposed to the risk that the deal will not be completed. As a result, this trade performs worst when announced deals are canceled. The strategy can offer poor returns when merger activity declines.

Event Driven—Bankruptcy

Most investors seek to avoid investing in companies that become bankrupt. Hedge funds may invest in securities of companies that face likely

TABLE 4.1 Hedge Fund Profit from Company A Acquisition of Company B

$100,000	Gross profit on shares
–$ 12,500	Dividend 4/15
$ 5,000	Dividend 5/15
–$ 12,500	Dividend 7/15
$ 5,000	Dividend 8/15
–$ 23,000	Interest on borrowed money
$ 15,333	Interest on collateral
$ 77,333	Net profit

bankruptcy because the securities are undervalued even in light of the risk of default. Typically, hedge funds buy debt securities at deep discounts from face value. Upon entering bankruptcy, these debt holders frequently become the de facto shareholders, and the return on the hedge fund investment is determined by the liquidation value of the assets and the skill of the debt holders at renegotiating other obligations.

Bankruptcy trades rely very little on the credit risk analysis described in the risk management chapter (Chapter 11). Instead, the analysis hinges on estimating the current liquidation value of all the assets plus the expected value of other liabilities after negotiation. Performance is best when investors are concerned about credit risks (because the funds have the chance to buy bonds at attractive spreads) and when the economy is improving (because the prospects of the borrowers improve). Performance is worst when defaults rise and the value of the assets supporting the debt falls.

Event Driven—Divestiture

One of the unique strategies surrounding change of control involves divestitures. Companies sell divisions for a variety of reasons. Often, a division will fall out of favor because it doesn't fit into a revised corporate strategy. When that occurs, the company often finds that the highest price for the division can be realized by selling the unit to the managers currently in charge of that division.

When the transactions are not completely arm's-length, there is no pressure to get the highest possible price for the assets. In fact, when the division is spun off as shares given to shareholders, there is little harm to investors, because they are given shares, not cash. However, many investors immediately sell shares of spin-offs. For example, a mutual fund that invests only in companies in the S&P 500 index often must sell shares of a division distributed to shareholders if the new company is not part of the S&P 500 and hence is not consistent with the investment strategy of the fund. In fact, many portfolio managers will sell shares of spin-offs simply because the daily volume of trading is too small for the liquidity requirements of the portfolio.

As a result, many assets are spun off at low prices and often shares decline further in value. Hedge funds invest in these securities knowing that managers of the newly separated company are highly motivated to improve results.

Hedge funds may invest in a completely different type of spin-off. Sometimes, a larger company will spin off a hot new product as an initial public offering (for example, the sale of Palm, Inc., by 3Com). Here, the hedge fund might speculate (short-term) in the offering, invest (medium- or long-term) in the new technology, or sell short a overpriced offering.

The techniques used to analyze spin-offs involve standard equity valuation methods. The hedge fund has divisional data, perhaps available for the first time as pro forma financial statements. The division can be valued using discounted cash flow analysis and by comparing the newly independent division to comparable companies in the same sector.

Equity Market Neutral—Pairs Trading

The pairs trading strategy begins as the most intuitive of equity trading. Identify two equity issues that should track one another closely. Then look for times when the issues fail to track one another.

In its purest form, the pairs strategy involves different issues of the same company. For example, Berkshire Hathaway has two classes of shares that differ in minor ways except that class B shares own one thirtieth as much of the company as class A shares. The shares should behave nearly identically, adjusted for the proportional difference in value.

Another example of a pairs combination is the American depositary receipt (ADR) market. For example, shares of Sony trade in Tokyo in the local currency. Shares of ADRs supported by shares of Sony trade on the New York Stock Exchange in U.S. dollars. The value of the shares in Tokyo differs from the value of the shares in New York primarily because of the exchange ratio between the Japanese yen and the U.S. dollar. A pairs trading strategy might involve buying the shares in one market, selling the equivalent amount short in another market, and hedging the currency exposure.

As the match between the long and short shares becomes looser, the number of trading opportunities increases along with the risk. Some companies have multiple classes of shares, reflecting different business lines. A pairs trade between these shares relies on predicting the relative success of the divisions.

Pairs trading may also involve trading two companies in the same industry. Differences in product mix, financial leverage, and other factors affect how closely two stocks track one another. The challenge with pairs trading of separate companies is distinguishing short-term aberrations from differences in performance that are sustainable due to differences with the companies.

Pairs traders can cross check the performance of a pair of stocks using a variety of statistical methods. Taken one step further, the statistical analysis can identify candidate pairs based solely on the past performance of the share prices. By opening up the makeup of pairs to statistically similar pairs, a hedge fund can choose from a practically unlimited number of pairs. With each step away from pure arbitrage, the hedge fund assumes greater risks. The fund manager may face a market environment in which the statistical relationships break down.

The success of a pairs strategy depends on being able to identify which stocks to buy and which to sell. The pairing of longs and shorts significantly reduces the risk from general movements of stocks and the performance of particular sectors. By carrying a portfolio of pairs positions, the hedge fund also benefits from diversification, which reduces the volatility of hedge fund returns.

Equity Market Neutral—Index Arbitrage

Hedge funds may employ several strategies to take market neutral positions in common stocks. One popular strategy involves trading a basket of stocks versus an index of stock returns. In its purest form, arbitrage involves simultaneously buying an asset in one market and selling it in another. The markets may be separate geographically (gold in London versus gold in Tokyo) or at different times (spot versus forward).

Index arbitrage begins with buying or selling the individual stocks that make up an index and simultaneously hedging with a derivative instrument that tracks the index (for example, a futures contract). Traders might buy all 500 issues in the S&P 500 index and sell the futures contract. When the futures contract is fairly priced relative to the index, the hedge fund can sell the long positions in the individual stocks and buy back the futures position.

A wide number of derivatives exist that track stock indexes. Index arbitrage also includes trading among different equity derivatives, including futures, options on futures, index options, exchange-traded funds, and over-the-counter derivatives.

Spreads between certain indexes are not market neutral. For example, a hedge fund that buys an equity derivative that tracks the Nasdaq Composite index and sells an equity derivative that tracks the S&P 500 will likely make money most of the time that markets rise and lose money most of the time that markets decline, unless the hedge fund takes steps to remove the market sensitivity from the position.

Equity Market Neutral—Dividend Capture

Dividend capture is usually not conducted with market neutral positions but, because of the short holding period, the performance of the strategy does not closely track stock market indexes.

Stock prices reflect the timing and magnitude of dividend payments (among other factors). Corporations announce a dividend payment to be paid to all holders on a particular future date (the ex-dividend date) payable a short time later (the dividend payment date). Prices of stocks move down on the ex-dividend date because buyers of the stock will not receive the announced dividend and sellers of the stock will nevertheless keep the dividend.

Pending orders on most stock exchanges are lowered by the amount of the dividend on the ex-dividend date. However, stocks generally decline on the ex-dividend date by less than the amount of the dividend. If all investors paid tax at the same rate, the decline in price should on average equal the after-tax amount of any announced dividend. In practice, investors pay many different tax rates, ranging from zero for pension funds, foundations, and endowments to the maximum tax rate on ordinary income (35 percent in the United States for 2003). Taxable U.S. investors may pay a lower tax rate for capital gains than for income. Offshore investors may also have a preference for gains over income. The price of a stock tends to fall by less than the amount of the pretax dividend but more than the after-tax dividend, using the maximum personal income tax rate.

A hedge fund can capture a dividend by buying the shares near the end of the day preceding the ex-dividend date and selling the stock early the next trading day. For this overnight exposure, the hedge fund can expect to receive a dividend in a few weeks and an immediate capital loss slightly smaller than the dividend. U.S. hedge fund investors would pay the same tax rate on the short-term capital gain or loss as they pay on ordinary income. Similarly, offshore investors pay no U.S. tax on either the price difference or the dividend income.

The hedge fund is also exposed to gains and losses during the time the fund holds the shares. The hedge fund can hedge the general direction of stock prices by selling an index future but will generally not hedge movements in the specific securities. Over time, if index prices are flat, the hedge fund can expect to accumulate capital losses and ordinary income. The hedge fund must be careful not to produce losses that cannot be deducted on the tax returns of hedge fund investors.

Convertible Arbitrage

Convertible bonds and convertible preferred stock are hybrid securities, having many of the characteristics of debt and many of the characteristics of equity. Investors have a built-in option to convert from the debtlike instrument to regular common stock. This option can be very valuable. Often, convertible bonds or preferred shares are issued by young companies whose common stock is capable of significant gains or losses.

The option may be difficult to value because the issue may contain other provisions. The option grants the right to convert for a specific period beginning in the future and continuing to a specified expiration date. The terms of the conversion may change over time. The issuing company may also own a call option or other provisions to force the owner of the convertible security to convert.

To complicate the valuation, realize that the conversion option gives the owner the right to exchange one asset (the bond or preferred shares) for common stock. Frequently, the value of the bond or preferred stock moves up and down along with the value of the common stock. If the company is successful, its stock rises because of the prospect of higher earnings. The value of its debt also rises because bondholders face lower risk of default. If a company does poorly, its stock declines. The value of its debt may also decline because of the heightened risk of default.

The convertible arbitrage fund usually buys the convertible issue and sells short the underlying common stock as a hedge. As constructed, this combination will generally be profitable if the common stock moves up or down significantly but will usually lose money if prices remain steady.

Hedge funds may design an option hedging strategy to increase the consistency of performance. The fund may sell listed or over-the-counter stock options to approximate selling the option rights in the convertible security. Properly constructed, the strategy may enable the hedge fund to expect to make money regardless of whether the common shares rise or decline and whether the movement is great or small.

Fixed Income Arbitrage

Fixed income arbitrage incorporates a number of strategies. The largest risk factor for most bonds is the general level of interest rates. Most interest rates tend to move up and down together, so a short position can closely hedge a long position for most fixed income securities.

Like the equity index arbitrage strategy, a hedge fund may buy bonds and sell futures. This trade is called the bond basis and has optionlike characteristics. The combination is a low- risk strategy and is profitable when interest rates move up or down significantly from the beginning level. The trader profits from the optionality of the relationship when large movements occur.

Fixed income arbitrage funds may also hedge long positions in cash securities by selling combinations of Eurodollar futures. Generally, traders seek out bonds with somewhat higher yields because they are not free from default. Then, the hedge fund makes money over time, as long as yield spreads remain steady or narrow to smaller spreads.

Fixed income hedge funds may also buy and sell combinations of securities, hoping to profit from changes in the relationship between the long positions and the short positions. For example, a fund might buy short-term securities and sell short long-term securities, hoping that the yields on the short instruments will decline relative to the yields on the longer issues. This trade is called "buying the curve." Although these trades may be constructed to be neutral to a general rise or decline in rates, the positions make or lose money based on the performance of the individual sectors.

Mortgage/Asset-Backed Arbitrage

Fixed income arbitrage hedge funds may use mortgage-backed securities or asset-backed securities to construct market neutral portfolios. Mortgage-backed securities are securities that are created from pools of mortgages. Most of these securities are issued as pass-through securities by Freddie Mac and Fannie Mae, although many have been reissued as collateralized mortgage obligations (CMOs), interest-only (IO), and principal-only (PO) notes, and other mortgage derivatives. Mortgage-backed securities present a challenge in constructing and maintaining a market neutral portfolio because these securities reflect the prepayment option granted to the homeowner on the underlying mortgages.

Asset-backed securities are created from a wide variety of loans, although most asset-backed securities are created from consumer loans, such as credit card receivables and automobile loans. Asset-backed securities do not present the hedging challenge of mortgage-backed securities. Instead, the investor faces the risk of default.

Several hedge funds have faced challenges running mortgage-backed strategies, including the well-publicized bankruptcy of the Granite Fund and financing challenges at Ellington[3] and MKP Capital. The first essential ingredient needed to run either mortgage-backed or asset-backed arbitrage strategies is to have a robust valuation model. If the valuation model is sound, then the hedge fund can measure the sensitivity of the positions to changes in interest rates, credit spreads, volatility, and other factors. The second essential ingredient is having a strategy for surviving periods when these types of securities go out of favor with investors. It is important for hedge funds to maintain some borrowing capacity for times when these assets are subject to distress pricing and lenders raise margin requirements.

Fund of Funds

The fund of funds is a hedge fund that invests in other hedge funds. These portfolios offer several advantages over investment directly in hedge funds. First, the funds of funds diversify the returns and reduce the volatility of performance. Second, the fund of funds manager investigates the funds it invests in and may be able to reduce the chance of losses to fraud or mismanagement. The fund of funds manager may also be able to identify funds likely to have superior performance.

Most funds of funds are skilled marketing organizations. Not surprisingly, the composition of funds of funds tends to migrate toward the popular hedge fund strategies. A small number of fund of funds managers make forward-looking asset allocations, based on internal forecasts of profitability of various strategies. Other fund of funds managers emphasize diversification strongly and are less likely to overweight particular strategies.

The classic method of portfolio selection first identified by Harry Markowitz[4] involved searching for the optimum trade-off between risk and reward. It is fairly easy to build a model to select hedge funds to get a portfolio with high expected returns and controlled risk. Many fund of funds managers have models or seek to build similar portfolios in other ways.

Unfortunately, the realities of fund of funds management and administration prevent managers from implementing their model portfolios. Many hedge funds impose significant lockups, preventing the fund of funds manager from removing funds from one hedge fund to redeploy in another. Even when exit is permitted, hedge funds won't redeem investments until the next accounting break period (the monthly or quarterly intervals when investors can enter or exit) and other funds won't accept new investments until they reach a break period. Finally, even if a fund of funds is permitted to exit, the manager will usually try to remain in the existing hedge funds because it may be difficult to reenter a hedge fund after withdrawing funds from a particular hedge fund.

As a result, the typical fund of funds manager at best implements an approximation of the model portfolio. The manager must rebalance by reducing the weight of the most successful strategy, which will be overweighted. If the fund of funds manager is growing, the manager may direct money to a small number of managers and partially rebalance, rather than making a proportionate investment in all managers. If the fund of funds is losing investment funds, the manager will raise cash from the hedge funds that permit withdrawals, even at the expense of distorting the balance in the portfolio.

SUMMARY

The introductory chapter presented a definition of hedge funds, despite the lack of clear divisions between hedge funds and other types of investment accounts. This chapter on investment techniques reflects the grayness of that definition. All the techniques described in this chapter are used by other types of investors as well as hedge funds. Notably, many of the techniques were developed by proprietary traders within broker-dealers.

Hedge funds have adopted these techniques along with conventional investment techniques to create desirable returns for their investors. The techniques described are more sophisticated and often require trading that is either prohibited or untypical of mutual funds, trust accounts, and conventional investment advisory accounts. Because the techniques create a pattern of returns that don't track stock and bond returns closely, they provide a way for the hedge fund investor to improve the return and risk characteristics of a traditional portfolio.

QUESTIONS AND PROBLEMS

4.1 A hedge fund manager claims to have a "black box." None of the investment decisions are left to the discretion of the hedge fund traders. Is the black box a technical trading strategy?

4.2 A hedge fund hears a rumor that Company X is considering making a takeover bid for Company Y. The hedge fund buys shares in Company Y, hoping to profit from a run-up in price when the bidding is announced. Is this a merger arbitrage trade?

4.3 Suppose Company X announces a bid for Company Y to be paid in cash. Should the merger arbitrage trader sell Company X shares to hedge a purchase of Company Y shares?

4.4 A trader estimates that he can make $5 per share after financing costs and commissions if the merger is completed at $105. However, if the deal is not completed, the position could lose $10. Explain why the trader might justify risking a 10 percent loss to try to capture a 5 percent gain.

4.5 XYZ L.P. operates as a merger arbitrage hedge fund. Is it likely that the manager of XYZ prefers to enter into takeover events where the acquiring company has a high dividend and the target company has a low dividend?

4.6 Why is a hedge fund a good structure for investing in bankruptcy-prone companies?

4.7 You run a multistrategy hedge fund. An employee proposes trading pairs of stocks. Is that a good strategy to add to a complicated mix of hedge fund strategies?

4.8 Would an endowment or foundation be interested in a hedge fund that relies on a dividend capture strategy?

4.9 What are the major risks taken by a convertible bond arbitrage hedge fund?

4.10 Many investors worry that the fixed income arbitrage strategies involve a pattern of many small profits over and over followed by a large and unpredictable loss. Explain why this pattern may or may not be an attractive pattern of return for a hedge fund investor.

4.11 Problems with mortgage trades have occurred when interest rates have been rapidly declining. If you believe interest rates will rise, should you invest in mortgage strategies?

4.12 Why might it be desirable to overweight a fund of funds into the popular hedge fund strategies?

NOTES

1. By convention, securities loans use an actual/360 day calendar, meaning that interest accrues for 184 actual days from March 15 to September 15 and the 5 percent annual rate is allocated over a 360-day year:

$$\$900,000 \times 5\% \times 184/360 = \$23,000$$

2. As in note 1:

$$\$1,000,000 \times 3\% \times 184/360 = \$15,333$$

3. Michelle Pacelle, "Hedge Funds Face Tougher Times—As Ellington's Vranos Discovers, Less Leverage and More Scrutiny Pose New Challenges for Managers," *Wall Street Journal*, February 12, 1999.

4. Harry Markowitz, "Portfolio Selection," *Journal of Finance*, Volume 7, Issue 1, March 1952, pages 77–91.

CHAPTER 5

Hedge Fund Business Models

Although a hedge fund is viewed by an investor as the portfolio of investments that provide a return, it may in fact be composed of two or more separate businesses. The structure and division of labor of the businesses are not arbitrary. The design of the hierarchy creates a limited liability investment for all investors and is tax efficient.

TYPES OF BUSINESS UNITS

To understand the typical hedge fund business structures, it is necessary to first discuss the building blocks. Bear in mind that small variations exist from state to state in the United States because the individual states authorize the creation of business units. Fortunately, the rules are similar in most states; these business structures have been adopted by all or nearly all the 50 states. The structures commonly used to create hedge funds are generally available in international locations, as well, although the makeup of offshore hedge funds typically combines these business types differently.

C Corporation

The most familiar business structure to most people is the C corporation. Most of the large companies in the United States and many of the small and medium-sized companies are structured as C corporations. This type of structure is also commonly used in many other countries.

The C corporation sells ownership stakes called common stock. A C corporation can have practically an unlimited number of owners. These owners can be spread over many classes of common stock plus preferred stock.

The C corporation could be used to structure a hedge fund investment so that investors could not be called upon to invest more than their original paid-in investment. In fact, this type of structure is usually used for hedge funds when the funds are located in areas with low or no income taxation. In the United States, however, the C corporation is seldom used to structure a hedge fund due to the double taxation of investment returns. Hedge fund management companies (the actual employees who invest the money) are organized separately from the investment assets and may be structured as a C corporation.

Professional Corporation

The professional corporation is used to structure businesses comprised of certain professionals—medical, legal, financial services, architectural, and other professionals. The laws governing the professional corporation differ from state to state. Some state laws might allow a manager to structure the management company as a professional corporation, rather than a C corporation, but it is unlikely that a hedge fund (the investment assets) would be structured as a professional corporation.

Limited Liability Corporation

The limited liability corporation (LLC) is a relatively new business structure; it has been approved in 48 of the 50 states in the United States. It may be taxed as a corporation or a partnership. Nearly all businesses structured as LLCs elect to be treated as partnerships to receive flow-through tax treatment. The LLC structure also allows all investors, including the fund sponsors and managers, to limit their liability to their committed investment.

Sole Proprietorship

The sole proprietorship is the default structure an individual ends up with if no effort is made to structure a business as a partnership or corporation. The owner of the sole proprietorship also retains unlimited liability for the liabilities of the business. So, despite a possible tax advantage over a corporation, a sole proprietorship is not used in the hedge fund industry.

Partnership

There are several variations on the partnership structure. The variations are fairly similar and closely resemble the general partnership in most regards. In particular, all partnerships (and several other business structures) are taxed the same as a general partnership. A partnership may be created formally, but a partnership is the default business structure when two or more individuals or businesses cooperate to create a business. A partnership receives flow-through tax treatment and may or may not report the business income as self-employment income.

The two most important partnership structures are described next. The differences primarily involve the scope of liability of the investors.

General Partnership   A general partnership has only one category of partners, and there must be at least two partners. The general partnership receives flow-through tax treatment, avoiding the double taxation of the returns. All partners are wholly liable for the obligations of the partnership. For hedge funds, this means that investors could be required to assume liabilities beyond their investments in the hedge fund, if the fund loses more than 100 percent of the capital under management.

General-Limited Partnership   A general-limited partnership (also called limited partnership) resembles a general partnership, except that one class of partners (the general partner or general partners) has unlimited liability for the obligations of the partnership and a second class of partners (the limited partner or limited partners) has no liability for the obligations of the partnership beyond the investment committed to the partnership. A limited partnership must have at least one general partner and one limited partner.

The limited partnership is a good structure for a hedge fund in a taxable domicile because the structure avoids double taxation of investment returns and can create a limited liability for the hedge fund investors. The general partners assume unlimited liability for the obligations of the hedge fund, but, as described in Chapter 5, the general partner can be a business entity with a limited capital base that effectively removes the general liability risks.

Limited Liability Partnership   The limited liability partnership (LLP) is very similar to an LLC but is used to organize the professional practices of accountants, lawyers, and architects. California first created the LLP structure, and to date very few states allow for the LLP structure. Although the structure has flow-through tax status and limited liability, it cannot be used for the hedge fund assets because that business unit has few or no employees who are accountants, lawyers, or architects. The management company could arguably be structured as an LLP in some cases, but the LLP is not an important business model for hedge fund managers.

CREATING LIMITED LIABILITY INVESTMENT POOLS

Investors who buy certain types of assets (notably real estate) may borrow money that could create a situation where investors must commit additional capital or otherwise repay debt obligation. In contrast, when buying a common stock, bond, or mutual fund, an investor can rely on losing no more than the committed investment. Hedge fund investors would also like to limit their exposure to their committed capital.

Need for Limited Liability

An investor in a common stock has made an equity investment in a corporation. The corporation may have issued debt in addition to stock. This debt creates leverage because the value of the assets is greater than the value of the equity. In the absence of default, equity holders receive all the gains if the assets rise in value and suffer all of the losses if the assets decline in value. Assets, however, sometimes decline in value by more than the total amount of equity. If losses exceed the capital of the corporation, lenders begin to share in the losses because equity holders cannot be required to invest more than their original paid-in investment.

This corporate structure would seem to work well as a structure for a levered pool of investments. Structured as a corporation, a hedge fund would be a limited liability investment that could use leverage, but the investors would never be required to make additional investments, even in the event of default. Further, the borrowings to finance levered hedge fund positions resemble corporate borrowings.

Indeed, the corporation is a common structure to use to organize hedge funds located in low-tax or no-tax domiciles. In areas with substantial corporate taxation, this structure often results in double taxation of investment returns. For this reason, hedge funds organized where the investment returns are subject to corporate taxation (certainly, the United States and Europe) use partnerships or other business structures that pass taxable income through to investors without paying tax as a fund (see Chapter 10). Those partnerships or other limited liability entities may leave the hedge fund sponsors with considerable liability losses from bad investment returns in the investment portfolios.

Who Bears the Loss in a Hedge Fund Default?

Hedge funds often invest more than their capital in assets and may have short positions. For either reason, hedge funds may lose more than the capital invested in the fund. If a hedge fund loses more than the investors' capital, other parties must bear part of the loss, because the fund investors are treated like equity investors in a corporation. They cannot be required to invest more money beyond their committed amount.[1]

When hedge funds lose more than 100 percent of their capital, the loss is shared by the secured and unsecured creditors. The secured creditors have the benefit of collateral, which may greatly reduce the chance of loss due to the bankruptcy of a hedge fund customer. The losses in excess of paid-in capital are generally shared by the unsecured creditors and the secured creditors (to the extent that their security is insufficient).

Liability of a C Corporation

Figure 5.1 shows the way losses are shared in a C corporation. The area of the boxes represents the relative size of the assets, liabilities, and equity (also called capital in a hedge fund).

If the assets decline in value, the loss is borne by the equity holders. Just as debt holders do not participate in the rise in asset values, they also don't participate in the losses, as long as there is sufficient equity in the company (see Figure 5.2).

If the losses continue, the debt holders may be exposed to risk that they will not be completely repaid. Figure 5.3 shows how a loss may exceed the equity and result in losses for the debt holders, as well. In Figure 5.3, losses have exceeded the value of the paid in capital. Liability holders share in the loss because the equity holders cannot be required to infuse additional capital and (except in circumstances involving fraud by the equity

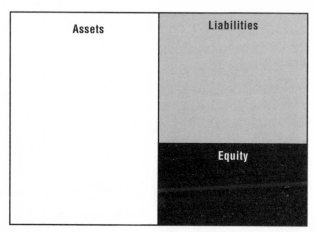

FIGURE 5.1   Starting Levels for Asset Values

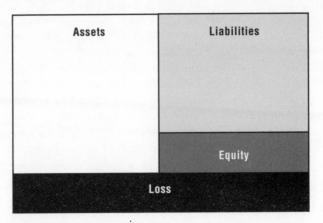

FIGURE 5.2   Balance Sheets after Loss

holders) can't be held liable for losses greater than their capital. This C corporation is bankrupt and the liability holders have effectively become the equity owners of the company.

Limited Partnership

In contrast to a C corporation, the general partners are held liable for the obligations of the partnership. Further, all partners remain liable for all the

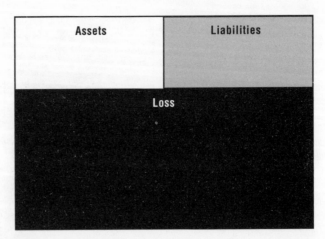

FIGURE 5.3   Balance Sheet after Loss Exceeding Capital

losses up to the total of their net worth regardless of the size of their commitments as partners before the loss.

Figures 5.4 to 5.6 shows the balance sheet of a limited partnership. With a limited partnership, the general partners must pay in additional capital if losses exceed the paid-in capital. Limited partners cannot be required to invest additional capital.

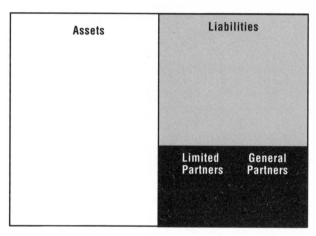

FIGURE 5.4   Balance Sheet for Limited Partnership

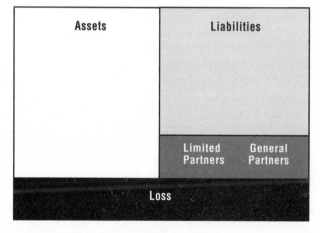

FIGURE 5.5   Limited Partnership Balance Sheet after Loss

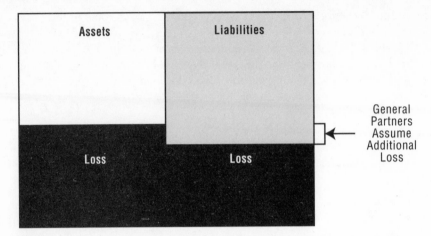

FIGURE 5.6 Limited Partnership Balance Sheet after Loss Exceeding Capital

Using Two (or More) Business Units to Alter Liability

If a corporation serves as the general partner of a limited partnership, the general partner still has unlimited liability. However, the owners of the corporation can't be required to put more money into that business. As a result, the ultimate owners of the partnership have liability limited to their capital investment in the corporation.

Figure 5.7 shows the organizational structure of a limited partnership that has a corporation as its only general partner. The structure may look unnecessarily complicated. It is not necessary if the hedge fund is located in a low-tax domicile. As you will see, structures similar to Figure 5.7 are typical in offshore funds. For a domestic fund organized in the United States or any other country with a substantial corporate income tax, the structure in Figure 5.7 avoids double taxation of investment returns at least for the limited partners. If the general partner is organized as a limited liability corporation or a subchapter S corporation, the general partner also avoids double taxation of investment returns.

Simple Hedge Fund Structure

A simple hedge fund must have a business entity to hold the investments plus at least one other business entity to act as manager. The manager usually contains all the employees involved with managing, marketing, and operating the business. Figure 5.7 resembles a typical hedge fund organized

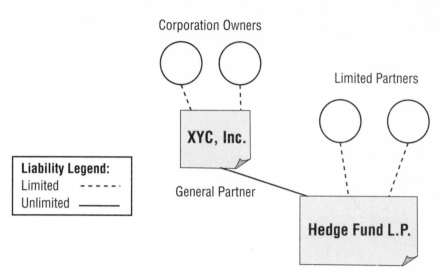

FIGURE 5.7   Basic Structure to Create Limited Liability

in the 1990s or earlier in the United States. The corporation served as both the manager and the general partner of the fund. Investors invested in the fund as limited partners.

Several variations to the structure in Figure 5.7 have become common. First, fund managers may be organized separately from the business that acts as the general partner because a manager may run more than one fund. Each fund is backed by a different general partner, so that the general partnership capital of other funds is protected from the failure of another fund. Second, with the development of the limited liability structure, the fund may be structured without any general partners. Instead, all the investors, including the insiders, invest as shareholders and have limited liability.

Who Is Liable?

Hedge funds as a group are less risky than an unlevered investment in common stocks. Some funds do fail because of the risks they have taken, because of failure to effectively control risk, or because of fraud. If none of the investors in a hedge fund have liability for losses beyond their committed investments, who bears the loss when hedge funds lose more than the paid-in capital? Refer again to Figure 5.6. If general partners do not make up losses, the decline in value falls on the liability holders.

A hedge fund has many creditors. Broker-dealers are liable on unsettled trades. Financing counterparties generally have collateral to secure
their lending, but rapid changes in asset values can leave secured lenders
exposed to default. Derivatives counterparties also margin their exposure
to hedge fund default, but the margin may be inadequate. If a hedge fund
fails, the losses cascade beyond the hedge fund investors.

When a hedge fund has investors from many different countries, it is
usually efficient to organize the fund in a low-tax or no-tax domicile. This
is a tax avoidance strategy but it is not a tax evasion strategy. The difference is important. By structuring a hedge fund offshore, a French investor
avoids paying taxes to the United States but does not avoid paying taxes to
the French government.

Figure 5.8 shows a simple structure for an offshore hedge fund. In
this master-feeder structure, a corporation is created in a low-tax or no-

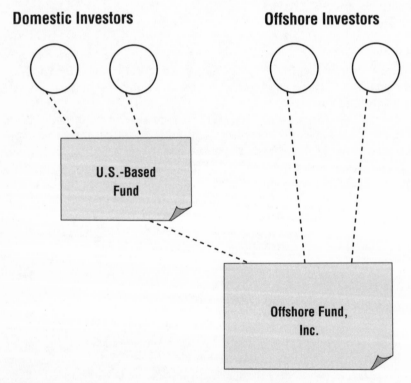

FIGURE 5.8   Offshore Hedge Fund Structure

tax domicile to avoid double taxation of investment returns. Some investors may invest directly in the offshore fund as shareholders. This offshore fund is not controlled by U.S. or other securities laws and regulations. In order to be accepted as an offshore entity for U.S. tax purposes, the fund does not accept investments from U.S. citizens. However, a U.S. hedge fund can invest in another hedge fund that happens to be a foreign asset. If constructed carefully, the U.S. hedge fund can channel U.S. investments into the offshore fund without compromising the offshore tax status of the main fund. Most hedge funds organized today resemble Figure 5.8.

Master-Feeder versus Mirror Funds

The master-feeder fund is also sometimes called a spoke and hub fund. Before this structure was developed, hedge fund sponsors frequently created separate funds in the host country and offshore (mirror funds; see Figure 5.9). The manager ran each fund so that each pool contained the same positions, adjusted proportionally to the size of the fund. Maintaining a mirror fund is very difficult because every flow into either fund requires the manager to rebalance all the investments in both funds.

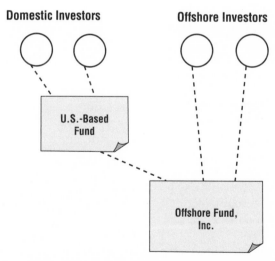

FIGURE 5.9 Mirror Hedge Fund Structure

Futures positions and over-the-counter derivatives are very difficult to re-balance. The rebalancing process is time-consuming and creates the opportunity for the performances of the funds to diverge.

QUESTIONS AND PROBLEMS

5.1   Why is a C corporation not a good choice for the business structure of a hedge fund in the United States?

5.2   Why is a corporation a sensible choice for an offshore hedge fund domiciled in a tax-free haven?

5.3   With a C corporation, who suffers a loss when the value of the assets decline below the value of the liabilities?

5.4   With a general-limited partnership, who suffers a loss when the value of assets decline below the value of the liabilities?

5.5   What is a flow-through tax entity?

5.6   Explain how a general partner can create a limited liability investment in a partnership.

5.7   What is the advantage of setting up a business as the general partner of a general-limited partnership?

5.8   Why is corporate or limited partner ownership *not* complete protection against liability above the capital committed to a business?

5.9   Why might a hedge fund sponsor create a separate business unit to act as the manager and another unit to act as general partner of a hedge fund?

5.10 What is the main objective of a mirrored hedge fund structure?

5.11 Why would a fund sponsor seek to get similar returns in the domestic and offshore mirrored funds?

5.12 Why is a corporate structure often used for an offshore fund, instead of a limited partnership?

5.13 What advantage does a master-feeder structure have over a mirrored structure for a fund sponsor needing both a U.S. and an offshore fund?

5.14 Why would anyone set up a mirrored structure, given the advantages of a master-feeder structure?

5.15 What is the correct domicile for setting up a business in the United States?

5.16 What is the best domicile for an offshore fund?

5.17 What is the key advantage of administering a hedge fund offshore?

NOTES

1. In reality, the commitments can be more complicated due to contractual obligations. For example, venture capital funds generally receive commitments to make additional capital contributions. These commitments may be enforceable in the event of bankruptcy. Also, some partnerships require the partners to sign commitments to put in additional money. These commitments act to strengthen the creditworthiness of the business.

CHAPTER 6

Hedge Fund Leverage

Over the centuries, many societies have frowned on borrowing money. It's not hard to find evidence of this displeasure in religion and literature. In Shakespeare's *Hamlet*, Polonius advises his son to "neither a borrower nor a lender be." Islam retains the prohibition against interest rates. Outside of the financial community (especially broker-dealers, hedge funds, and futures traders), modern society fears selling an asset short (selling an asset with the intent of repurchasing at a lower price in the future) and reproaches those carrying short positions. Yet borrowing to buy assets has become much more acceptable. Corporations rely on debt. Consumers finance houses with mortgages. Credit cards give individuals the ability to borrow on demand.

BACKGROUND ON LEVERING SECURITIES POSITIONS

Securities regulations have historically limited the ability of regulated investment companies (mutual funds, common trusts, etc.) to borrow money to buy assets or sell securities short. While some of these restrictions have been relaxed over the past several decades, hedge funds sidestep the limitations by organizing in ways that exempt the pools from borrowing restrictions (see Chapter 8). Certain strategies require no borrowing or short selling to produce attractive returns; these funds may use none of the techniques described here. Many hedge funds, however, either borrow cash to carry positions, sell securities short, or invest in derivative securities that create the same effect in their portfolios. In the past, some hedge funds have carried positions more than a hundred times their capital. After the collapse of Long-Term Capital Management, counterparties began to limit the ability of hedge funds to carry positions so far in excess of their capital.[1] Hedge funds that primarily invest common stocks (more than half the hedge fund assets) rarely carry positions more than about twice their capital.

Leverage is operationally defined as borrowing cash to carry long positions in excess of capital or borrowing securities to carry short positions. A fund that carries long and short positions twice as large as capital may be described as using leverage of 2:1.

Investors may measure leverage in a variety of ways. Investors may look at the debt/equity ratio or the debt to total capital ratio. One intuitive measure sums the market value of the long assets with the market value of the short positions (treated as a positive number) divided by the partner's capital.

The most commonly accepted way to measure leverage (nearly universal in the fund of funds industry) is to divide the total assets on the balance sheet by the equity (capital). This method of course includes the market value of the long positions but also approximates the value of the short positions because every short position also has a financing position that gets carried as an asset.

REASONS HEDGE FUNDS USE LEVERAGE

Hedge funds use leverage for a variety of reasons. First, a fund borrows money to carry assets greater than the capital on deposit. The manager usually believes that the assets will earn a higher return that the cost of borrowing the money to carry the assets. A hedge fund may carry a position in volatile technology stocks, believing the sector will earn much more than the borrowing rate. A stock picker may handpick the stocks to buy and create a hedge to remove the general market risk. In conjunction with the hedging strategy, borrowing money may be used to increase the return from this stock selection strategy. Similarly, borrowing can be used to magnify the return on any lower-risk strategy.

Hedge funds can also use leverage to create short positions. Some hedge funds create positions to benefit from price declines. The short positions allow the fund to profit from the decline of particular stock prices and, when accumulated into a portfolio of short positions, the general decline in stock prices. Other hedge funds will create short positions to combine with long positions. The combined portfolio may be less risky than either an unlevered long position or an outright short position.

Finally, a hedge fund may use leverage because trading is more efficient when structured as derivatives transactions. For example, it is not very easy to store electricity, so hedge funds that want to trade electricity use energy derivatives. These derivatives create leverage.

WAYS HEDGE FUNDS CREATE LEVERAGE

Hedge funds can create leverage in a variety of ways. Day trading is the simplest way to carry positions larger than capital. The fund can buy securities during the day and sell the position on the same day. Or the fund can sell short an asset and buy it back later in the same day. In both cases, the purchase and the sale are netted, no delivery of securities is required, and the fund can make or lose money without posting capital.

Day Trading to Create Leverage

Day trading by individuals made headlines during the large rally in the stock market in the 1990s. In fact, these methods have been used (and are still being used) by traders at broker-dealers, futures exchanges, and hedge funds. Brokers do require a certain amount of capital to be carried in the day trader's account. Most brokers monitor intraday positions and many have set limits to the size of unsettled positions.

Leverage from Unsettled Positions

Several assets can be bought or sold for delayed delivery. Most mortgage securities must be traded for deferred settlement of several weeks while waiting for monthly principal and interest amounts to be tallied. By buying or selling for settlements delayed one month, two months, or longer, the hedge fund can trade mortgage-backed securities without using the cash on hand to pay for them immediately. This deferred settlement creates leverage for the buyer and allows the hedge fund to sell short mortgage assets.

The foreign exchange market also trades for both immediate settlement (spot) or for later settlement (forward). For most currencies, trading for forward delivery is more liquid than trading in the futures markets. In fact, outside the currencies of the largest economies of the world, it is rarely possible to find a futures market for the exchange rate, but banks with currency trading desks will buy or sell most currencies for forward delivery.

Stock Loan and Repo Financing

One simple way to create leverage is to borrow money to finance securities trades. Broker-dealers have lent money to investors in regulated margin accounts. Banks will grant loans secured by equity positions or banks. Outside these regulated financial institutions, a fairly unregulated market developed to finance government securities positions. This market, called the "repurchase" market or "repo" market, allows institutions to borrow money at favorable rates because the loans are secured by extremely high-quality collateral. Hedge funds can borrow money to finance Treasury bond positions at rates very close to the U.S. Treasury bill rates. Traders can borrow nearly 100 percent of the market value of some types of bonds. Less liquid bonds and less creditworthy bonds can be financed at slightly higher rates and are subject to excess collateralization (called a "haircut") of 10 percent or more.

The stock loan market evolved based on the model of the government securities markets. Like the repo market, the stock loan market allows borrowers to finance positions at rates close to Treasury bill rates. Rates in the stock loan market are typically 50 basis points higher (100 basis points equals 1 percent) than repo rates. Stock traders can typically borrow up to 90 percent of the market value of liquid equity positions. Other limitations on leverage (including regulations such as the U.S. Federal Reserve's Regulation T and credit limits imposed by counterparties) may limit hedge fund position size.

Suppose a hedge fund owns a position in a particular common stock worth $1 million. If the fund must maintain a haircut of 10 percent, it can borrow $900,000 in the stock loan market. The fund delivers the shares to the lender to hold as collateral. At the end of the loan period, the lender returns the shares to the owner, who repays the loan plus interest.

Typically, interest is calculated based on the actual/360 convention whereby interest is calculated based on the actual number of days in the loan but the annualized interest rate is prorated as if a year had 360 days. For example, a $900,000 loan at 5 percent to finance a stock position would cost the hedge fund $875 ($900,000 × 5% × 7 days/360 days).

The repo market works similarly except the value of the bond position includes accrued interest. For example, if the hedge fund owned $1 million face value of bonds with a current price of $102 and accrued interest of a half point, the value of the position is $1,025,000 ($1,000,000 face × 102.5% of face). Also, haircuts are much lower on bonds than on equities. The haircut for a U.S. Treasury with a maturity of five years or less may be a quarter of 1 percent or less. The hedge fund may be able to set a repo balance as high as $1,022,437.50 ($1,025,000 × 99.75%). Also, financing rates are somewhat lower for bonds, especially for Treasury and agency bonds. Assuming the fund can borrow money at 4.5 percent, interest on this repo for a week would equal $894.63 ($1,022,437.50 × 4.5% × 7/360).

In practice, the hedge fund would finance a significantly lower portion of the total value of stocks or bonds in the portfolio than in the example. Usually, the principal amount would also be set to a rounded amount.

Also, the length of the financing is often one day, with the financing terms renegotiated daily. Finally, when a prime broker finances many positions for a hedge fund, the principal and interest are often based on portfolio values, rather than individual positions.

Hedge funds can also borrow securities sold short in the repo market (for bonds) and the stock loan market (for equities). The owner of a security (stock or bond) lends the security to the hedge fund. In return, the hedge fund transfers cash to the security lender as collateral until the securities are returned. The lender of the securities pays the borrower interest (called the "rebate rate") on these cash deposits at a rate somewhat below prevailing interest rates. The lender may reinvest the cash and earn a fee for lending the securities equal to the difference in interest. Borrowers must also collateralize the stock and bond loans with somewhat more cash than the market value of the securities. This excess collateral (also called a haircut) is generally small in the fixed income market but may be 50 percent of the value of some stock positions if the stock is volatile or illiquid.

The procedure to borrow securities closely resembles the procedure to borrow money secured by securities. Suppose a hedge fund has sold short 50,000 shares of stock at a price of $22. The fund expects to receive $1,100,000 ($22 × 50,000) three business days later. On the settlement date, the fund needs to borrow the shares, because the fund must satisfy its obligation to deliver and will get paid the cash only if it settles the trade. Suppose the price of the stock has declined to $21 per share. The lender of the shares has a position worth $1,050,000 (50,000 × $21). The lender will demand cash collateral in excess of the current value (the lender pays no attention to the sale proceeds even if the lender is the same broker-dealer that handled the original sales transaction). If the lender requires excess collateral equal to 25 percent of the value, the hedge fund must post $1,312,500 ($1,050,000 × 125%). The securities lender pays interest on the cash collateral, but at a bargain rate. Interest on the cash collateral is calculated the same way as the interest on borrowed money described earlier.

Leverage Using Derivative Securities

Derivative securities allow hedge funds to create leverage. Derivative securities (or derivatives) provide a return based on the performance of other assets. Generally, derivatives require a smaller payment of cash than a direct investment in the underlying assets.

Using the Futures Market The futures market is the best-known derivatives market that provides an additional way for a hedge fund to create leverage. Starting in the 1980s and 1990s, there has been a steady increase in the number and types of assets that can be carried as a future as exchanges have proliferated products in a wide range of assets worldwide. The futures markets resemble the forward markets described earlier. However, the terms of the trade are standardized. This standardization makes it simple for a hedge fund to buy a future one day and sell it later even if the counterparties of the trades are different. Also, a third party called a clearinghouse acts as the counterparty for all trades on the exchange and assumes the responsibility for making or taking delivery. Finally, each party must pay in unrecognized losses daily and may withdraw unrecognized gains.

Options Markets   Hedge funds can use a second kind of derivative called options to create leverage. An option gives the holder the right but not the obligation to buy or sell an asset in the future. A call gives the holder the right to buy the underlying asset. A put gives the holder the right to sell the underlying asset. Hedge funds can almost always buy an option for less cash than an outright purchase of an asset. Hedge funds that invest a particular amount in calls or puts will generally have greater gains or losses than they would have gotten from an equal investment in the underlying asset.

Swap Derivatives   A third type of derivative that can be used to create leverage is called a swap. A swap is a contract to receive cash flows derived from one financial instrument and pay cash flows derived from another financial instrument. Swaps are traded over-the-counter between customers and swap dealers. The swap agreements vary greatly as parties can negotiate any kind of agreement agreeable to both parties. Most swaps, however, closely resemble an outright investment in a conventional asset plus funding of that position. Swaps, therefore, create leverage for a hedge fund, often requiring little or no capital.

LIMITS ON HEDGE FUND LEVERAGE

Margin requirements limit the amount of leverage hedge funds can create with futures, options, or margin loans.

Initial Margin

Hedge funds face many limits on leverage they can employ. Most investors know Regulation T or at least know something about margin that is required by Reg T. To read the regulation, see www.access.gpo.gov/nara/cfr /waisidx_03/12cfr220_03.html. A series of regulations was promulgated by the Federal Reserve Bank. Reg T limits lending by a broker or dealer to customers secured by securities. Regulation U extends to provisions to banks and other lenders; to read the regulation, see www.access.gpo.gov/nara /cfr/waisidx_03/12cfr221_03.html. Regulation X extends the provisions to U.S. entities that seek such loans from financial institutions exempt from Reg U and Reg T; to read the regulation, see www.access.gpo.gov/nara/cfr /waisidx_03/12cfr224_03.html.

The regulations impose initial margin requirements on these securities loans. Margin is the part of the security value that is funded by capital (i.e., the value of the position minus the debt extended). The portion that may not be financed with borrowings is formally one of the tools the Federal Reserve Bank may use to implement monetary policy. In practice, the margin amounts have not changed for decades, as the central bank has focused on other policy tools.

Different initial margin requirements apply to different assets. A margin percentage of 50 percent applies to most exchange-traded common stock. Smaller initial margin requirements exist for fixed income securities. Certain types of assets (options owned and nonmarginable stock) may not be used as collateral.

For example, a hedge fund with $1 million could buy no more than $2 million of common stock to comply with a 50 percent initial margin requirement. It is important to note that once this initial margin requirement is met the requirement does not apply to subsequent market values. The hedge fund would not be in violation of the initial margin requirement even if the value of the position dropped to $1 million and the value of the securities just matched the loan amount. As noted in the next subsection, other limitations would require the hedge fund to post additional margin if this happened, but Reg T (and Reg U and Reg X) would not require adjustments.

Maintenance Margin

The Federal Reserve imposes only initial margin requirements. However, the major stock exchanges require their members to hold minimum maintenance margin (the minimum margin required based on updated values). Maintenance margin is recalculated frequently to account for the updated market value of the positions securing the lending. These requirements establish only the lowest margin that members must require. Broker-dealers are free to require maintenance margin in excess of exchange minima.

If the broker carrying the $2 million in common stocks required maintenance margin of 35 percent, the fund would get a margin call if the value of the positions fell below $1,538,461.54. The remaining value of the margin is $538,461.54 after subtracting the $1 million loan balance from the total value. This margin exactly equals 35 percent of the position. If the value of the position fell below $1,538,461.54, the hedge fund would need to either post additional margin in cash or sell part of the position until the maintenance requirement is met. If the fund failed to meet this margin maintenance voluntarily, the broker would sell positions to satisfy the requirement.

More generally, suppose the margin maintenance requirement was Maintain%. The current loan amount is Loan, and the minimum margin for that loan amount is Margin. The margin requirement can be stated algebraically as:

$$\text{Maintain\%} = \frac{\text{Margin}}{\text{Margin} + \text{Loan}} \tag{6.1}$$

which is reordered as follows:

$$\text{Maintain\%} \times \text{Margin} + \text{Maintain\%} \times \text{Loan} = \text{Margin} \tag{6.2}$$

$$\text{Maintain\%} \times \text{Loan} = (1 - \text{Maintain\%}) \times \text{Margin} \tag{6.3}$$

$$\frac{\text{Maintain\%} \times \text{Loan}}{(1 - \text{Maintain\%})} = \text{Margin} \tag{6.4}$$

The maintenance margin imposes a limitation on the amount of leverage available to a hedge fund if the hedge fund holds assets subject to margin requirements and if the hedge fund must observe the requirements (many offshore hedge funds bypass margin requirements by financing positions with dealers or subsidiaries of dealers located outside the United States). Maximum leverage is equal to the total value of the positions that can be carried divided by the margin required to carry those positions. The margin maintenance percentage can be readily converted into the leverage possible under that margin requirement:

$$\text{Maintain\%} = \frac{\text{Margin}}{\text{Total Value}} = \frac{\text{Margin}}{\text{Margin} + \text{Loan}} \tag{6.5}$$

$$\text{Leverage} = \frac{\text{Margin} + \text{Loan}}{\text{Margin}} = \frac{1}{\text{Maintain\%}} \tag{6.6}$$

Of course, funds generally run leverage below this amount to avoid margin calls for routine changes in market value of the positions carried.

Equity Option Margin

Exchanges collect margin for equity options. Buyers of puts and calls on individual stocks must fully pay for all options and cannot use the value of the options as collateral on a loan. Short option margin is calculated two ways and the seller is charged the higher of the two amounts. First, the proceeds of the sale plus 20 percent of the underlying stock price are reduced by the amount (if any) that the option is out of the money. Second, the proceeds of the sale are combined with 10 percent of the share price. Margin is somewhat lower for index options than the margin for individual options.

Options offer a way to participate in the price of a stock but options, generally move less than the underlying asset. The delta of an option measures the sensitivity of the option price relative to the underlying common stock. An option with a delta of .5 moves only half as fast as the stock. Accounting for this delta, options can create leverage of about 2:1 relative to an equally responsive position in the underlying stock. The amount of leverage is also subject to change, depending on the level of the stock relative to the strike, the time to expiration, and other factors.[2]

Futures Margin

Futures exchanges also impose margin requirements on hedge funds. Futures margin differs somewhat from margining of stocks and bonds. When a new trade is created, both the buyer and the seller must post initial margin. This amount is a good-faith deposit and makes it possible for a third party, a clearing corporation, to guarantee performance to both the buyer and seller. The initial margin is set by the exchanges and varies from time to time. The exchange may raise initial margin requirements when a futures contract becomes volatile. This margin may be satisfied by depositing cash but the exchange pays no interest on the balances. Most futures traders deposit short-term Treasury bills, which are also accepted as initial margin and earn a return.

Futures exchanges also impose a maintenance margin on both the buyer and seller. Futures are revalued daily and customers must post cash if the margin value falls below the maintenance level. The maintenance margin must be in cash because much of this money will be deposited in the accounts of traders who are making money, and those traders have the right to withdraw the cash immediately.

Because futures margin is considerably less than the value of the assets underlying the futures contract, the hedge fund creates leverage when the fund buys or sells a future. For example, the S&P futures contract (based on the Standard & Poor's 500 index) is valued at 250 times the level of the index. If the S&P index is 1,120, the futures contract represents $280,000 worth of stock. This amount is 77 larger than the initial margin of $3,625. Although this future creates considerable leverage, it does demonstrate that futures margins place limits on hedge fund leverage.

SPAN Margin

Futures margin has historically been calculated individually for various futures positions (and options on futures). Futures exchanges allow brokers to collect lower margin for positions with less risk than an outright long or short position. As the variety of futures products has risen, exchanges have adopted a more comprehensive way to allow for the combined riskiness of a futures portfolio. The margin method is called standardized portfolio analysis of risk (SPAN). SPAN margin equals the largest likely loss on the entire position for a one-day horizon. For hedge strategies, this can be substantially less than the margin calculated in the traditional way. Brokers may require more margin that the minimum SPAN margin. See the futures exchanges for more information about how their SPAN margin is calculated.

IMPACT OF LEVERAGE ON RISK OF HEDGE FUND PORTFOLIOS

Leverage may increase the risk of a portfolio compared to a long-only unleveraged portfolio of assets. A leveraged long position can lose more than 100 percent of a hedge fund's capital, while an unleveraged long position can lose only 100 percent. Similarly, any short position can appear to be more risky than a long position even if neither position is larger than the capital base of the hedge fund because short positions can lose more than 100 percent of capital. There is no absolute limit on the losses because an asset can double (losing 100 percent of capital), triple (losing 200 percent of capital), or more.

Hedge funds are structured so that individual investors cannot lose more than 100 percent of their capital, so potential losses on the portfolio that exceed 100 percent don't necessarily affect hedge fund investors. However, the use of leverage may increase the probability of a loss of a certain magnitude. Investors are concerned about the impact leverage has on the probability of these losses (of all sizes). Creditors, in turn, are interested in the probability of losing more than the hedge fund's capital, so creditors monitor hedge fund leverage.

Risk in Unlevered Portfolio

The normal distribution provides a convenient way to study the impact of leverage on hedge fund risk. The standard bell curve is actually a probability curve and displays the probability of a range of outcomes.

In Figure 6.1, the normal distribution is displayed for an asset having an expected return of 15 percent and a standard deviation of return equal to 18 percent. The area to the left of 0 percent on the x-axis shows the times when this asset produces a loss. In this case, the investment would lose money 20.2 percent of the time.[3]

Risk in Leveraged, Unhedged Portfolio

A hedge fund that borrows money to buy more of the same asset can increase the expected return of the fund if the expected return of the asset is higher than the borrowing rate. This kind of levered trading can increase risk. Risk is often described as the standard deviation of return. Figure 6.2 shows the impact of leverage when the borrowed money is used to buy more of the asset held in the fund.

The leftmost point on the line is an unleveraged position. A portfolio

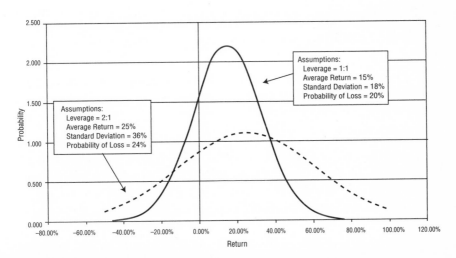

FIGURE 6.1 Distributions of Returns

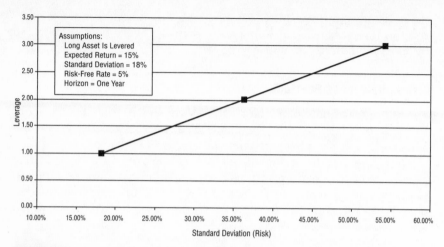

FIGURE 6.2 Impact of Leverage on Portfolio Risk

containing this asset has a standard deviation of return equal to 18 percent. As the fund borrows money to buy more of the same asset, leverage rises from 1:1 to 2:1. The standard deviation of return rises proportionally to 36 percent.

The expected return on the portfolio is just the weighted average of the returns of the assets in the portfolio, adjusted for borrowing costs if the portfolio is leveraged:

$$\text{Return}_{\text{Portfolio}} = \sum_{i=1}^{N} w_i \text{Return}_i - \text{Borrowing Rate} \times \left(\sum_{i=1}^{N} w_i - 1 \right) \quad (6.7)$$

Note that the weights need not sum to 1 (or 100 percent of the portfolio) and will exceed 1 for a levered portfolio. Financing applies only to the portion that exceeds the capital. For the return on the two-asset portfolios shown in the figures in this chapter, equation (6.7) simplifies to:

$$\text{Return}_{A,B} = w_A \times \text{Return}_A + w_B \times \text{Return}_B \\ - \text{Borrowing Rate} \times (w_A + w_B - 1) \quad (6.8)$$

It is possible to derive the portfolio standard deviation of return using standard statistical formulas found in many statistics books. The standard deviation of a portfolio is calculated from the variance covariance table:

$$\sigma_{\text{Portfolio}} = \sqrt{\sum_{i=1}^{N} \sum_{j=1}^{N} w_i w_j \sigma_{i,j}} \qquad (6.9)$$

for N variables and weights of w_1 to w_N. For two assets, this reduces to:

$$\sigma_{\text{Portfolio}} = \sqrt{w_A^2 \sigma_A^2 + 2 w_A w_B \sigma_{A,B} + w_B^2 \sigma_B^2} \qquad (6.10)$$

Stated in terms of the correlation statistic (ρ):

$$\sigma_{A,B} = \sqrt{w_A^2 \sigma_A^2 + 2 w_A w_B \sigma_A \sigma_B \rho_{A,B} + w_B^2 \sigma_B^2} \qquad (6.11)$$

The impact of this leverage can be seen in Figure 6.1. The expected return rises to 25 percent (15 percent on the unleveraged part of the portfolio and 15 percent – 5 percent borrowing rate on the leveraged portion). Notice that the higher expected return means (all other things being equal) that a loss is less likely. Of course, things are not equal, but the doubling of portfolio risk as defined by the standard deviation of return leads to a probability of loss equal to 24.4 percent.[4] Under this particular set of assumptions, leverage significantly increases the expected return but increases the chance of losing money less significantly.

The reader should not conclude that risk of loss is a superior measure of risk than the standard deviation. Hedge fund investors measure risk in a variety of ways. Also, the chance of losing greater amounts (say 25 percent or 50 percent) may be higher in the levered portfolio. Without leverage, the portfolio cannot lose more than 100 percent of the capital, but the levered portfolio in Figure 6.1 can lose up to twice the capital (and perhaps a little bit more because of financing costs and transactions costs).

In going from an unlevered to a levered portfolio, a hedge fund may use the borrowed funds to buy a different asset. If the assets added to the unlevered portfolio provide diversification to the portfolio, the increase in risk caused by the leverage is mitigated by the risk-reducing impact of diversification. Correlation measures the degree to which two assets move together. Suppose a second asset was bought that was only 40 percent correlated with the unleveraged portfolio. That is, for every dollar in capital, the fund buys $1 of one asset and $1 of a second asset that is correlated 40 percent to the first (leverage 2:1).

Although the portfolio contains as much leverage as the examples shown in Figures 6.1 and 6.2, the diversification reduces the standard deviation of the portfolio to 30.12 percent, down from 36 percent. As can be seen in Figure 6.3, the portfolio has about the same probability of loss (20.3 percent)[5] as an unleveraged portfolio (20.2 percent). It is clear, however, that the chance of large losses is higher on the levered portfolio. In return, this levered portfolio also has a considerably higher probability of large gains.

Risk in a Levered, Hedged Portfolio

Hedge funds commonly construct portfolios so that the risk of the long positions is significantly mitigated by the risk of the short positions. (This kind of position is called a hedge or arbitrage.) Two nearly identical positions behave almost exactly opposite each other if one position is held long and the other is held short. When analyzing the returns of

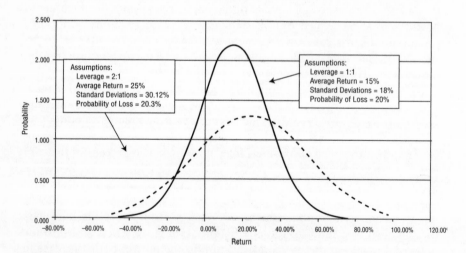

FIGURE 6.3   Distribution of Returns

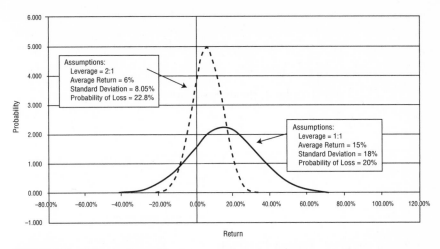

Assumptions:
Leverage = 2:1
Average Return = 6%
Standard Deviation = 8.05%
Probability of Loss = 22.8%

Assumptions:
Leverage = 1:1
Average Return = 15%
Standard Deviation = 18%
Probability of Loss = 20%

FIGURE 6.4 Distribution of Returns

the assets, these are generally described as being highly correlated (near 100 percent).

The assets in Figure 6.4 are constructed to be equal in value and 90 percent correlated. However, the first asset is held long and the second asset is short. The combined portfolio has an expected return of 6 percent (in part by design because the expected return on the long is assumed to be 15 percent and the expected return on the asset held short is 14 percent).[6] The standard deviation of the combined returns is 8.05 percent. While the standard deviation is much lower than the unhedged portfolio, the risk of loss is 22.8 percent,[7] higher than the unhedged portfolio. Nevertheless, the probability of a large loss is much smaller for the levered, hedged portfolio than for the outright long, unlevered, and unhedged portfolio.

Because it is possible to remove much of the aggregate market risk from a portfolio, it is not accurate to presume that more leverage leads to more risk. In fact, the least volatile hedge funds are the funds following arbitrage strategies. These funds also have the highest leverage of all hedge fund investment styles. A highly levered, well-hedged portfolio has other risks that are not easy to measure with standard measures of risk. These risks, including the risk of losing financing capacity, are discussed in Chapter 11, which deals with risk management.

CONCLUSIONS

Hedge funds use leverage to construct portfolios that differ significantly from conventional long, unlevered portfolios. While leverage often creates a riskier portfolio than the assets that make up the portfolio, there is no simple relationship between leverage and risk. Investors and creditors need to understand the nature of the positions to understand the impact of the leverage on the risk in a hedge fund portfolio.

QUESTIONS AND PROBLEMS

A hedge fund has $40 million in common stock long and $50 million in common stock short. It has stock loan agreements of $60 million as assets and $30 million as liabilities. The fund has $40 million is capital (including both limited partner and general partner capital). Answer questions 6.1 and 6.2 about this hedge fund's positions:

6.1 How do the stock loan amounts relate to the stock positions held as assets and liabilities?

6.2 What is the leverage in this hedge fund?

6.3 A hedge fund is reviewing a stock or bond. It appears that the asset should have a return equal to 3 percent. The fund can borrow or lend the security at the rate of 5 percent. Why might a hedge fund use leverage with this instrument?

6.4 One fund holds assets equal to its capital and is using no margin or other techniques to create leverage. A second fund has no long positions but carries short positions in a margin account equal to its capital. Which fund has higher leverage?

6.5 A fund has assets equal to $100 million, including $25 million common stock carried in a cash margin account. The fund has $50 million in capital. What is the leverage on the fund?

6.6 Another fund has assets equal to $100 million, including $2 million in margin at futures exchanges. The fund has long positions in futures contracts representing an additional $50 million in assets. The fund has $50 million in capital. What is the leverage of this fund?

6.7 During the day, an entity carries up to $20 million in securities. All positions are liquidated by the close of day each day. The entity has

$5 million in capital. What are the limits on leverage for this company?

6.8 A hedge fund has positions (long and short) in stocks, index futures, commodity futures, and currencies. The fund's prime broker finances all the cash positions and carries all the futures positions. To what extent can SPAN margin rules reduce the margin required for the positions?

6.9 How can a hedge fund exceed the limit of 50 percent margin required on cash stock positions?

6.10 Your hedge fund has long positions in U.S. Treasury securities totaling $50 million and short positions worth $35 million. You pay an average repo rate of 4.5 percent to finance your longs and receive an average reverse repo rate of 4 percent on your cash collateral covering your short positions. You post haircuts averaging 0.25 percent on the long positions and 0.5 percent on the short positions. What amount of capital is tied up in haircuts?

6.11 How levered is the Treasury part of the portfolio in question 6.10?

6.12 A hedge fund has $100 million in capital levered approximately 20:1. It maintains a position of long notes and bonds roughly equal to its position in short bonds. The financing rate on the long positions averages about 0.5 percent (50 basis points) higher than the rate on the short positions. How much does the fund need to make trading (annually) to break even after financing costs?

6.13 You borrow 25,000 shares of XYZ common and deliver the shares to satisfy a short sale. While you are carrying the short, the stock pays a dividend of $1 per share. Who receives the dividend?

6.14 You borrow 25,000 shares of XYZ common and deliver the shares to satisfy a short sale. While you are carrying the short, the stock splits 2:1. How does this affect the stock loan transaction?

6.15 You borrow 25,000 shares of XYZ common and deliver the shares to satisfy a short sale. While you are carrying the short, a proxy fight develops over control of the company. How do you restore the vote to the lender of the shares?

6.16 What is the tax treatment of a Treasury coupon or stock dividend received as a replacement payment from a securities borrower?

6.17 Why might it be reasonable to allow a hedge fund greater leverage for risky positions held as outright futures (long or short) than for levered positions in the underlying cash instruments?

6.18 Why would the U.S. Federal Reserve Bank want to limit the amount of leverage possible on securities loans?

6.19 A hedge fund has $10 million in marginal positions and has loans totaling $8 million. The fund is subject to maintenance margin of at least 30 percent. How much new cash would the hedge fund need to deposit to satisfy a margin call?

6.20 If the hedge fund in question 6.19 chose to liquidate positions rather than deposit additional margin, how much would need to be liquidated?

6.21 A hedge fund buys a six-month call on a common stock at a price of $5. The strike of the option is $102. The current price of the stock is $100. The short-term rate of interest is 5 percent. The current value of the call is $5.25. How much margin must the hedge fund put up to carry the call?

6.22 What margin would the hedge fund need to post if it wrote (sold) an option like that described in question 6.21? Assume the sale is a naked short sale (i.e., you have no position in the stock).

6.23 What is the standard deviation of the return on a hedge fund portfolio that is 100 percent invested in stock A and also carries an equal amount of stock B on leverage. Stock A has a standard deviation of return equal to 22 percent. Stock B has a standard deviation of return equal to 25 percent. The two stocks have a correlation of 75 percent.

6.24 What is the expected return on the leveraged portfolio in Question 6.23 if the expected return on each stock is 20 percent (unleveraged) and the risk-free rate is 5 percent?

6.25 What is the probability of loss for the portfolio in questions 6.23 and 6.24?

6.26 What is the probability of losing 25 percent or more for the portfolio in questions 6.23 and 6.24?

NOTES

1. "Hedge Funds, Leverage, and the Lessons of Long-Term Capital Management: Report of the President's Working Group on Financial Markets, April 1999," www.ustreas.gov/press/releases/reports/hedgfund.pdf.
2. For additional reading on options, see John Hull, *Options, Futures, and Other Derivatives,* 5th Edition, Pearson Education, 2002.
3. The cumulative probability is the area under the curve. This value can be calculated using the Excel function NORMDIST(Threshold Return, Expected Re-

turn, Standard Deviation of Return, TRUE or 1). {=NORMDIST(0%, 15%, 18%, 1)} returns 20.2 percent.

4. (=NORMDIST(0%, 25%, 36%, 1)} returns 24.4 percent.
5. (=NORMDIST(0%, 25%, 30.12%, 1)} returns 20.3 percent.
6. The cash generated by the short sale is also reinvested at the short-term rate of return equal to 5 percent.
7. (=NORMDIST(0%, 6%, 8.05%, 1)} returns 22.8 percent.

CHAPTER 7

Performance Measurement

Competitive investors seek attractive returns. Beauty remains in the eye of the beholder, though. Clearly, higher returns are better than lower returns. Investors would prefer to accept less risk to achieve a given return.

It is important to understand performance measurement. First the reader may be called upon to conduct a performance return. Second, the reader should be able to review critically the performance measurement calculated by others. Finally, the hedge fund returns are not directly comparable to the yields on alternative assets.[1] However, hedge fund returns can be readily adjusted to facilitate comparison to bond and money market returns.

CALCULATING RETURNS

Investors commit funds to a particular investment for a variety of reasons. The return on the investment is usually very important. Yet return is calculated many different ways to serve different purposes. Investors need to know how return is calculated to properly understand the investment results they receive.

Nominal Return

The nominal return is the simplest type of return calculation and is a component of most of the other return measures. To calculate nominal return, divide the gain in value by the starting value of the investment.

$$\text{Nominal Return} = \frac{\text{Gain}}{\text{Initial Investment Value}} \qquad (7.1)$$

Restating equation (7.1) slightly:

$$\text{Nominal Return} = \frac{\text{Final Investment Value} - \text{Initial Investment Value}}{\text{Initial Investment Value}} \quad (7.2)$$

This simplifies to:

$$\text{Nominal Return} = \frac{\text{Final Investment Value}}{\text{Initial Investment Value}} - 1 \quad (7.3)$$

Sometimes, this nominal return is modified slightly to acknowledge that the return shown in the numerator increases the investment base in the denominator as in equation (7.4):

$$\text{Nominal Return} = \frac{\text{Final Investment Value}}{(\text{Initial Investment Value} + \text{Final Investment Value})/2} - 1 \quad (7.4)$$

In equation (7.4), the return is divided by the average value of the investment.

Annualized Return

It is difficult to compare the nominal returns of different assets. Clearly, higher returns are better than lower returns, but it also matters how long it takes to achieve a particular return. Without some adjustment for time, it is not possible to compare returns. Generally, nominal returns are adjusted to a period equal to one year.

$$\text{Annualized Return} = \frac{\text{Gain}}{\text{Initial Investment Value}} \times \frac{1}{\text{Fraction of Year}} \quad (7.5)$$

Incorporating equation (7.1):

$$\text{Annualized Return} = \frac{\text{Nominal Return}}{\text{Fraction of Year}} \quad (7.6)$$

This method of converting a nominal return to an annual return presumes that you can repeat an investment over and over successively, until a year has passed. The return earned in a full year is the sum of the returns earned in all the subperiods of the year. In its simplest form, returns partway through the year are not available for reinvestment during the period. This annualized return can be compared with simple interest rates on investment alternatives.

Compound Returns

Many investments pay interest regularly during the life of the investment. Investors prefer to receive frequent partial payments of interest because this interest is then available for reinvestment. Compound returns account for this potential to earn interest on interest. Also, compound returns calculated from hedge fund returns that may not make periodic payments are important because this return can be compared directly with other investment alternatives.

Semiannual Compound Return Most bonds pay periodic interest payments during the life of the investment. In the United States, most government and corporate bonds pay half the annual income in two installments per year. Interest from first payments can be reinvested in the second period, so the gain to the investor is greater than in stated coupon rate.

Consider the following specific example. A bond pays 10 percent interest and repays principal at the end of one year. The repayment in one year (per $100 bond) is $100 principal plus $10 ($100 × 10 percent) or a total of $110. This value is sometimes called the future value. Equation (7.7) shows the future value of an annual-pay bond:

$$\text{Future Value} = \text{Principal} + (\text{Principal} \times r) \qquad (7.7)$$

which factors down to:

$$\text{Future value} = \text{Principal} \times (1 + r) \qquad (7.8)$$

$$= \$100 \times (1.10) = \$110 \qquad (7.9)$$

If the bond paid half the coupon after six months, the investor could reinvest that amount for the second half of the year. The future value of the semiannual bond will slightly exceed the future value of the annual bond.

Suppose for simplicity that the coupon could be reinvested in an identical bond. The future value is given by equation (7.9):

$$\text{Future Value} = \left(1+\frac{r}{2}\right) \times \left[\left(1+\frac{r}{2}\right) \times \text{Principal}\right] \qquad (7.10)$$

$$= \left(1+\frac{r}{2}\right)^2 \times \text{Principal} \qquad (7.11)$$

$$= (1.05)^2 \times \$100 = \$110.25 \qquad (7.12)$$

Using Excel:

$$= 1.05\wedge2*100 \qquad \text{produces } \$110.25$$

The semiannual bond has the same future value as an annual-pay bond with a 10.25 percent coupon. This means that a 10 percent semiannual bond has an effective annual yield of 10.25 percent.

Daily Compounding   In the 1970s, savings institutions used this interest-on-interest effect to pay a higher effective rate than the allowable ceiling. If a bank paid 10 percent interest compounded daily, the investor would have a balance (future value) of $110.5156 at the end of one year. The formula for daily compounding is shown in equation 7.13:

$$\text{Future Value} = \left(1+\frac{r}{365}\right) \times \left(1+\frac{r}{365}\right) \times \left(1+\frac{r}{365}\right) \ldots \left(1+\frac{r}{365}\right) \qquad (7.13)$$

$$= \left(1+\frac{r}{365}\right)^{365} \qquad (7.14)$$

$$= \left(1+\frac{10\%}{365}\right)^{365} \times \$100 = \$110.5156 \qquad (7.15)$$

Using Excel:

= (1 + 10%/365)^365*100   produces $110.5156

Therefore, a 10 percent interest rate paid daily is equivalent to an annual payment of 10.5156 percent.

Continuous Compounding   The logical limit to compounding in an accounting system is daily. Most interest accrual systems don't break down a year any finer than daily. However, mathematicians followed this progression from annual to semiannual to daily to the mathematical extreme. If interest could be paid every infinitesimally small fraction of a second and that interest was available for immediate reinvestment, the formula for the future value is given by equation (7.16):

$$\text{Future Value} = e^{rT} \tag{7.16}$$

where T is the time until repayment in years.

$$\text{Future Value} = 2.71828^{10\% \times 1} \times \$100 = \$100.5171 \tag{7.17}$$

Using Excel:

= exp(10%)*100   produces $100.5171

Notice that nearly all the benefit of interest on interest has already been realized under daily compounding.

Monthly and Quarterly Compounding   Hedge fund performance is generally reported monthly or quarterly. The mathematics follows the same pattern as already described. See equations (7.18) to (7.21) for details:
    Quarterly:

$$\text{Future Value} = \left(1 + \frac{r}{4}\right)^4 \tag{7.18}$$

$$= \left(1 + \frac{10\%}{4}\right)^4 \times \$100 = \$110.3813 \tag{7.19}$$

Monthly:

$$\text{Future Value} = \left(1 + \frac{r}{12}\right)^{12} \qquad (7.20)$$

$$= \left(1 + \frac{10\%}{12}\right)^{12} \times \$100 = \$110.4713 \qquad (7.21)$$

Using Excel:

$= (1+ 10\%/4)\wedge 4*100$	produces \$110.3813
$= (1+ 101\%/12)\wedge 12*100$	produces \$110.4713

Finding Equivalent Interest Rates for Different Compounding Frequencies It should be clear that a particular rate can imply different economic returns, depending on the frequency of compounding. For this reason, it is not possible to compare rates of different compounding frequencies without further analysis. Fortunately, it is possible to convert a rate using one compounding frequency to the equivalent rate using any other frequency. In the previous examples, a 10 percent rate was converted to the annual equivalent. The examples that follow find the rates required to attain the same effective annual rate.

For example, suppose that a hedge fund has been providing an annualized monthly return of 10 percent. To find a semiannual rate that is equivalent, find a rate that creates the same future value after one year. Equations (7.22) to (7.25) derive the equivalent rate relative to equal future values.

Find the future value from the monthly return:

$$\text{Future Value} = \left(1 + \frac{10\%}{12}\right)^{12} = 1.104713 \qquad (7.22)$$

Find the semiannual rate giving the same future value:

$$1.104713 = \left(1 + \frac{r_{\text{Semiannual}}}{2}\right)^{2} \qquad (7.23)$$

$$\sqrt{1.104713} = 1 + \frac{r_{\text{Semiannual}}}{2} \tag{7.24}$$

$$10.210\% = r_{\text{Semiannual}} \tag{7.25}$$

Using Excel:

=(SQRT(1.104713) − 1) × 2   produces 10.210%

It is also possible to convert the annualized monthly performance numbers to continuously compounded returns. See equations (7.26) to (7.27):

$$1.104713 = e^{r_{\text{Continuous}}T} \tag{7.26}$$

Take the natural logarithm of each side. Recall that $T = 1$, so it drops out:

$$\ln(1.104713) = r_{\text{Continuous}} = 9.9586\% \tag{7.27}$$

Using Excel:

ln(1.10473)   produces 9.9586%

Effect of Taxes

Suppose an individual investor paid a 40 percent income tax (federal plus state tax) on the return. Suppose that the investor made a $100 investment that provided a nominal return of $30 or 30 percent. The $30 return would create a $12 tax liability, reducing the after-tax return to $18 or 18 percent. The after-tax return is approximated by equation (7.28):

$$r_{\text{AfterTax}} = r_{\text{BeforeTax}} \times (1 - \text{Tax Rate}) \tag{7.28}$$

Notice that it is also possible to calculate the after-tax return directly, by reducing the future value in equation (7.18) by the amount of the taxes paid and resolving for the return consistent with this reduced future value.

Equation (7.18) is only an approximation because the timing of the tax payment may affect the true return. Certain taxes like the capital gains tax can be postponed indefinitely. Other taxes are payable several months after the end of a tax year. For the investor who makes estimated tax payments quarterly, the approximation may be accurate.

AVERAGING RETURNS

Hedge fund investors generally want to know how well a fund has performed over a period of time, so that the return is not overly influenced by short-term performance. This performance may be the basis of comparison between two hedge funds of the same strategy or between two hedge fund strategies, or comparison of a hedge fund against a benchmark return.

Calculating the Arithmetic Average Return

The simplest way to generate an average return is to add up a series of returns and divide by the number of periods in the sum. This method is called the arithmetic average return. Refer to the performance of a hypothetical hedge fund in Table 7.1.

The arithmetic average is calculated in the way most familiar to readers. First, the 12 monthly numbers are totaled (22.15 percent). Next, this total is divided by 12, the number of data points in the table. This arithmetic average (1.85 percent) is also called the simple average or unweighted average.

TABLE 7.1 Monthly Hedge Fund Performance

Month	Return
1	1.50%
2	–3.00%
3	3.75%
4	7.50%
5	7.20%
6	9.00%
7	–5.80%
8	1.80%
9	6.90%
10	–1.80%
11	0.20%
12	–5.10%
Total	22.15%
Arithmetic Average	1.85%

Calculating the Geometric Mean Return

Table 7.2 extends the monthly performance from Table 7.1. The "Wealth Relative" column represents a $1 investment in the fund with reinvestment.

At the end of one year, $1 grows to $1.2282. Obviously, the fund has produced an annual return of 22.82 percent. This information is sufficient to determine the geometric average monthly return. Equations (7.29) to (7.32) show how the monthly average is calculated:

$$\text{Future Value} = \left(1 + \frac{r_{\text{GeometricAverage}}}{12} \right)^{12} \tag{7.29}$$

To simplify, take the 12th root of both sides:

$$\sqrt[12]{1.2282} - 1 = \frac{r_{\text{GeometricAverage}}}{12} \tag{7.30}$$

$$1.73\% = r_{\text{GeometricAverage}} \quad \text{(Monthly)} \tag{7.31}$$

$$20.73\% = 1.37\% \times 12 \quad \text{(Annual)} \tag{7.32}$$

TABLE 7.2 Monthly Performance with Wealth Relatives

Month	Return	Wealth Relative
January	1.50%	1.0150
February	−3.00%	0.9846
March	3.75%	1.0215
April	7.50%	1.0981
May	7.20%	1.1771
June	9.00%	1.2831
July	−5.80%	1.2087
August	1.80%	1.2304
September	6.90%	1.3153
October	−1.80%	1.2916
November	0.20%	1.2942
December	−5.10%	1.2282

Using Excel:

$$= 1.2282\char`^(1/12) - 1 \qquad \text{(Monthly)} \qquad \text{produces } 1.73\%$$

Notice that the geometric average is lower than the arithmetic average. The geometric average will generally be below the arithmetic average when the returns differ from month to month. Consider an example that may be familiar. Suppose a hedge fund made 50 percent in one month and lost 50 percent in the second month. The arithmetic average return is zero because $(50\% - 50\%)/2 = 0$. The geometric return is negative. A \$1 investment would grow to \$1.50 at the end of the first month then decline to \$.75 after the second month.[2]

Time-Weighted Returns

Investors often hear about time-weighted returns. Portfolio managers like to publish the time-weighted returns because the results are not influenced by whether investors made additional investments just before a good or a bad month. Instead, the time-weighted returns reflect a constant investment in the fund, changing only by the amount reinvested each period.

In fact, the time-weighted return is nearly the same as the geometric average return. For hedge fund returns averaging evenly spaced time intervals (months or quarters), they are identical.

Dollar-Weighted Returns

Investors may prefer to see the performance they have experienced with a particular hedge fund. The investor may have not made a single investment. Instead, the investor may have made additional investments over time and have greater sensitivity to recent performance. The dollar-weighted return reflects the economics of a particular investor and specifically considers the impact of the timing of the investments.

Suppose an investor contributed \$1 million to a hedge fund that experienced the returns in Table 7.1. After six months, the fund had experienced monthly returns of over 4 percent (by both the arithmetic and geometric means). In fact, based on Table 7.2, the \$1 million investment would have grown to \$1,228,200. Suppose that the investor put in an additional \$1 million on June 30. At the end of the year, the combined investment was worth \$2,185,466 (less than the value on June 30) because the fund lost around 0.75 percent per month in the final six months of the year.

The dollar-weighted return is the rate that makes equation (7.33) true:

$$-\$1,000,000 \times \left(1 + \frac{r_{\text{DollarWeighted}}}{12}\right)^{12} - \$1,000,000 \times \left(1 + \frac{r_{\text{DollarWeighted}}}{12}\right)^{6} = \$2,185,466 \qquad (7.33)$$

Equation (7.33) is true at a return of 11.82 percent compounded monthly or 12.49 percent compounded annually.[3] This return is considerably below the 22.82 percent reported in Table 7.2 because more money was invested during the later, losing period than the earlier months that produced gains.

MEASURES OF INVESTMENT RISK

Hedge funds measure risk in a variety of ways. In this chapter, risk measures will be derived from the reported performance values. Other measures of risk can be calculated from the characteristics of the positions. For additional reading, review material discussing value at risk (VaR), RiskMetrics, CreditMetrics, bond duration, and option "Greeks."

Standard Deviation as a Measure of Performance Risk

The most common measure of portfolio risk used by both practitioners and academics is the standard deviation of return. The measure applies the textbook definition of this summary statistic; see equations (7.34) and (7.35):

$$\sigma = \sqrt{\frac{\sum\limits_{i=1}^{N}\left(r_i - \bar{r}\right)^2}{N-1}} \qquad (7.34)$$

or the more efficient formula:

$$\sigma = \sqrt{\frac{N\sum\limits_{i=1}^{N}r_i^2 - \left(\sum\limits_{i=1}^{N}r_i\right)^2}{N \times (N-1)}} \qquad (7.35)$$

Using Excel:

   = sstdev(a1 : a12)   or   = stdeva(a1 : a12)   produces sample
                                                                     standard deviation

The standard deviation of returns from Table 7.1 or Table 7.2 was 5.11 percent. Typically, this monthly standard deviation would be annualized. To annualize, multiply this monthly standard deviation by the square root of the number of time periods per year: $5.11\% \times \text{sqrt}(12) = 17.70\%$.

The standard deviation is a powerful, concise measure of risk if the returns of the portfolio are normally distributed and if the standard deviation is constant or predictable. Refer to Figure 7.1, which shows the distribution of returns for two portfolios. One portfolio has an expected return of 10 percent and a standard deviation of return of 10 percent. The second portfolio has a higher expected return of 15 percent and a standard deviation of return of 20 percent. Assuming the returns of the two portfolios are indeed normally distributed, the standard deviation contains detailed information about the chance of virtually any outcome. For example, the chance of losing money on the first portfolio is 15.9 percent in the next year, while the second portfolio should lose money 22.7 percent of the time. This kind of information is available because the familiar bell curve is, in fact, a map of probabilities of such outcomes.[4]

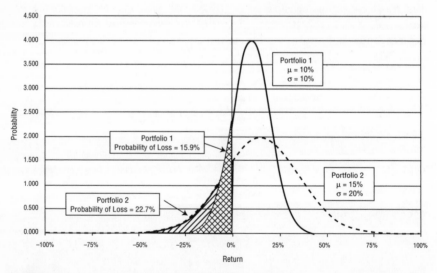

FIGURE 7.1   Normal Distributions

Other Statistical Models of Risk

Standard deviation has historical precedence as a risk measurement, but most investors worry less about very good performance than very bad performance. Realizing that investors are more concerned about outcomes on the left sections of the bell curves in Figure 7.1, researchers have constructed a number of measures to focus on the bad performance.

The measure called "downside deviation" is essentially the formula for standard deviation with the favorable deviations omitted. This concept is stated more formally in equation (7.36):

$$\text{Downside Deviation} = \sqrt{\frac{\sum_{i=1}^{N} \min(r_i - r^*, 0)^2}{N-1}} \qquad (7.36)$$

Note that a variable r^* substitutes for the mean return in equation (7.36). This threshold return is the break point. When r_i is below r^*, the deviation is included; and when r_i is above r^*, the deviation is ignored. When r^* equals zero, the downside deviation includes only the losing returns for each month or quarter. The data from Tables 7.1 and 7.2 have a downside deviation of 2.56 percent (not annualized) using a threshold return of 0 percent.

A related measure called downside semivariance corresponds to the variance of returns. Just as the standard deviation is the square root of variance, downside deviation is the square root of downside semivariance. See equation (7.37):

$$\text{Downside Semivariance} = \frac{\sum_{i=1}^{N} \min(r_i - r^*, 0)^2}{N-1} \qquad (7.37)$$

The data in Tables 7.1 and 7.2 have a downside semivariance of 0.07 percent (not annualized) using a threshold return of 0 percent.

Other Measures of Portfolio Risk

Not all distributions are normal, but the statistical methods just described may still provide useful information about the risk of a hedge fund portfolio. Hedge fund practitioners have developed several alternative measures of hedge fund portfolio risk.

Largest Losing Month and Drawdown   This measure calculates the largest cumulative loss on a hedge fund portfolio. In the example in Table 7.1, the largest loss was 5.8 percent. Usually, these loss statistics are calculated from inception, so if additional performance data was available, it would also be analyzed to find a larger loss.

In addition, if an additional loss occurs before an earlier loss is made back, the cumulative effect of the losses is measured as a drawdown. Table 7.3 extends the performance calculations from Table 7.1 and Table 7.2 and demonstrates one way that the drawdown can be calculated.

The monthly returns and the wealth relative columns in Table 7.3 are the same as they appeared in the previous tables. The new column labeled "High-Water Mark" preserves the previous wealth relative after a loss. (If the net asset value of the hedge fund is known, that value may be substituted for the wealth relative values because these wealth relatives are just normalized net asset values.) The column labeled "Drawdown" measures the cumulative loss from the previous high-water mark.

Months to Earn Back Loss   Another measure of risk is to track the number of months before a loss is made up by later gains. In our sample data, the loss in February lasted only one month because the gain in March restored the value of the fund to levels greater than the value at the beginning of February. The loss in July lasted two months. The loss that began in October has stretched to three months and continues to be a loss period.

Investors look at a variety of statistics related to these measures of time. How long did it take to recover the largest monthly loss? What was

TABLE 7.3   Drawdown Calculations

Month	Return	Wealth Relative	High-Water Mark	Drawdown
January	1.50%	1.0150	1.0150	0.00%
February	−3.00%	0.9846	1.0150	−3.00%
March	3.75%	1.0215	1.0215	0.00%
April	7.50%	1.0981	1.0981	0.00%
May	7.20%	1.1771	1.1771	0.00%
June	9.00%	1.2831	1.2831	0.00%
July	−5.80%	1.2087	1.2831	−5.80%
August	1.80%	1.2304	1.2831	−4.10%
September	6.90%	1.3153	1.3153	0.00%
October	−1.80%	1.2916	1.3153	−1.80%
November	0.20%	1.2942	1.3153	−1.60%
December	−5.10%	1.2282	1.3153	−6.62%

the average length of time that a drawdown persisted? What is the longest period of time that a drawdown persisted?

Percent of Months with Losses   Hedge fund investors may wish to predict the probability that a given month will be a loss. With the usual caveat that past performance may not be indicative of future performance, this indicator provides a way to separate hedge funds that have been more likely to show losses from hedge funds that have been more likely to show gains.

One measure of this probability is the percent of past months that have been losses. In our example, the hypothetical fund lost money in 4 out of 12 months (33 percent). If this performance provides a fair prediction of future performance, investors can expect to lose money one-third of the time. There is also a 1 in 3 chance that the next month will be a loss, and 2 in 3 chances or 67 percent of breaking even or receiving a gain. There is a 44 percent probability that both of the next two months will be gains (66.7% × 66.7%).

A technique called resampling can be used to generate a variety of probability statistics similar to the "probability of loss" statistic. This method generates a distribution of future returns from the past returns. The previous months are equally likely to recur. By generating many samples in random order, it is possible to discern the probability of a loss in a particular month, the chance of losing two or more months in a row, the chance of losing 10 percent or more, and so on.

TRADE-OFF BETWEEN RISK AND RETURN

Financial theory argues that investors can increase the returns on their portfolios by assuming greater risk. Of course, investors prefer higher returns to lower returns. Investors also prefer a portfolio with less risk to a portfolio with more risk. Investors face a trade-off, where it is possible to increase the expected return on their portfolios only by assuming greater portfolio risks. Consequently, investors want a measure of how different hedge funds perform in the trade-off between risk and return.

Sharpe Ratio

The Sharpe ratio measures the excess return on a portfolio versus the standard deviation of return (reward divided by risk).

$$\text{Sharpe Ratio} = \frac{r_{\text{Average}} - r_{\text{RiskFree}}}{\sigma_{\text{Return}}} \qquad (7.38)$$

The Sharpe ratio is calculated over an interval of time. Usually, the arithmetic mean return is used in the numerator because the arithmetic mean return is used to calculate the standard deviation in the denominator.

The Sharpe ratio for the hypothetical performance used in this chapter is 1.02522 using a risk-free rate of 4 percent:

$$\text{Sharpe Ratio} = \frac{22.15\% - 4\%}{17.70\%} = 1.02522 \qquad (7.39)$$

Sortino Ratio

The Sortino ratio substitutes downside deviation for the standard deviation in the denominator. The Sortino ratio for the sample data is 2.0495 as calculated in equation (7.40) (again using a 4 percent risk-free rate):

$$\text{Sortino Ratio} = \frac{22.15\% - 4\%}{8.86\%} = 2.0495 \qquad (7.40)$$

Treynor Ratio

One of the problems with using the Sharpe ratio or the Sortino ratio to manage the risk-return trade-off is that the measure ignores the effects of diversification. In fact, the amount of risk present in a component of a portfolio is less important than the effect that component has on the risk of the entire portfolio. For this reason, financial theory argues that investors should not be paid for assuming risks in general, but only those risks that cannot be diversified.

The risk measure beta ignores the diversifiable risks and measures only the broad market returns. The Treynor ratio modifies the Sharpe ratio by substituting this measure of risk for the standard deviation in the denominator in equation (7.41):

$$\text{Treynor Ratio} = \frac{r_{\text{Average}} - r_{\text{RiskFree}}}{\text{Beta}} \qquad (7.41)$$

$$\text{Absolute Risk-Adjusted Return} = \text{Treynor Ratio} + r_{\text{RiskFree}}$$

Jensen's Alpha

Jensen's alpha also focuses on undiversifiable risk. The statistic focuses on the excess return above the return expected on the portfolio by virtue of the risks taken in the portfolio. The formula for that excess return is in equation (7.42):

$$\text{Jensen's Alpha} = r_{\text{Portfolio}} - r_{\text{RiskFree}} - \text{Beta}_{\text{Portfolio}} \times (r_{\text{Market}} - r_{\text{RiskFree}}) \qquad (7.42)$$

The return on the portfolio is reduced by the risk-free rate. The return is also reduced by the amount demanded by the market for a portfolio with a beta equal to the hedge fund's beta.

While Jensen's alpha is used in hedge fund analysis, there are several problems that the user should note. First, unlike conventional long-only portfolios, many hedge funds seek returns that are independent of stock and bond returns. It may be misleading to benchmark this type of performance against market returns. To the extent the fund succeeds in producing a low correlation to market returns, it may produce a beta of zero (all risks are nonsystematic or diversifiable risks). That would mean that all the return above the risk-free rate is alpha. As desirable as this performance may be, many investors would not agree that a hedge fund that was as volatile as the stock market and underperformed stock returns was producing substantial positive alpha.

It is possible to define the market narrowly. If a hedge fund pursues an identifiable strategy, it might be possible to compare the fund performance to a benchmark based on the performance of several managers pursuing the same strategy. Measured in this way, Jensen's alpha would measure the extent a manager performed well within a strategy and would not confound the alpha with the performance of the style.

SUMMARY AND CONCLUSION

Hedge funds are intensely interested in performance measurement. Because fees are high in hedge funds, funds are pressured to perform well. Some investors may be willing to experience high levels of risk with their hedge fund assets, but all investors want to get as high a return as possible for the amount of risk assumed.

Performance is the largest motivator influencing investors to make an investment in a hedge fund or to close out an investment. For this reason, hedge funds use performance measurements prominently in their marketing literature.

QUESTIONS AND PROBLEMS

7.1   Why might it be desirable to annualize nominal returns?

7.2   Why would an investor be interested in nominal return, which ignores the amount of time required to produce a return?

7.3   Sometimes, return is calculated by dividing the gain by the average of the beginning investment and the ending value. Why would an investor favor this formula for return over a simpler formula that considers only the beginning investment?

7.4   Why would an investor prefer a compound return over simple annualized return?

7.5   Nominal returns are annualized by multiplying by number of times this return could be achieved in a year (i.e., number of days in a year divided by the number of days in the return period). Why is 360 often used for the number of days in a year?

7.6   Why is it necessary to sometimes assume a year has 360 days and other times use 365 (or even 366) days?

7.7   What is meant by present value?

7.8   Describe the meaning of future value.

7.9   Explain why a geometric average return is generally below the arithmetic average return for the same data.

7.10 Measures of risk based on statistics frequently assume that returns follow a normal distribution. Other statistics, such as percent of winning months and probability of loss, can be calculated without assumptions about the return distribution. What major limitation do distribution-free measures have as measures of risk?

7.11 A hedge fund net asset value on June 30, 20XX, was 1,010.50. The NAV on July 31 was $1,111.55. What was the nominal return on the fund for the month of July?

7.12 What is the annualized return on the fund described in question 7.11?

7.13 You are offered two investments. One will pay 10 percent in a year. The second will pay 9.65 percent (annualized), but payments will be compounded monthly and paid after one year. Which investment would you prefer?

7.14 You must pay $1 million three years from now. What is the present value (PV) of the payment if interest rates are at 8 percent (compound annually)?

7.15 Your marginal tax rate (federal plus state) is 39.6 percent. How would your answer to question 7.14 change if you incorporated an after-tax return in your PV analysis?

7.16 What is the future value (FV) of a $10.00 cash flow in 2.5 years at an interest rate of 9 percent semiannually compounded?

7.17 What is the FV of a $10.00 cash flow in 2.5 years at an interest rate of 9 percent continuously compounded?

7.18 What are the arithmetic and geometric averages of the following monthly returns?

January	2.25%
February	−1.75%
March	8.15%
April	−4.40%
May	−3.30%
June	3.55%
July	9.15%
August	1.85%
September	3.65%
October	2.25%
November	−3.60%
December	2.95%

7.19 What is the standard deviation of return for the return series in question 7.18?

7.20 What is the semiannually compounded equivalent to the geometric average return calculated in 7.18?

7.21 What is the continuously compounded equivalent to the geometric average return calculated in 7.18?

7.22 Calculate the downside deviation from the returns in question 7.18 and a threshold rate of 0 percent.

7.23 Calculate the Sharpe ratio and the Sortino ratio from the data in question 7.18 (using the results in 7.18 to 7.22). Assume a risk-free rate of 5 percent.

7.24 What is the largest drawdown in the performance in question 7.18?

7.25 Based on the 12 months of data in question 7.18, what is the probability of loss in a given month?

NOTES

1. Performance measurement of traditional portfolios also differs from the stated returns on bonds and money market instruments.
2. In fact, it doesn't matter if the returns occur in the opposite order. In this case, $1 declines to $.50 at the end of the first month (that is, − 50 percent), then rises to $.75 (that is, + 50 percent) at the end of the second month.

3. The dollar-weighted average was also calculated using the XIRR function in Excel. This calculation resulted in a dollar-weighted return of 22.75 percent if only a single investment is made at the beginning of the period (compared to 22.82 percent calculated from Table 7.2) and 12.43 percent if the investor made the additional contribution as per this example (compared to 12.49 percent as reported in the text). These values differ slightly because of details such as the way the fraction of time is calculated within the year and how monthly rates are annualized.

4. To retrieve these probabilities in Excel, use the NORMDIST function:

=NORMDIST(Return, Expected rReturn, Standard Deviation of Return, TRUE)

Note: The fourth parameter, TRUE, directs the function to return the cumulative probability. This function will return the probability that the outcome will be zero (on the verge of loss) and worse.

CHAPTER 8

Hedge Fund Legislation and Regulation

The laws and regulations affecting a hedge fund represent one of the most complex topics addressed in this course book. One law firm that sets up hedge funds and provides legal services to hedge funds created a handbook[1] for its clients totaling 563 pages, with promises to produce at least a second volume to complete the tutorial. In contrast, this course book presents only a summary of the major legal issues.

INTRODUCTION TO FUND REGULATION

Hedge funds are affected by many laws and regulations even when they are exempt from certain provisions. Hedge funds must comply with these rules or make certain they are able to take advantage of exemptions.

Reasons for Regulating Securities Markets

Many of the laws and regulations governing securities markets trace their origin to the stock market crash of 1929 and the resulting depression. The laws passed in 1933 and 1934 as well as more recent rules and regulations have attempted to reform the securities markets for all investors. The state and federal securities laws seek to make the markets fair for all participants. The legislation also is designed to prevent abuses and punish offenders when abuse occurs. The rules are designed to protect naive investors from harm that less naive investors escape. Finally, the rules require adequate disclosure as one of the primary means of accomplishing these goals.

Reasons for Granting Exemptions

The legislators who drafted the securities markets legislation have generally provided exceptions to individuals and institutions with substantial income, wealth, investment experience, and investment sophistication. The rationale for these exemptions is that this group gets little benefit from paternalistic protection and would be better off with greater freedom to invest as they see fit. The exemptions arbitrarily draw a line (actually several lines) separating investors who qualify for exemption from investors who do not.

There are several reasons why certain investors should be exempted from some protective provisions of the securities laws. Investors in this group, if properly identified, should have sufficient resources to be able to afford to lose all of their investments in a particular exempt investment. This group should have sufficient knowledge to make sound investment decisions. This group can hire experts on accounting, tax, law, or other specializations if their own expertise is insufficient to evaluate an exempt investment. Many in this group could invest in hedge fund products in some way by establishing offshore investment vehicles that could sidestep rigid regulations. Finally, it may be easier to permit some financial products to exist as unregulated products rather than trying (perhaps unsuccessfully) to regulate them.

INVESTMENT COMPANY ACT—FUND REGISTRATION

The Investment Company Act of 1940 requires investment companies to register with the U.S. Securities and Exchange Commission (SEC) and submit to SEC regulation. Hedge funds are investment companies and would have to register but for the exemption described next.

Hedge fund organizers gain exception by selling ownership as a private placement, which means, in part, that the manager must not make a public offering of securities anywhere in the world. So-called accredited investors may buy private placements and thereby be exempt from most of the Investment Company Act of 1940 and the Securities Act of 1933. Accredited investors are defined in Section 3(c)(1) of the Investment Company Act and include individuals who earn at least $200,000 ($300,000 with spouse) both in the current year and the previous two years or have net worth of at least $1 million or are certain institutions worth at least $5 million. Hedge funds can sell to not more than 100 investors under the Section 3(c)(1) exemption. The investor count is subject to certain integration rules and look-through provisions that affect how the number of investors is counted.

Hedge funds that limit sales to "qualified purchasers" may admit not more than 499 investors. Section 3(c)(7) defines a qualified purchaser as an individual, family corporation, or family trust having net worth of at least $5 million or various businesses with net worth of at least $25 million made up entirely of qualified purchasers.

Finally, commodity pools may be exempt from the Investment Company Act as long as they trade only futures (they may own and trade government securities to maintain margin on the futures positions).

SECURITIES ACT OF 1933

The Securities Act regulates the issuance of securities. Hedge funds accept money from investors by selling stock or partnership interests in an investment company. However, those investment sales are exempt from the Securities Act as long as the interests are sold as private placements.

Regulation 506 of Regulation D provides a safe harbor definition of a private placement. In addition, Regulation 506 significantly lowers the so-called blue sky requirements (the collection of state laws affecting security issuance). The hedge fund must make no general solicitation and may not advertise. The regulation created the "reasonable beliefs test," which means that the manager may approach an investor only if there is a reasonable basis for believing the investor is accredited and knowledgeable based on a prior relationship. The regulation allows the manager to sell only to accredited investors, although the manager may sell to no more than 35 nonaccredited investors in return for higher disclosure requirements.

INVESTMENT ADVISERS ACT OF 1940

The Investment Advisers Act requires the investment advisers to register with the SEC and regulates the employees working for the investment adviser. Recall that a hedge fund usually has no employees but is instead a pool of cash and investments. The business organization that contains the employees and occupies office space is the hedge fund management company. This management company is an investment adviser hired by the fund and paid management and incentive fees for investment services.

Most hedge fund managers are exempt from registration because the Investment Adviser Act exempts advisers with fewer than 15 relationships from regulation. The hedge fund may have 100 or 499 investors, but the Investment Advisers Act acknowledges that the manager usually has only one customer (i.e., one hedge fund).

Some managers sponsor more than one hedge fund. In particular, a manager may have mirror funds in the United States and offshore that carry nearly identical positions. Some managers may also run separate accounts for certain investors with positions that closely resemble the hedge fund managed in parallel. These relationships could require a hedge fund manager to register as an investment adviser, but most managers limit the number of relationships to preserve their exemption. However, the SEC recently proposed requiring all hedge fund managers to register.

SECURITIES EXCHANGE ACT OF 1934

The Securities Exchange Act created the SEC, defined the duties of the SEC, and empowered the agency. The Act also defined certain illegal activities and required market participants to make certain disclosures.

The SEC is responsible for registering securities and registering and regulating securities market participants. But for the exemptions written into individual securities acts, a hedge fund would be regulated by the SEC in many ways. The sale of interests to investors (at least in the United States) would be controlled by the Securities Act of 1933 and enforced by the SEC. The day-to-day management of the investments by the management company would be controlled by the Investment Company Act of 1940 and enforced by the SEC. Finally, the marketing of hedge fund interests (unless outsourced) would require a hedge fund to register as a broker-dealer, as provided by the Securities Exchange Act.

The Securities Exchange Act established a policy of handing off a substantial portion of the monitoring and enforcement to self-regulating agencies. The Commodity Exchange Act (see next section) follows this pattern of mixing governmental and industry regulation, with the SEC regulating the securities markets and Commodity Futures Trading Commission (CFTC) regulating the futures and cash commodity markets. The New York Stock Exchange (NYSE), the Nasdaq over-the-counter market, and the National Association of Securities Dealers (NASD) all operate as self-regulating bodies.

COMMODITY EXCHANGE ACT

The Commodity Exchange Act regulates commodity pool operators and the commodity pools they manage. The Commodity Exchange Act will define a hedge fund as a commodity pool if a hedge fund trades futures or commodities. Many hedge funds therefore register as commodity pools and their managers register as commodity pool operators. There is no exemption used by hedge funds to escape regulation under the Commodity Exchange Act, except not trading futures and commodities (which really isn't an exemption).

However, if all investors are qualified eligible participants (QEPs), the fund may take an election in Section 4.7, which eases reporting requirements. A QEP is defined as an individual with $2 million in investments or $200,000 in margin (or a combination). Certain organizations with $5 million in assets, accredited individuals or organizations (under SEC Regulation D, Rule 501), or offshore individuals or organizations are also QEPs.

The Commodity Exchange Act charges the CFTC with regulating the industry. The Act also requires a self-regulating agency to regulate the individual participants. The National Futures Association (NFA) was created to implement the regulations required by the Commodity Exchange Act.

The CFTC imposes disclosure requirements and procedures for commodity industry participants. The CFTC and NFA require the hedge funds that register as commodity pools to submit audited financial statements to each agency. Each agency may subject the hedge fund to on-site audits.

EMPLOYEE RETIREMENT INCOME SECURITY ACT OF 1974

The Employee Retirement Income Security Act (ERISA) regulated qualified retirement accounts in the United States, including pension funds, various types of individual retirement accounts (IRAs), Keogh plans, simplified employee pension (SEP) plans, and other tax-deferred accounts. These retirement accounts are sometime called plan assets.

ERISA regulates the investment management of plan assets in many ways, including disclosure requirements, use of leverage, and risk tolerance, and holds the manager to the high standards of a fiduciary relationship. In contrast, investors in an exempt hedge fund are only protected from fraud, and managers are charged with few duties beyond honesty and fairness.

Not surprisingly, hedge fund managers avoid being classified as managers of plan assets. If plan assets comprise 25 percent or more of a hedge fund, the hedge fund is deemed to be plan assets and the manager and the fund are controlled by ERISA. Hedge funds monitor the portions of their funds attributable to plan assets and most managers reserve the right to return any money to investors if the investment puts them at risk of being regulated as a pension fund.

UNRELATED BUSINESS TAXABLE INCOME

Congress created a tax called the unrelated business income tax (UBIT) to prevent tax abuse and to promote fair play in the business community. The Internal Revenue Service was concerned that individuals or companies might form a tax-exempt entity (for example, a church, foundation, or endowment) and run an otherwise taxable business through the tax-exempt organization solely to avoid being taxed. Taxpaying businesses also complained that tax-exempt businesses had an unfair advantage in competing with taxable businesses because the tax-exempt businesses didn't pay tax on the profits of their businesses.

The tax was not meant to apply to investments made by tax-exempt businesses, so the law made an effort to distinguish investing activities from business activities. The nature of some hedge fund investments, coupled with the flow-through tax treatment of hedge fund returns (partnership or limited liability corporation) can trigger UBIT.

Hedge funds that have significant interest expenses may force an otherwise tax-exempt investor to pay UBIT. Income expenses exist primarily as borrowing expenses for hedge funds that use leverage. Strategies that use leverage, including many arbitrage strategies and most bond strategies, may produce large enough interest expense to require tax payments.

Tax-exempt investors can usually avoid UBIT by not using strategies that might generate interest expenses or by investing in offshore hedge funds instead of domestic (U.S.) funds. Because the offshore funds are generally organized as corporations, they do not flow interest expense on to their investors. Instead, the tax-exempt investor receives dividends (possibly) and capital gains or losses.

USA PATRIOT ACT

The Uniting and Strengthening America by Providing Appropriate Tools Required to Intercept and Obstruct Terrorism Act (USA Patriot Act) was passed by Congress shortly after the terrorist attack on the World Trade Center on September 11, 2001. The Act contains many provisions, but the sections that affect hedge funds most are the parts of the Act restricting money laundering.

The Act specifies many procedures and requires the manager to train employees to ensure compliance. The Act imposes a duty on hedge funds to know quite a bit about their investors. Prior to the existence of the Patriot Act, hedge funds only had to have a reasonable basis to believe their investors were suited to invest, and the Section 3(c)(1) or Section 3(c)(7) exemptions described earlier provided a basis. The duties required by the Patriot Act will become clearer over time, but advisers recommend that hedge funds gather considerably more background information than previously and probably should take steps to verify the information to assure compliance with the Act.

QUESTIONS AND PROBLEMS

8.1 Considering the complications imposed on hedge funds to take advantage of registration exemptions, why don't hedge funds just register their securities and register their management companies as investment advisers?

8.2 You run a hedge fund organized under the exemption Section 3(c)(1). You currently have 99 investors. Are you permitted to admit a senior trader as a partner in your hedge fund?

8.3 Suppose the trader in question 8.2 does not have enough income or wealth to be an accredited investor. Is this employee permitted to invest in your hedge fund?

8.4 A wealthy investor has a net worth of $10 million but admits to having little or no knowledge of investments. He invests in a hedge fund as a limited partner. The hedge fund admits the investor as a qualified purchaser on the basis of the investor's net worth. Later, the investor loses his hedge fund investment because of losses in the position of the hedge fund. Can he sue for restitution based on the argument that due to his inexperience as an investor he was not a qualified purchaser?

8.5 An offshore hedge fund has nearly 499 investors. What can the manager do to permit it to accept additional investors into the fund?

8.6 A domestic hedge fund has nearly 499 investors. What can the manager do to permit it to accept additional investors into the fund?

8.7 Under what circumstances does a tax-exempt investor need to worry that an investment in a hedge fund would require the hedge fund to pay unrelated business income tax?

8.8 What are some of the problems for hedge funds complying with the USA Patriot Act?

8.9 How do exemptions affect a hedge funds' exposure to fraud rules?

8.10 Is it always true that investors receive less disclosure from a privately placed hedge fund investment than from a registered investment account?

NOTES

1. Gardner Carton and Douglas, LLP, *The GCD Hedge Fund Handbook, Volume 1: Organizational and Marketing Matters*, September 1, 2003.

CHAPTER 9

Accounting

The first written descriptions of accounting methods appeared 500 years ago.[1] Double-entry accounting methods have evolved to accommodate the specialization that has developed in the economy, the new technologies that have been created, and the tremendous increase in size of businesses. The accounting principles and methods used for manufacturing and service firms are used with little change to account for leveraged investments in stocks, bonds, and commodities denominated in a variety of currencies.

ACCOUNTING PRINCIPLES APPLIED TO HEDGE FUND ACCOUNTING

Double-entry bookkeeping is used to account for hedge fund transactions and ownership interests of the investors. Hedge funds adopted methods from other types of portfolio investors and from broker-dealers to meet their special needs.

Consistency

Most of the principles of accounting found in standard accounting text-books apply with little or no reinterpretation. Take, for example, the principle of consistency. An accounting system should use consistent methods to calculate results from different periods. For an industrial corporation, the need for consistency rests on assuring that comparisons between periods result from the operation of the company and are not an artifice of changing methods. Results from several periods over time allow an investor to monitor the success and forecast results. The hedge fund investor must also track fund performance and cannot do so without a consistent accounting. More important, the investor contributes capital, receives allocations of performance, and redeems capital. It is even more important that the hedge fund accounting is consistent because the investor's return is based on changes in the accounts during the investment period.

Disclosure

Similarly, the principle of disclosure also applies to hedge funds. In general, the financial statements should disclose adequate information so that readers of the statements can make informed decisions about the company. Managers of manufacturing or service companies may prefer to make incomplete disclosures to make the results look favorable, but auditors, regulators, and readers of the financial statements pressure the companies to make adequate disclosures. Likewise, hedge fund managers often resist making adequate disclosure, especially about the nature of investment positions. These managers argue that the information cannot be disclosed without putting the investors at risk that others will use this information to the detriment of the hedge fund investors. Hedge funds sometimes received qualified opinions from auditors because they fail to disclose enough information in their financial statements. For all but the largest hedge funds, auditors, regulators, and investors prevail on the fund managers to make adequate disclosures.

Materiality

The materiality principle also applies to hedge fund accounting. A hedge fund may violate most generally accepted accounting methods if doing so creates no impact on financial statements large enough to affect any user of the statements. This is not an invitation to falsify records, ignore data, or mislead investors. Nevertheless, financial statements are acceptable despite errors and shortcuts that create tiny discrepancies.

Conservatism

When a difference in method might result in more than one result, financial statements should reflect the least favorable result. The principle of conservatism presents no clear standard for hedge fund accounting. In general, conservatism calls for accounting policies that lead to lower revenues, higher expenses, lower asset values, higher liability values, and lower equity. The principle of conservatism cannot be used to justify undervaluing assets in an early period to create gains in later periods when less conservative methods are used. New investors should not be able to buy into the fund at bargain prices, just as existing investors should not be redeemed at a low net asset value to assure that the financial statements are conservative.

Revenue Principle

The revenue principle determines when revenues are recognized. Some companies have trouble defining when revenue is recognized because it is difficult to point to a specific date when the service has been performed or the good has been delivered. This ambiguity doesn't generally exist for hedge funds. The positions are repriced each statement period, and the income, expenses, gains, and losses are tallied. Since the service provided by the hedge fund is the production of investment returns, revenues (and all components of investment performance) are recognized at the end of each period.

Some hedge funds have trouble revaluing certain kinds of assets at the end of each period. For example, a fund that invests in venture capital and other private equity may find it difficult to identify prices that are objective enough to use to calculate investment returns and assess performance fees. These funds may hold such assets at historical cost until resold and assess no incentive fees on unrealized gains.

These funds use a method called side-pocket allocations. The hedge fund that acquires assets that are difficult to value will segregate those assets and establish the ownership percentages based on the capital positions of the investors. These percentages remain fixed until the assets are liquidated, unaffected by capital contributions and withdrawals. In other words, a new investor does not participate in returns on existing assets, and old investors are not permitted to withdraw capital committed to assets in side-pocket allocations. As a result, revenues are timed to either the liquidation of assets or a time when the price of the assets becomes easier to determine (for example, after an initial public offering).

Matching Principle

The matching principle is the main basis for accrual accounting (see later). Corporations accumulate the costs of production as inventory or in other accounts that postpone recognizing a cash outflow as an expense. Hedge fund income statements recognize revenue each accounting period, so they likewise recognize most expenses in the current period. As will be noted, the revenues and expenses are accrued, not necessarily the timing of the cash flows.

Lower of Cost or Market Rule

Accounting values are generally based on historical cost. Both as a reality check and as a reasonable effort to control fraud, most accounting entries (including assets, liabilities, equity, revenues, and expenses) are based on the actual cash value at the time of the entry. In order to keep financial statements conservative, a corporation will sometimes be required to recognize a loss if an asset permanently falls below historical cost. In general, assets are not written up when fair value exceeds historical cost.

The lower of cost or market rule does not apply to portfolios. The rule may apply to office equipment or supplies, but these assets would generally be carried on the books of the fund manager, not the fund. In any case, the fund investments will comprise most of the assets (and liabilities) on the balance sheet.

Many of the rules about valuation are controlled by the tax code. These rules are covered in Chapter 10. For financial reporting purposes, stocks, bonds, commodities, and derivatives are valued at the current market value of the assets. The portfolio accounting measures the changes in value of the fund caused by realized and unrealized changes in prices of the individual positions.

Finally, the definition of market value can influence the performance of the fund. A fund may be able to choose to price positions based on the last price, a closing price, offer, bid, or some combination. Within a range of reasonable alternatives, managers are not required to choose the most conservative pricing. Rules and regulations do, however, require a hedge fund manager to apply a pricing strategy consistently.

Accrual versus Cash Accounting

Like nearly all corporations, hedge funds use accrual accounting to time the recognition of accounting entries. It is difficult to imagine how cash accounting would treat limited partners fairly. In fact, tax reporting requires the hedge fund to accrue unrecognized gains and losses (see Chapter 10).

The managers of hedge funds are organized into business units separate from the business unit that contains the assets. The manager may compile these accounting records using either accrual or cash accounting. If a fund is organized as a flow-through tax entity such as a partnership, a limited liability corporation, or an S corporation, the accounting records probably must be compiled using the same basis as the owners. As a result, many hedge fund managers use cash accounting because their owners are individuals who use cash accounting.

Using Double-Entry Bookkeeping

Portfolio accounting is a specialized form of double-entry bookkeeping. A hedge fund could produce an income statement and balance sheet using mass market general ledger software. Funds would not use many types of accounts commonly used in manufacturing and service companies, however. In practice, most funds use software designed to keep track of extra data that isn't preserved in the general ledger records. The software may port information to portfolio management software, risk management software, tax reporting software, and other specialized applications.

Types of Accounts

Hedge funds use the same categories of accounts as other types of businesses: assets, liabilities, equity, revenues, and expenses. The assets, liabilities, and other accounts differ markedly from those of a manufacturing or service company because a hedge fund is little more than a legal wrapper around a pool of investment assets. Because the fund contracts the management duties to a separately organized management company, the fund generally has no employees. A hedge fund has no physical plant and may have no office equipment and supplies.

On the income side, a hedge fund has no cost of goods sold. Interest expense may be large. Realized gains and losses may show no pattern from month to month and may not relate closely to investment performance.

Assets The assets of a hedge fund are primarily investments plus cash balances. In particular, the fund will carry long positions in stocks, bonds, and commodities as assets, predominately long-term assets. In addition, the asset section of the balance sheet will contain financing transactions as short-term assets. The mechanism of financing a levered long position is described in Chapter 6.

Suppose a hedge fund started with $100 million cash at inception. At that point, the fund would have short-term assets of $100 million and the same amount of equity or partnership capital. If the fund buys $80 million in stocks, the short-term asset (cash) goes down by that amount, to be replaced by an equal amount in a long-term stock investment.

Suppose, too, that the fund sells short another issue for $70 million. The proceeds of the sale generate $70 million in cash. However, the only way to settle the short sale is to borrow the shares to make the delivery. The fund posts $75 million in collateral, receives the shares, and makes the delivery. After all this has settled, the fund has $15 million in cash ($100 million minus $80 million paid for stock plus $70 million proceeds from a short sale less $75 million in collateral). The fund also has a short-term, interest-bearing asset of $75 million (the collateral) and $80 million in stock. The fund has a reserve of cash plus $5 million in collateral in excess of the value of the short positions.

This example does not include other assets that might appear on a hedge fund balance sheet. These assets are likely not large, compared to the assets described. If the fund buys bonds, part of the value of the position will appear as accrued interest. The fund may also have margin on deposit at futures brokers. The fund may invest the excess cash balances in money market instruments. The fund may also have receivables reflecting dividends declared but not paid or funds deposited by partners awaiting investment. The fund may also carry past expenditures (professional fees, for example) as assets to delay recognizing the expense.

Liabilities   If a hedge fund carries short positions, those positions show up as liabilities. It may seem counterintuitive to classify a short as a liability instead of a negative asset, but accountants go to great lengths to avoid showing negative values in any account. In fact, a short sale of a bond looks very much like a loan, which is clearly a liability. In both cases, the lender gives the fund a loan balance (also described as the proceeds of the short sale). In both cases, the hedge fund makes periodic interest payments to the other party. Finally, the loan repayment of principal corresponds with buying back the bond.

A short sale of a stock doesn't correspond with a conventional liability but represents a liability all the same. Because the short represents a future obligation to pay out cash (buy back the position), it is carried as a liability even though common stock would clearly be considered an asset out of the context of levered trading.

The short sale of $70 million worth of stock in the previous example would appear as a liability on the books of the hedge fund. The fund could also create leverage by borrowing against the long position. Suppose, to extend the example, the hedge fund pledges $80 million worth of stock and borrows $50 million. The $50 million would show up as a higher cash balance and also as a short-term liability because the loan balance would need to be repaid at the end of the financing term.

In this example, the hedge fund would no longer possess the $80 in common stock because it is delivered to the lending counterparty. However, the lender only holds the collateral (stock) to assure repayment of the loan and must return the shares to the hedge fund when the loan is repaid. In other words, the hedge fund still owns the stock even though it is being held by the lender. As a result, the lending trade does not reduce the size of the long-term assets. Similarly, the fund continues to show a short position of $70 million in the second issue after making delivery on the sale because the financing trades do not affect the number of shares the fund must buy in the future.

Equity The accountants use the word *equity* to describe the third category of balance sheet accounts. Hedge fund investors call it capital. In both cases, it is the value of the fund assets in excess of the fund liabilities. It is also called net asset value (NAV) but shouldn't be confused with assets.

Hedge funds may be organized as corporations, especially outside the United States (see Chapter 5). The equity or NAV of a hedge fund organized as a corporation is common stock. Practitioners generally think of NAV more like net liquidating value in a margin account at a broker. It is possible to have more than one class of common stock, which creates the opportunity to treat investors differently (different fees, for example).

Hedge funds organized within the United States are often organized as limited partnerships. Capital is called partnership capital and the fund distinguishes between general partners' capital and limited partners' capital. The rights of the two classes of partner are laid out in the partnership agreement. If identical fees are assessed for limited partners' capital as for general partners' capital, the return on the two types of capital would generally be equal. Because limited partners cannot lose more than their committed capital, it is possible for the general partners to lose more than the limited partners lose. The general partners may have a prior claim on performance when recovering from a loss if the general partners have lost more than their committed investment.

Revenue The revenue of a hedge fund includes dividend income and coupon income on long positions. The revenue for a particular period includes income accrued but not yet paid. For example, suppose a fund holds 10,000 shares of stock in a company that declares a quarterly dividend of $1 per share. In particular, on March 20 the company announces that the dividend will be paid to the shareholders registered as owners on March 25 but will not be paid until March 30. Assuming the fund still owns the position on March 25, it will receive dividend income of $10,000, which is included in revenue in calculating net income. Even if the payment date was April 2, the entire amount of revenue is recognized in March and benefits the owners of the fund in March. However, none of the dividend income is accrued for the benefit of investors of the fund for January or February, even if the income could be predicted accurately.

The revenue is handled differently if the fund also owns a bond that pays interest semiannually at the end of March and September. The fund must prorate (i.e., accrue) the coupon to the investors in each statement period. As a result, the fund would recognize roughly the same income in March whether the coupon is paid on March 30 or April 2.[2]

Much of the return to hedge fund investors may come in the form of gains. Individual gains are classified as short-term and long-term and accumulated in separate accounts. Gains on futures and commodities are tallied separately from gains on securities. These gains, called Section 1256 gains, are taxed at a blended rate as if 60 percent of the results was long-term and 40 percent was short-term. The fund must report these gains to investors, who in turn include this income on their tax forms. The mechanics of this tax reporting are described in Chapter 10.

Expenses   Hedge funds pay commissions to execute trades. The fund is also charged management and incentive fees that are included as expenses on the income statement. The interest paid to finance a leveraged position is a typical expense for a hedge fund. Note that a corporation does not deduct the dividends it declares and pays to its shareholders, but a hedge fund includes payments paid for dividends declared by other companies if the hedge fund carries a short position in a security that pays a dividend (this is the scenario posed by question 6.13). The hedge fund must make substitute dividend and interest payments on all short positions in stocks and bonds, which are reported as expenses.

Hedge funds accumulate short-term losses, long-term losses, and Section 1256 losses. These losses are included on the hedge fund income statement. The losses are also reported to investors, who include the amounts on their individual or corporate income tax forms. The losses reduce income and usually reduce the taxes investors must pay. Chapter 10 includes a brief description of these tax rules related to gains and losses.

Accruals

Hedge funds accrue many accounts to fairly allocate investment returns and expenses to investors.

Interest on Bonds   Hedge funds accrue income on bonds exactly the same way corporations and unleveraged portfolios accrue income. However, hedge funds may carry either long or short positions, so accruals on individual positions may be treated as either an asset or a liability.

Hedge funds generally don't report accrued interest as an individual item on the balance sheet. Frequently, the value of the accrued interest on long positions is included in the market value of the long positions and the accrued interest on short positions is included in the market value of the short positions. The net amount carried in accrued interest may also appear either as an asset (when the sum of accruals on long positions exceeds accrued interest on short positions) or a liability (when the sum of accruals on short positions exceeds accruals on long positions).

If a hedge fund buys $10 million face value of a bond with a 6 percent semiannual coupon, the total paid for the position must reflect both the price paid for the face value plus accrued interest. Assume for this example that the bond maturing on May 15, 2009, was purchased to settle on February 15, 2004, at a price of $103 (or 103 percent of face value). The principal amount of the trade is $10,300,000 (103% × $10 million). The accrued interest would be approximately $151,648.[3] The following entries might be used to book the purchase:

XYZ Corporation 6 Percent Debenture Due 3/15/XX

XYC 6 percent bond	$10,300,000	
Accrued interest	$ 151,648	
Cash		$10,451,648

At the end of the month, the accrued income would rise by $23,077.[4] The increase in the value of the asset on the balance sheet would show up as income and be included on the income statement.

February Month-End Journal Entries

Accrued interest	$23,077	
Coupon income		$23,077

As a result, investors would get credit for the income, even though no cash flow was received during the month.

A slightly more complicated set of transactions is required when a bond actually pays a coupon. The fund would continue to recognize income and increase the accrued interest. On April 30, 2004, the balance sheet would reflect $275,275 for the bond and the fund would have recognized income of $51,099 in March and $49,451 in April.[5] On May 15, 2004, the fund receives a semiannual interest payment of $300,000 ($10 million × 6%/2). The fund must now journal the incremental $24,725[6] of income:

May 15, 2004, Journal Entries

Cash	$300,000	
Coupon income		$ 24,725
Accrued interest		$275,275

After these entries, this bond will show no accrued interest on the balance sheet and the fund will have recognized income on the position for half the month. On May 31, if the fund still carries the position, it recognizes $26,087[7] in income, reflecting 16 more days of income at a new accrual rate.

Suppose the fund sells the bond at 104.375 on June 15. The fund must book an additional 15 days' worth of income totaling $24,457[8]. The fund must also journal a gain of $137,500 (1.375 percent of $10 million) and remove the position from the balance sheet:

Cash[9]	$10,488,043	
Coupon income		$ 24,457
Short-term gain		$ 137,500
Accrued interest		$ 26,087
XYC 6 percent bond		$10,300,000

Notice that the asset account for the bond is credited (reduced) by exactly the amount debited when the position was established, not the current value. This accounting differs from when the position was established so that the asset account is reset to zero. The difference between that cost amount and the sale price is entered as the gain. Notice, too, that the accrued interest amount as of May 31, 2004, is credited to remove this amount from the balance sheet. The accrual from May 31, 2004, through June 15, 2004, is booked as income at the time of sale.

Interest on short bond positions is accrued the same way as long positions. However, the initial interest on the bond at the time of sale is a liability, not an asset. Also, the interest in each accounting period is recognized as an expense, not as revenue. The expense debited is booked against an equal credit to the accrued interest liability each period.

Dividends on Stock Positions   Stock dividends are not accrued, even if the timing and the amount of the dividend are predictable. Instead, the entire amount of the dividend is booked as revenue for long positions or as expense for short positions after the dividend is declared, probably on the record date.

Interest on Financing   The hedge fund accrues the interest expense paid to borrow money and the interest income received on the collateral supporting borrowed securities. Most financing transactions are short-term. These trades originate and end within a single accounting period. The fund should monitor those items daily but there is no need to accrue the interest on these positions.

Generally, the journal entries to establish a financing trade are created when the financing is created. For simplicity and to increase the verifiability of the accounting records, the income and the termination entries are created at the same time. These entries must be created in light of the dates financial statements are produced.

Consider the financing trade related to the bond purchase described earlier. Recall that a long position was purchased for $10,451,648, including principal and accrued interest. Suppose the hedge fund agreed to borrow $10 million secured by this position. The hedge fund must deliver the position to the lender on February 15, 2004, and receives the loan amount of $10 million on that date. If the lender agrees to lend the funds for 30 days at 5 percent, the fund would book the interest expense at the time of the trade:

On February 15, 2004

Cash	$10,000,000	
Short-term borrowing		$10,000,000

For March 16, 2004 (but Entered on February 15, 2004)

Interest expense[10]	$ 41,667	
Short-term borrowing	$10,000,000	
Cash		$10,041,667

These journal entries would be perfectly adequate for a hedge fund that publishes financial statements quarterly. However, if the fund produces statements at each month-end, it should accrue the expense incurred but not yet paid. To recognize 14 days' worth of interest expense in February, the fund could substitute a more complicated accrual of the interest expense:

For February 29, 2004 (but Entered on February 15, 2004)

Interest expense[11]	$19,445	
Accrued financing expense		$19,445

This accrual is removed when the actual interest expense is made:

For March 16, 2004 (but Entered on February 15, 2004)

Interest Expense[12]	$ 22,222	
Accrued financing expense	$ 19,445	
Short-term borrowing	$10,000,000	
Cash		$10,041,667

Accruing Management Fees   Management fees accrue steadily on the assets under management. Hedge funds need to accrue management fees to reflect this progressive expense. This accrual is not generally necessary at the end of each accounting period because a prorated amount of the annual management expense is journaled each accounting period.

However, most hedge funds calculate their net asset value (NAV) much more frequently than they publish formal financial statements. Because the NAV is little more than a simple balance sheet, it is necessary to accrue management fees whenever NAV is calculated.

Financial Statements

Hedge funds can produce the standard collection of accounting statements that are used by nonfinancial businesses. Usually, the hedge fund discloses the balance sheet to trading and financial counterparties. The hedge fund generally discloses the income statement and balance sheet to investors. Other statements such as the statement of cash flow are less useful to hedge fund investors.

Balance Sheet   The balance sheet or statement of financial positions lists the assets and liabilities of the fund. This is the only financial statement routinely published and shared with investors and creditors. The balance sheet can be used to determine the sizes of positions carried by the hedge fund. The statement does not review specific positions because the assets and liabilities are aggregated to obscure the details of the hedge fund's positions.

Income Statement   An income statement lists the types of revenues and expenses that make up net income. It is generally not possible for analysts to extrapolate income accounts into the future. Dividends and interest income reflect the particular positions held by the fund and are subject to change. A major component of performance is unrealized gains and losses, which are particularly difficult to extrapolate.

If the income statement includes unrecognized gains and losses on securities positions in addition to recognized gains, losses, revenues, and expenses, it would be possible to derive performance from the income statement. In practice, because much of the investment community does not see the income statement, investors calculate performance from the NAV, based on the balance sheet for the fund.

Statement of Cash Flow   Generally accepted accounting practice requires a hedge fund to produce a statement of cash flow that reconciles the change in cash or cash equivalents to the accounts in the income statement and balance sheet. Hedge funds may not circulate the statement of cash flows. The statement can be useful to the fund manager to track how cash is being used in its various strategies and to measure the adequacy of liquid cash balances.

UNIQUE ASPECTS OF HEDGE FUND ACCOUNTING

Although hedge funds follow the general procedures used by any user of double-entry accounting, the unique needs of hedge funds present a series of challenges. Accountants have developed methods to satisfy these unique accounting requirements.

Distinguishing the Fund from the Manager

It is typical for a corporation to conduct business in several distinct business units. Usually these businesses are organized hierarchically. The results of subsidiaries are consolidated into parent's results. A hedge fund may have subsidiaries. A fund may carry some or all of its assets as investments in other hedge funds. See Chapter 5 to learn more about motives for these kinds of structures.

It is important to contrast this parent/subsidiary structure with the two business units universally associated with hedge funds. A hedge fund is a business unit that exists to hold the financial assets. It generally has no physical operations. A hedge fund manager contains the employees who make investment decisions, market the fund, and account for performance. In principle, these can be completely independent legal entities. In practice, the management company may have a considerable investment in the hedge fund and may act as the general partner of a hedge fund. It would be wrong, however, to consolidate the positions and income of the hedge fund with the positions and income of the manager, because the two businesses do not fit the model of a parent/subsidiary relationship.

Flow-Through Entity Hedge funds within the United States are generally organized as limited partnerships or limited liability corporations (see Chapter 5). There are substantial tax advantages to these structures and tax regulations strictly control tax reporting of the fund results. Chapter 10 presents some of those tax requirements. In general, the fund is not considered an economic entity. Instead, the financial results of the fund are allocated to the fund's investors and taxed only at that level.

Surprisingly, this flow-through tax status has little effect on financial reporting. The financial statements present the income statement and balance sheet accounts without regard to the tax treatment of the fund.

Inventory Accounting   Hedge funds don't carry inventory in the same sense that a manufacturing firm carries inventory. The manufacturer uses inventory accounting to postpone expenses so that the timing of the expenses matches the timing of the revenues. A retailer uses inventory accounting to reflect the investment the company carries in merchandise.

A hedge fund, in contrast, carries a portfolio of investment securities. It is tempting to treat these positions as inventory. Indeed, the positions fit well into the methods used to account for inventory. However, the tax code, not generally accepted accounting principles (GAAP), defines the ways a hedge fund can determine the cost of positions that are sold.

Mark to Market   In general, accountants rely on historical cost. There are exceptions where a corporation must mark down the carrying value of assets if they fall below historical cost. The tax reporting of hedge fund results resembles this type of accounting. In contrast, the financial records of a hedge fund rely on current market prices of the securities. The differences between financial or performance accounting and tax accounting create major accounting burdens for the hedge fund accounting system.

Futures and Other Derivatives   Hedge funds don't treat futures and derivatives differently than do manufacturing companies or financial corporations (banks, broker-dealers, and insurance companies). However, like many financial companies, hedge funds may carry substantial positions in these derivatives. These positions don't appear on the balance sheet, although the fund must disclose the positions in footnotes. These footnotes disclose the notional amount of the derivatives positions. The fund does not detail these positions or the economic significance of the positions.

The Financial Accounting Standards Board (FASB) prescribed the GAAP treatment of derivatives transactions in its Financial Accounting Standard 133 (FAS 133).

The derivatives positions are consistently carried at current market value, like the securities positions. As a result, hedge funds are not significantly affected by FAS 133, which controls which derivatives are marked to market with other types of businesses.

Hedge funds can deliver securities to satisfy initial margin in a futures account. No accounting entry is required because the securities are still owned by the hedge fund. The accounting system does not record the change in the location of the securities or the encumbrance granted to the futures broker (unless, of course, the broker seizes the positions to satisfy a margin deficit).

However, the hedge fund may also deposit initial margin in cash. This transfer would generally enter the accounting system because the accounting records contain an account for cash held at the broker:

When Cash Is Transferred to the Broker

Cash held at broker	$10,000	
Cash held in demand deposit account #123		$10,000

After the deposit of initial margin, the purchase or sale of contracts is not recorded in the general ledger system. The fund will no doubt keep track of this information outside the accounting ledger and must report information about the position in footnotes.

After the trade, the broker adjusts the margin balance daily. These adjustments enter the general ledger:

Daily Margin Maintenance on Futures Position

Section 1256 loss	$2,500	
Cash held at broker		$2,500

The debit holding the loss is a particular category for losses that is reported separately from securities gains. See Chapter 10 to learn more about Section 1256 gains and losses. As is clear from the credit record, the broker removes cash equal to the daily loss. The loss may require the hedge fund to restore margin to the minimum maintenance amount. If the loss is large enough, the hedge fund must transfer additional cash (not securities) and the entries are handled the same as a cash deposit.

Identified Straddles and Mixed Straddle Election Hedge funds, broker-dealers, and other trading businesses may be required to mark some or all of their positions to market for tax purposes. A hedge fund may identify a combination of trades as a straddle if gains on part of the position occur at the same time as losses on another part of the position (usually because the position contains both long and short trades). Hedge funds are not allowed to recognize a loss on one part and postpone realizing gains on another part of a straddle.

Some funds declare in advance that all trades should be treated as if they were part of a straddle (mixed straddle election). In both cases, the fund must calculate unrecognized gains and losses on all positions and include them in taxable income. These tax calculations more or less match the calculation of NAV, but it means that financial statements must reflect current market prices rather than historical cost.

Nonledger Accounting Information The hedge fund must keep track of a large amount of data that doesn't fit into the debits and credits of a general ledger. For example, the fund needs to know how many shares it is long or short. It probably needs to know the cost basis of individual lots and the dates the lots were acquired. This data is maintained by a portfolio accounting system and can be passed to position-management routines or risk management routines, or used for tax reporting.

Maintaining Capital Accounts The hedge fund must keep track of many details concerning the ownership interests of the partners investing in the fund. It is possible to use the general ledger to record some of this information. For example, the fund's accountants could establish a unique capital account for each investor (or even distinguishing multiple lots for investors). A hedge fund may have hundreds of different investors, so this could require many separate accounts. In contrast, a corporation may have only a few capital accounts: common stock, additional paid-in capital, retained earnings. Frequently a hedge fund will establish a capital account for general partners and a capital account for limited partners. Details, including ownership percentages, cost, and tax information, can be preserved in subledgers or subsidiary ledgers. A portfolio accounting system should handle this information automatically, but a hedge fund may also track this portfolio data in many spreadsheets maintained by hand outside the general ledger system.

ACCOUNTING AND CONTROL

Perhaps the most important job of any accountant is control. Chapter 11 describes risk management as it pertains to hedge funds, but the accounting records, the accountants, and the auditors have a role in corporate control that differs somewhat from risk management, which focuses on position risks, financing risks, and counterparty risks.

Accountants are the first line of defense against loss of control. The accounting process must assure that all tickets have been written. The accountants should monitor trading to ensure that all trades are authorized and consistent with trading limits.

The accountants are responsible for making sure that positions are fairly valued. These valuations are important to investors entering and exiting the fund. They also affect the return of the fund. Traders, risk managers, and investors are all interested in getting accurate return information, and inaccurate pricing can lead to bad decisions.

Accountants should make fair allocations. Traders have no concern over costs that are not allocated. For example, if commission expenses or financing costs are not allocated, traders are tempted to enter into uneconomic trades that nevertheless show up as profitable to individual traders. Similarly, if traders are not held accountable for their individual contributions to the risk in the portfolio, traders may be tempted to take excessive risks. Finally, the firm should associate the cost of trading capital with the positions of individual traders, so that traders are motivated to treat capital as a scarce resource.

Accountants are responsible for maintaining deposits for the hedge fund. These deposits include cash balances for liquidity needs, investment balances held for medium-term investing, and margin balances. The accountants must be sure that balances in these accounts are adequate for the possible needs the hedge fund positions might create. The accountants, too, should work with the risk managers to monitor the hedge fund's exposure to counterparties.

The accountant is responsible for monitoring the money flows. The accountants must have procedures in place to prevent and detect fraud. The procedures should include cross-checks to prevent collusion.

CONCLUSIONS

Despite their unique nature, hedge funds record accounting information in general ledgers and use most of the same conventions and principles that are adopted as generally accepted accounting principles (GAAP). Like a manufacturer or retailer, the hedge fund must also keep track of additional data. This data must be accurate and available on a timely basis to be useful to the managers of the hedge fund.

QUESTIONS AND PROBLEMS

9.1   A hedge fund has a debt-to-equity ratio of 3:1. What is the leverage on this hedge fund?

9.2   A hedge fund buys $25 million in common stock and finances 50 percent of the position in the stock loan market. How much does this stock position and financing contribute to the total assets of the hedge fund?

9.3 A hedge fund sells $10 million in common stock and posts $12 million to borrow the shares. How much does this stock position and financing contribute to the total assets of the hedge fund?

9.4 A hedge fund buys 10,000 shares of XYZ common at $10 per share (net of commissions). The fund later buys 15,000 additional shares of XYZ common at $12.50. The fund sells 5,000 shares of XYZ at $15. What value appears on the balance sheet for the value of 20,000 shares of XYZ?

9.5 What factors would influence the hedge fund to use the cost of the $10 shares or the cost of $12.50 lot to determine the gain for financial reporting?

9.6 What problems would a hedge fund have creating its accounting records on a cash basis?

9.7 A hedge fund manager disagrees with his auditor on the issue of disclosure. The auditor believes some information must be disclosed to comply with generally accepted accounting practices. The manager argues that disclosing the information to investors could cause damage to the investors because the information is sensitive. Does this mean that the principle of disclosure doesn't apply to hedge funds?

9.8 A hedge fund mispriced some assets at year-end. Some assets were priced too high and other assets were priced too low. No investor had redeemed capital and the fund accepted no new capital at that time. Based on the argument of materiality, the fund argued to its auditor that it didn't need to restate the fund's results. Should the auditor require the fund to restate the year-end results?

9.9 An auditor told a hedge fund to use the bid-side prices to value long positions and to use offer-side prices to value short positions. The fund manager said this violated the principle of consistency. Is the fund manager right?

9.10 A particular hedge fund carries a position of long and short assets. The positions roughly hedge the major movement of the market. The fund auditor announces that all of the long positions must be carried at the lower of cost or market. The hedge fund manager objects, saying that this would lead to misleading and spurious gains and losses. Should the auditor prevail in requiring the fund to adhere to the lower of cost or market accounting principle?

9.11 A particular hedge fund is designed to profit from lower prices. The fund has no long positions and a portfolio of short positions. Would the leverage of this fund be zero because the firm has no assets?

9.12 A corporation declared a dividend of $1 per share of common stock on April 22 for holders of record April 29 to be paid May 5. A hedge fund holds 50,000 shares of the stock on April 30. How should it treat the dividend payment?

9.13 A particular hedge fund has $100 million is assets and $50 million in liabilities. The fund is a limited partnership that has sold 28,000 partnership units at $1,000 each. What is the current NAV of a partnership unit?

9.14 A hedge fund has long and short Treasury positions. During the year, it receives $25 million in Treasury interest. The fund also makes $20 million in substitute interest payments on the fund's short Treasury positions. The Treasury interest on long positions is exempt from state income taxes when allocated to taxable investors. How is the interest expense treated for financial reporting?

9.15 A hedge fund has $100 million under management on April 30. The hedge fund manager charges a management fee of 1 percent of the assets under management. To calculate NAV on May 5, how much should the manager deduct for the fraction of the month that has passed?

9.16 A hedge fund is able to create long and short positions exclusively with futures contracts. It is carrying long positions equivalent to 100 percent of partner's capital. It carries short positions approximately equal to its long positions. What is the leverage of the hedge fund?

NOTES

1. Frater Luca Bartolomes Pacioli published a mathematical treatise called *Summa de Arithmetica, Geometria, Proportioni et Proportionalita* in 1494. It contained a description of the accounting methods in use at the time. An earlier work written by Benedetto Cotrugli called *Delia Mercatura et del Mercante Perfetto* also contained a description of prevailing accounting methods but was not printed until well after Pacioli's work. For more information on the early history of accounting, see the web site for the Association of Chartered Accountants in the United States (www.acaus.org).

2. The reader who is familiar with bond mathematics should realize that the accrual rate in March depends on the dates the payments are scheduled. The accrual is calculated from the number of days in the coupon period, and two bonds with different payment dates would accrue at slightly different rates. Readers interested in learning more about coupon accrual can find several good reference books, including Marcia Stigum and Franklin L. Robinson, *Money Market & Bond Calculations*, Chicago: Irwin Professional Publishing, 1996.

3. The accrued interest would equal $151,648 for a bond that uses the actual number of days to determine accrued interest (different types of bonds use dif-

ferent protocols). To calculate this amount, determine what portion of the semiannual coupon has already been earned by the previous owner of the bond. There are 182 days between 11/15/2003 and 5/15/2004. Between 11/15/2003 and 2/15/2004, 92 days have passed, so the previous holder earned 92/182 times the semiannual payment (92/182 × $10 million × 6%/2).

4. The position accrues interest for 14 days. The fraction of the semiannual coupon is 14/182. The accrual on a $10 million position is:

$$\$10 \text{ million} \times 6\%/2 \times 14/182 = \$23,077$$

5. By April 30, 2004, the bond has accrued 167 days' worth of interest:

$$(167/182 \times \$10 \text{ million} \times 6\%/2) = \$275,275$$
$$\text{March (31 days)} = 31/182 \times \$10 \text{ million} \times 6\%/2 = \$51,099$$
$$\text{April (30 days)} = 30/182 \times \$10 \text{ million} \times 6\%/2 = \$49,451$$

Cross-check:

$$\$151,648 + \$23,077 + \$51,099 + \$49,451 = \$275,275$$

6. The fund must recognize 15 days of accrued income:

$$\text{May (15 days)} = 15/182 \times \$10 \text{ million} \times 6\%/2 = \$24,725$$

Cross-check:

$$\$275,275 + \$24,725 = \$300,000$$

7. There are 183 days between 5/15/2004 and the next payment on 11/15/2004. Therefore, the accrual for the 16 days from 5/15/2004 to 5/31/2004 is:

$$\text{May (16 days)} = 16/183 \times \$10 \text{ million} \times 6\%/2 = \$26,087$$

8. The fund must book 15 additional days of accrued income:

$$\text{June (15 days)} = 15/183 \times \$10 \text{ million} \times 6\%/2 = \$24,457$$

This amount must reconcile with the interest calculations on the sale:

$$\$10 \text{ million} \times 6\%/2 \times 31/183 = \$50,543$$

Cross-check:

$$\$26,087 + \$24,457 = \$50,543 \text{ (net of small rounding error)}$$

9. The principal value equals $10 million times 104.375 percent of face = $10,437,500. Accrued interest is $50,543 (see note 8). Total proceeds from the sale equal $10,437,500 + $50,543 = $10,488,043.

10. The interest expense is based on the actual number of days (30) but the annual rate is adjusted as if a year has 360 days. The interest expense is:

$$\$10,000,000 \times 5\% \times 30/360 = \$41,667$$

11. The interest period from 2/15/2004 to 2/29/2004 is 14 days. The interest expense is:

$$\$10,000,000 \times 5\% \times 14/360 = \$19,445$$

12. The interest period from 2/29/2004 to 3/15/2004 is 16 days. The interest expense is:

$$\$10,000,000 \times 5\% \times 16/360 = \$22,222$$

CHAPTER 10

Hedge Fund Taxation

AVOIDING U.S. FEDERAL TAXATION

It is natural to want to avoid paying more tax than necessary. A loophole to someone may be a provision providing greater tax equity to someone else. Whether everyone agrees with the state of the U.S. tax law, it is important to emphasize that this chapter will be talking about legal tax strategies, not (illegal) tax evasion. In fact, the courts are clear that it is permissible to make decisions that result in lower taxation. Hedge funds are generally structured to minimize the tax burden on the investors.

Some investors pay income tax to countries other than the United States. These investors may get little or no credit for taxes paid to the United States. As seen in Chapter 5, offshore hedge funds are structured so that nonresident investors can invest in a manager's fund without creating a tax liability in the United States. These investors don't escape income tax. The income must still be reported to the investor's taxing authority (to the extent required by the laws governing the investor), but the offshore structure allows the offshore investor to avoid taxation by the United States.

Note that the U.S.-based hedge fund manager must report income in the form of management and incentive fees generated by managing offshore pools of money. The offshore structure allows the investment process to occur outside the United States, but the business of managing the assets usually produces income that is taxable by the United States if the activity occurs within U.S. borders.

FLOW-THROUGH TAXATION

All businesses in the United States must report income to the U.S. Treasury. Many businesses pay corporate income tax on the profits of the business.

The dividends paid by these companies to their investors are taxable (if the investors are subject to tax) even though the dividends are paid from profits after tax. Companies may also retain profits left after paying taxes. These profits may make the shares more valuable and may result in capital gains taxes for investors who sell stock.

Other types of businesses also report income to the U.S. Treasury but pay no tax. Instead, the revenues and expenses are allocated to investors, who must report this income and pay tax on the income if they are taxable investors. These businesses are called flow-through tax entities.

Hedge funds located in taxable jurisdictions are structured (1) to avoid double taxation and (2) to make certain that investors can lose no more than 100 percent of their investment in the hedge fund. This chapter will briefly discuss how partnerships are taxed, because they avoid most corporate income taxes. Several of the flow-through entities are used as the business type for hedge funds.

DOUBLE TAXATION OF CORPORATE INCOME

Certain types of businesses file tax returns and pay income tax on the income of the business. Owners are later taxed on the returns. These profits are therefore taxed twice.

C Corporation

C corporations pay U.S. federal corporate income tax at a maximum rate of 35 percent. In addition, most states tax the income of the corporation. Investors may not deduct these corporate taxes or use the taxes paid by the corporation to reduce their tax liabilities in any way. However, investors do not include this corporate income on any tax form, and a corporation can usually postpone taxation at the investor level indefinitely by retaining all of the after-tax profits. When the corporation makes a dividend payment to investors, the investors must include this payment as income if they are taxable investors.

Limited Liability Corporation

If a limited liability corporation (LLC) elects to be taxed as a C corporation, the income of the business will be taxed twice. However, most LLCs elect to be taxed as a partnership and avoid double-taxation of income.

FLOW-THROUGH TAX TREATMENT

A variety of business types file income tax forms but pay no tax on business income. Instead, taxable items are passed through to investors, who must report them in their own taxable income.

Sole Proprietorship

The income from a sole proprietorship is reported on the individual's tax form. As a result, this business could be viewed as a flow-through tax entity. The income is, however, additionally taxed as self-employment income. The business is owned by one individual, which pretty much rules out this structure for the hedge fund. In addition, a sole proprietorship does not shield the owner from unlimited liability so it is not recommended as a hedge fund structure.

Partnership

All partnerships are taxed the same in the United States and most or all other countries. All the individual accounts (interest, dividends, interest expense, short-term gains, and so on are reported to investors, who must include all the results on their own income tax forms. Although this complicates tax filing, it avoids the double-taxation of investment returns.

Limited Liability Corporation

The limited liability corporation (LLC), as mentioned earlier, may be taxed as a corporation or as a partnership. Most LLCs elect to be treated as a partnership to get flow-through tax treatment. The LLC structure also allows all investors, including the fund sponsors and managers, to limit their liability to their committed investment.

TRADER VERSUS INVESTOR VERSUS DEALER

A hedge fund domiciled in the United States could be taxed as if it is an investor, a trader, or a broker-dealer. This distinction is not important to offshore funds because those investors generally don't pay U.S. income tax. To U.S. domestic funds, the impact on investors can be significant.

Hedge Funds Taxed as a Trader

Hedge funds generally prefer to be taxed as a business actively engaged in the business of trading (which primarily makes money by buying and selling as distinguished from an investor who primarily makes money by buying and holding). A fund is more likely to be classified as a trader if the turnover in the fund is higher, the gains and losses are primarily short-term (not long-term), and the return derives primarily from gains and losses, not dividends and interest.

If a fund is treated as a trader, certain expenses like interest costs on leveraged positions and management fees are included in net income. This net income is allocated to investors as described later. These expenses are not reported on individual taxpayers' schedules of itemized deductions.

Individual taxpayers benefit by not having to report gross income and investment expenses. First, these expenses are deductible only to the extent that they exceed 2 percent of adjusted gross income. Second, due to phaseout limitations on itemized deductions, these investment expenses may be capped at 5 percent of adjusted gross income (that is, only the expenses that fall between 2 percent and 5 percent of adjusted gross income are deductible). Third, as long as the hedge fund is treated as a trader, these investment expenses would reduce taxable income when calculating alternate minimum tax.

Hedge Funds Taxed as an Investor

A hedge fund characterized as an investor would have to allocate income before certain investment expenses to investors. The fund would also allocate investment expenses such as financing interest, management fees, and incentive fees. Investors would be able to reduce taxable income by the amount of these expenses, subject to the 2 percent and 5 percent limitations described earlier. Individuals would add back these deductions to calculate alternate minimum tax.

Foreign investors invested in a U.S. hedge fund would prefer that the fund was classified as an investor, not a trader. These foreign investors would be taxed only on the dividends received by the fund, not interest or gains and losses. These dividends would be subject to 30 percent withholding tax. Admittedly, this is a small market because a U.S. fund capable of attracting sizable offshore investments would probably organize an offshore fund to allow the offshore investors to sidestep U.S. taxation.

Hedge Funds Taxed as a Dealer

Some hedge funds seek to be treated as dealers to take advantage of more liberal margin rules under Regulation T (see Chapter 8). The hedge funds must mark all their positions to market for tax purposes. Some funds (notably arbitrage strategies) must mark their positions to market anyway because of tax straddle rules as described in Chapter 9. These funds make a mixed straddle election designed to prevent tax abuse because all positions are taxed annually at market value whether gains and losses are realized or unrealized. For hedge funds not required to make a mixed straddle election, the impact of being classified as a dealer is that the fund may not defer unrecognized gains to later tax years.

INTRODUCTION TO ALLOCATION

The general allocation provisions of a partnership are laid out in the partnership agreement. In the absence of special allocation rules, allocations are generally made equal to the relative ownership amounts of the investors. While a fund can use special allocation rules, the allocations must have economic substance. That is, the tax allocations must be consistent with the economic gains and losses realized by the investors.

Income items (including revenues, expenses, gains, and losses) must be allocated at least annually. Funds allocate each break period, that is, each time investors may enter or exit the partnership and the ownership percentage of the partners could change.

Most funds allocate these items as if the fund closed its books at each break period and issued quarterly or monthly income statements. This method is called the "interim closing of the books" method. As the name implies, the fund may generate equivalent allocations in portfolio software or in subledgers.

ALLOCATION OF REVENUES AND EXPENSES

The first kind of allocation involves most of the income accounts with the exception of gains and losses (the allocation rules for gains and losses are considerably more complicated and are described later). The fund first allocates the amount to each period. This allocation should be made daily. Second, the income amount is allocated to investors, generally proportionate to their ownership percentage.

For example, suppose a hedge fund estimates its annual audit expenses at $48,000 for the 2004 trading year. It would allocate $131[1] per day to the fund every day of the year in advance of the actual expense. The accountants would book $3,803[2] audit expense for February.

Suppose this hedge fund has three investors. The first partner holds 200 units, the second partner holds 300 units, and the third partner holds 300 units. Therefore, the fund has 800 units outstanding. The first partner owns 25 percent of the fund (200 units/800 units) and is allocated $951 (25% × $3,803) for February. The second partner owns 37.5 percent of the fund (300 units/800 units) and is allocated $1,426 (37.5% × $3,803) for February. The third partner owns 37.5 percent of the fund (300 units/800 units) and is allocated $1,426 (37.5% × $3,803) for February.

ALLOCATION OF GAINS AND LOSSES— LAYERED ALLOCATION

Partnerships and other entities that are flow-through tax entities must report income items to investors as if they hold proportional amounts of the business as a sole proprietorship. For most income items, this is relatively straightforward. If an expense is incurred in a month, it is booked in the same month that investors received the benefit of that expense. In the preceding example, accrual accounting may allow the accountant to time the recognition of the expense to match the benefits of the expense to the cash payment.

In contrast, gains and losses are not recognized for tax reporting until positions are liquidated. Therefore, the accounting gain or loss may be reported long after the gain or loss was achieved. This is true for individuals and it is true for the investors in a flow-through tax entity. So the realized gains must be allocated to the investors who were invested when the gains occurred, and the realized losses must be allocated to the investors who were invested when the losses occurred.

To illustrate layered allocation, consider a simple example before advancing to a more complete scenario. Suppose two investors formed a partnership that bought a stock. The stock appreciated, but the partnership retained the stock and carried an unrecognized gain on the position. A third partner was admitted and the stock was sold shortly thereafter at the previous appreciated price. The partnership must allocate the gain to the initial two investors and not to the new investor. The allocation should replicate the effect of the two investors individually owning proportionate amounts of the position and experiencing a gain (eventually realized). The newest investor's allocation should match buying a reapportioned amount of the stock and selling it for no gain or loss.

Layered Tax Allocation Example

Now consider a multiperiod example to demonstrate how the layered allocation is actually calculated. Suppose the partnership was owned 40 percent by investor 1 and 60 percent by investor 2 in January. The partnership buys 10,000 shares of XYZ common during the month of January at 25. The position is worth $30 per share at the end of January. The partnership has a $50,000 gain (10,000 × $5 gain) allocated 40 percent to investor 1 (40% × $50,000 = $20,000) and 60 percent to investor 2 (60% × $50,000 = $30,000).

Suppose the partnership admits a third partner at the beginning of February. After the new partner enters, investor 1 owns 25 percent of the fund[3] and investor 2 and investor 3 each own 37.5 percent. During February, XYZ advances to $35. This $50,000 unrecognized gain is allocated $12,500 to investor 1 (25% × $50,000) and $18,750 each to investor 2 and investor 3 (37.5% × $50,000).

During the month of March, XYZ stock is sold at $32. No changes have occurred in the partnership stakes. The $30,000 loss (at least, it is a loss on the month) is allocated $7,500 to investor 1 (25% × $30,000) and $11,250 each to investor 2 and investor 3 (37.5% × $30,000).

The scenario has three investors in the stock with a cost basis or layer each of three months (although investor 3 didn't participate in the first layer). As a result of these layers, investor 1 reports a gain of $25,000 ($20,000 plus $12,500 plus –$7,500). Investor 2 reports a gain of $37,500 ($30,000 plus $18,750 plus –$11,250). Investor 3 reports a gain of $7,500 ($18,750 plus –$11,250). The gain allocated to the three investors ($25,000 plus $37,500 plus $7,500) equals the $70,000 gain realized on XYZ common (from $25 to $32 on 10,000 shares). The partners are allocated gains as if they owned a proportionate position in XYZ directly.

Needless to say, this methodology puts severe demands on the tax accountants to keep track of each of these cost layers. If there are many investors and many positions, and if investments are held for many periods, the data needs and computational effort to produce tax returns can be enormous. To make matters worse, smaller funds in the past have done these calculations by hand in spreadsheets, requiring duplicate efforts to maintain positions and partnership allocations.

Problems with the Ceiling Rule

All three partners reported gains in our example. If the third investor had entered the fund at the end of February, the decline in price in March and subsequent sale would have caused a loss for that partner. The hedge fund would have had two partners reporting gains and a partner reporting a loss on the same position. This is a violation of the ceiling rule, which prohibits partners from reporting a loss greater than the loss on the securities.

The hedge fund might argue that the allocation does not violate the ceiling rule if all partners report gains or all partners report losses during the tax year. Other hedge funds would alter the layered allocation, first skipping the allocation to partners that would violate the ceiling rule and then adjust future allocations, realigning the tax allocations to match the economic gains of each investor overall.

AGGREGATE TAX ALLOCATION

Investors were granted some relief from the burden of layered tax allocation. The tax code now permits flow-through tax entities to develop shortcut methods to allocate gains and losses to investors. This shortcut is permitted only for "qualified financial assets," which include assets where price quotes or recent trading price information is readily available. The shortcut applies only to "securities partnerships." This group includes registered investment advisers, although not many hedge funds are registered in the United States. A hedge fund may also qualify as a securities partnership if at least 90 percent of its assets (excluding cash) are qualified financial assets and the hedge fund is marked to market at least annually.

Most hedge funds are thereby permitted to use aggregate tax allocation. Hedge funds that carry private equity positions may be prohibited from using aggregate tax allocation either because price information is unavailable or they don't mark positions to market until the positions are liquidated. Many of these hedge funds instead use side-pocket allocations (discussed later).

Partial Netting versus Full Netting Allocation

The tax code allows the hedge fund to allocate the aggregate gains separately from the aggregate losses (partial netting) or to aggregate the gains and losses together (full netting) and only allocate the net gain or loss to investors. Partial netting will tend to keep the allocations more in line with the economic gains of the partners. Nevertheless, most hedge funds use the full netting approach to tax allocation.

Using the "Interim Closing of the Books" Method

To use the aggregate allocation methodology, the hedge fund must track the economic gain or loss of each partner. It is not important to preserve

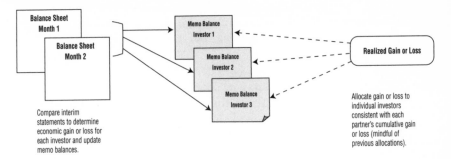

FIGURE 10.1 Aggregate Allocation Flow Chart

the details about how and when an investor experienced a gain or loss. It is not important whether a partner experience a gain in one month or another (except to maintain a paper trail for the auditors). It is not important which securities were responsible for creating the gain or loss. For all these reasons, the aggregate method reduces the effort required to perform tax allocations.

Most hedge funds create an interim closing to measure partner gain or loss. A hedge fund may create financial statements with interim securities prices to calculate the value of the capital positions. Alternatively, a portfolio accounting system might calculate the economic gains or losses as if interim statements were created. In either case, interim gains and losses are accumulated in memorandum accounts for each partner.

Figure 10.1 illustrates the aggregate allocation procedure.

Aggregate Allocation Example

Suppose two investors form a partnership. The first investor holds a 40 percent interest in the partnership and the second investor holds a 60 percent interest in the partnership. During January, the partnership buys two positions. The first position is 5,000 shares of common stock purchased at $9 and worth $12 at the end of January (an unrecognized gain of $15,000). The second position is 5,000 shares of common stock purchased at $16.50 and worth $19 at the end of January (an unrecognized gain of $12,500).

Table 10.1a summarizes the unrecognized gains for each investor in January.

TABLE 10.1a   January Positions

	Shares	Beginning Price	Ending Price	Gain (Loss)
Position 1	5,000	$ 9.00	$12.00	$15,000
Position 2	5,000	$16.50	$19.00	$12,500

These mark-to-market gains are recorded in a memorandum account for each partner. The calculations of the allocations are shown in Table 10.1b.

At the beginning of February, investor 3 is admitted as a partner. The new ownership percentages are: investor 1 (25 percent), investor 2 (37.5 percent), and investor 3 (37.5 percent). During the month, the partnership creates a short position of 15,000 shares in position 3 at a price of 9.25. At month-end, the prices of the three positions are: position 1 ($14), position 2 ($20.50), and position 3 ($11), as summarized in Table 10.2a. Notice that the beginning price for Table 10.2a equals the ending price from Table 10.1a, except for the new position, which begins at the cost established during the month.

TABLE 10.1b   Memorandum Balances (as of January 31)

	Partner 1	Partner 2
Position 1	$6,000[a]	$9,000[b]
Position 2	$5,000[c]	$7,500[d]

[a]$6,000 = 40% × $15,000.
[b]$9,000 = 60% × $15,000.
[c]$5,000 = 40% × $12,500.
[d]$7,500 = 60% × $12,500.

TABLE 10.2a   February Positions

	Shares	Beginning Price	Ending Price	Gain (Loss)
Position 1	5,000	$12.00	$14.00	$10,000
Position 2	5,000	$19.00	$20.50	$ 7,500
Position 3	−15,000	$ 9.25	$11.00	($26,250)

These gains and losses are entered into the memo balances for the three investors in Table 10.2b. For example, the $10,000 gain on position 1 is allocated 25 percent to investor 1 (an allocated amount of $2,500). This allocated amount is added to the previous memo balance ($6,000—see Table 10.1b). The memo balance of $8,500 reflects the pro-rated amount of unrecognized gain on position 1 during January and February. Similarly, the rest of Table 10.2b includes the unrecognized gains and losses plus any previous gains or losses in each position for each investor.

The ownership percentages do not change in March. The partnership sells the 5,000 shares of position 1 at $15. The ending price for position 2 is $22, and position 3 is marked to market at $11.25. Table 10.3a summarizes the new recognized and unrecognized gains and losses in the partnership. The beginning prices for the March table were the ending prices in February. The ending price for position 1 is the sale price and position 2 and position 3 are marked to market.

The memo balances are updated for the March gains and losses (including both the realized and unrealized amounts). Table 10.3b shows the updated memo balances for each investor. As before, Table 10.3b is the sum of the amounts carried over from Table 10.2b plus the allocation for March.

TABLE 10.2b   February Memo Balances

	Partner 1	Partner 2	Partner 3
Position 1	$8,500[a]	$12,750	$3,750
Position 2	$6,875	$10,313	$2,813
Position 3	($6,563)	($ 9,844)	($9,844)

[a]$8,500 = $6,000 + 25% × $10,000.

TABLE 10.3a   March Positions

	Shares	Beginning Price	Ending Price	Gain (Loss)
Position 1	5,000	$14.00	$15.00	$5,000
Position 2	5,000	$20.50	$22.00	$7,500
Position 3	−15,000	$11.00	$11.25	($3,750)

TABLE 10.3b   March Memo Balances

	Partner 1	Partner 2	Partner 3
Position 1	$9,750	$14,625	$ 5,625
Position 2	$8,750	$13,125	$ 5,625
Position 3	($7,500)	($11,250)	($11,250)

Allocating the Gain (Partial Netting)   The partnership realized a gain of $30,000 ($6 appreciation from $9 to $15 on 5,000 shares). Suppose the partnership chooses to allocate the gain using partial netting. The first step is to accumulate the gains for each investor. In Table 10.4a, the positions that created gains for each of the partners are totaled. Note that this includes all economic gains, both realized and unrealized.

Under this fairly typical allocation scheme, the realized gain is allocated according to the share each partner has of the total economic gains. The partners have experienced $57,500 in gains in the memorandum accounts. Investor 1 has received $18,500 of that gain, or 32.2 percent. Investor 2 has 48.3 percent of the gains, while investor 3 has 19.6 percent of the gains. These allocations are displayed in Table 10.4b.

TABLE 10.4a   Aggregate Gains and Losses

	Partner 1	Partner 2	Partner 3	Total
Gains	$18,500[a]	$27,750	$11,250	$57,500
Losses	($ 7,500)	($11,250)	($11,250)	($30,000)
Net	$11,000	$16,500	$ 0	$27,500

[a]$18,500 = $9,750 + $8,750.

TABLE 10.4b   Aggregate Allocation Ratios

	Partner 1	Partner 2	Partner 3	Total
Partial Netting Gain	32.2%	48.3%	19.6%	100.0%
Partial Netting Loss	25.0%	37.5%	37.5%	100.0%
Full Netting	40.0%	60.0%	0.0%	100.0%

TABLE 10.4c Aggregate Allocation Amounts

	Partner 1	Partner 2	Partner 3	Total
Partial Netting	$ 9,652	$14,478	$5,870	$30,000
Full Netting	$12,000	$18,000	$ 0	$30,000

The $30,000 realized gain is allocated 32.2 percent or $9,652. Investor 2 receives 48.3 percent or $14,478 and investor 3 receives $5,870. See Table 10.4c.

Full Aggregate Allocation Investor 3 has been invested in the partnership for two months. The gain in February disappeared in March, so investor 3 has made no money from the partnership. (See Table 10.4a.) Because investor 3 missed the gains in January, only 19.6 percent of the gains relate to investor 3, but the investor received 37.5 percent of the losses. Because the gain on positions exceeds the loss on positions, the partnership has economic profits but investor 3 does not. Yet this investor is nevertheless allocated 19.6 percent of the realized gains.

The partnership could also allocate the realized gain based on the net gains for each partner. Table 10.4a also shows the net gain for investor 1 and investor 2. Table 10.4b shows the allocation percentages using the net gain amount. Under the full netting approach, investor 1 receives a 40 percent allocation of the $30,000 realized gain because the $11,000 gain in the memorandum account for investor 1 represents 40 percent of the $27,500 net gain for all investors. Investor 2 is allocated 60 percent and investor 3 is allocated none of the gain because investor 3 has no net gain from the partnership.

Updating the Memorandum Balances Once the realized gains and losses have been allocated to the partners, the memorandum accounts must be updated to reflect that tax allocations that have been made, as shown in Table 10.5. For example, the memo balance for investor 1 in position 1 was $9,750 (Table 10.3b) at the end of March before the tax allocation. The tax allocation of $9,625 was applied (Table 10.4c). The memo balances are similarly updated for investor 2 and investor 3. The memo balances show that investor 1 and investor 2 were allocated slightly less than their share of the gains on position 1. The memo balances carry part of this gain until later realized gains are allocated. Investor 3 has been overallocated gains. This kind of overallocation is common and will be corrected

TABLE 10.5 Updated Memorandum Balances

	Partner 1	Partner 2	Partner 3
Position 1	$ 98[a]	$ 147[b]	($ 245)[c]
Position 2	$8,750	$13,125	$ 5,625
Position 3	($7,500)	($11,250)	($11,250)

[a]$98 = $9,750 (memo balance from February—Table 10.3b) – $9,652 (gain allocated in Table 10.4c).

[b]$147 = $14,625 (memo balance from February—Table 10.3b) – $14,478 (gain allocated in Table 10.4c).

[c]–$245 = $5,625 (memo balance from February—Table 10.3b) – $5,870 (gain allocated in Table 10.4c).

by later allocations, where investor 1 and investor 2 receive a larger portion of future realized gains. Hedge funds carry the amount in different ways, depending on the set of rules they apply to perform the allocation.

Need for More Complete Allocation Rules The allocation in the preceding example is relatively simple because all three partners had gains in their memo balances and because they collectively had larger gains than the $30,000 realized gain. Allocation rules must be complete enough to deal with all possible situations.

For example, it is typical to allocate gains to partners who have positive memo balances and omit partners from the allocation who have negative memo balances. Similarly, losses may be applied proportionately to partners having negative memo balances, omitting allocations to partners with gains in their memo balances.

Sometimes, partners have positive memo balances but the partnership realizes gains greater than the beginning memo balances. In the case, the partnership may allocate part of the gain to match gains in memo accounts. Realized gains allocated when no partners have positive memo balances are usually based the economic ownership percent of the partners. Similarly, realized losses may be allocated according to economic ownership when no partners have negative memo balances.

Other partners may apply the realized gains and losses to the partners with the oldest entries in the memo accounts. This method is sometimes called first in, first out (FIFO). In the preceding allocation example, investor 1 and investor 2 would receive some of the realized gain based on their memo gains in January. The realized gain ($30,000) exceeds the January memo entries ($27,500—the total of all the entries in Table

10.1b). The remaining unallocated amount of $2,500 ($30,000 – $27,500) would be allocated among the three investors based on the February results.

Hedge funds use many other allocation procedures. There is little discussion of these rules in the published press.[4] Investors may be unaware of the particular rules used to allocate taxable gains and losses even though the allocation rules can have a significant impact on the timing of tax liabilities for the investors.

Section 1256

The tax code offers a break to traders of futures and certain commodities. The provision requires the taxable investor to treat 60 percent of all gains (losses) on Section 1256 assets as long-term capital gains (losses), regardless of the holding period. The provision has the effect of lowering the effective tax rate on futures trades. The tax break extends some of the benefit of lower long-term tax rates to an industry that rarely holds an asset long enough to get the benefit of the lower tax rate.

Hedge Funds and Not-for-Profit Entities

The U.S. tax code exempts many kinds of investors from taxation on investment returns. Pension funds, endowments, and foundations may avoid income taxation on most of their activities if they follow the rules set down to grant them tax-exempt status. One of the requirements designed to prevent tax abuse is that not-for-profit organizations may not operate a business within the tax-exempt umbrella. If a tax-exempt entity runs a taxable business, the income from that business is subject to unrelated business income tax (UBIT).

Leverage in a hedge fund often triggers UBIT. Investment income in tax-exempt organizations is generally not taxed. However, if the investment vehicle borrows money, doing so may trigger UBIT.

To avoid UBIT, tax-exempt investors often invest in the hedge funds with very low leverage. Tax-exempt investors also prefer to invest in offshore hedge funds because the corporate structure stands between the tax-exempt entity and the interest.

Side-Pocket Allocations

Certain assets are easy to mark to market. When recent trade prices or market quotes are not available, hedge funds can establish fair value. However, the hedge fund must have a defensible basis for the valuations. When it is impossible to identify periodic mark-to-market value, it would be unfair to investors to allow partners to enter or exit the partnership based on unreliable values.

One solution to the problem is to prohibit investors from entering or exiting the fund. In effect, this is the way that venture capital funds operate because a large part of the portfolio is difficult to mark to market. Such a solution is too restrictive for most hedge funds that carry a portfolio comprised of many assets that can be readily revalued and a small portion that is difficult to price. Instead, those hedge funds might create side-pocket allocations.

To understand side-pocket allocations, imagine first that a hedge fund manager creates a new business unit to contain some private equity positions. The hedge fund awards ownership of this private equity portfolio proportional to the current ownership percentages in the hedge fund and diverts cash to the separate entity to fund the portfolio. As investors in the hedge fund enter and exit, the ownership of the hedge fund can start to diverge from the ownership in the private equity portfolio. Ultimately, the private equity positions are sold and the original investors are paid out based on the original, unchanging ownership percentages.

Finally, imagine that the hedge fund did not set up a separate business but created allocations of return to match the pattern described. That is, the ownership percentages of the assets in the side pocket are fixed. Entering investors gain no ownership stake in these assets, and exiting investors may not redeem their stake in the side-pocket assets. Further, any return on the side-pocket assets is due to the original owners of those assets. In summary, the accountants treat the side pocket the same as if there was a separate legal entity.

QUESTIONS AND PROBLEMS

10.1 One hedge fund manager receives a fee equal to 1 percent of the assets under management, which the fund reports as an expense to its investors. Another manager receives a distribution from the partnership equal to 1 percent of the assets under management paid to the general partners. Why might a fund manager prefer to receive a management fee as an allocation rather than the same payment as income?

10.2 Referring to the two funds in question 10.1, why might investors prefer to pay the manager a fee instead of granting a special allocation to the general partners?

10.3 Referring to the two funds in questions 10.1 and 10.2, why might investors prefer to pay the manager a special allocation instead of a fee?

10.4 A partner holds a 25 percent stake in an investment partnership. The partnership reports ordinary taxable income of $1 million and allocates $250,000 to this partner. Assume that this investor pays income tax at the rate of 35 percent and that the corporate income tax rate is also 35 percent. Calculate the tax penalty if the hedge fund had been structured as a C corporation instead of a partnership.

10.5 An investor invests in a mutual fund in December. A short time later, the mutual fund distributes a short-term capital gain to all shareholders equal to the short-term capital gains realized by the fund during the entire calendar year. The investor has experienced no appreciation in the value of the mutual fund shares at the time of the distribution. Explain how this tax allocation differs from the allocation at a hedge fund organized as a limited partnership.

10.6 A fund admits a new partner during the middle of a tax year. A short time later, the fund liquidates a position and generates a long-term gain. The fund makes a layered allocation to all investors, including the newest investor. Does the new investor receive a short-term or long-term gain?

10.7 You allocate gains and losses using the aggregate method. You must allocate a realized gain but all of your investors have losses. How should you allocate the losses to the investors?

10.8 A hedge fund pays $30,000 per month for a computer service. Does this mean that the fund should allocate out the expense at different daily rates for February (having 28 or 29 days) than for March (having 31 days)?

10.9 A fund has commissions equal to $1 million annually. How should the fund allocate the expense to the individual months?

10.10 An institutional investor has 10 percent ownership of a hedge fund for the first six months of the year. In the second six months, the institution has only 8 percent of the capital. The fund has an annual expense of $100,000 for a futures exchange membership. How much of the expense should you allocate to this investor for the year?

10.11 Refer to the aggregate allocation example in the text (including Tables 10.1a through 10.5). Allocate the gain on position 1 using the layered method of tax allocation.

10.12 Faced with the memorandum balances in Table 10.5, suppose the fund realized a gain of $245. How should the fund allocate the gain?

NOTES

1. $48,000/366 days (i.e., leap year) = $131
2. $48,000/366 days × 29 = $3,803
3. For example, suppose that investor 1 owned four units (40 percent) and investor 2 owned six units (60 percent) before investor 3 is admitted. Investor 3 buys six units. After admitting the new investor, investor 1 has 25 percent (4 units/16 units). Investor 2 and investor 3 each own 37.5 percent (6 units/16 units).
4. For more information, see Stuart McCrary, *How to Create and Manage a Hedge Fund*, Hoboken, NJ: John Wiley & Sons, 2002, pages 213–232.

CHAPTER 11

Risk Management and Hedge Funds

RISK IN HEDGE FUNDS

Risk is present in nearly every investment to differing degrees. Even default-free U.S. Treasury bills leave the investor with reinvestment risk. And risk (at least as it is often measured) is not inherently bad because it is usually associated with higher returns.

Nevertheless, it is important to measure risk, and that is the subject of this chapter. Chapter 7 shows ways to quantify the risk of the reported performance, using the standard deviation of return or volatility, downside deviations, the Sharpe ratio, the Sortino ratio, and other *ex post* measurements. In contrast, the methods presented in this chapter are forward-looking. Also, the measures in Chapter 7 rely only on the performance of the fund as a whole. This chapter presumes that the analyst has information about individual positions. In a time when investors frequently demand significant transparency, it is not unusual to have the details necessary for a robust risk analysis. Certainly, the funds have this position detail and often report results of risk analysis similar to those just described.

How Risky Is a Hedge Fund?

Many people believe hedge funds are extremely risky. Certainly, the risk disclosure documents don't discourage this attitude. It is important to realize, though, that the risks described are designed to be the worst case, not the most likely case. Since hedge fund sponsors face much greater litigation risk from failing to disclose potential risks than from disclosing implausible risks, the documents sometimes make it difficult for investors to assess the likely risk of a hedge fund investment.

The media reports about hedge funds also dwell on the risks of hedge fund investing. Disasters make for good copy, so it is reasonable that bad news makes the front page and other hedge fund news appears inside, if at all. Further, in the 1990s, the large global macro hedge funds were newsmakers, and this is one of the riskiest hedge fund strategies. Unnoticed by the press (but not by hedge fund investors), many hedge funds came into existence offering modest returns and lower risks. The penchant for secrecy at many hedge funds may create a situation where the public never hears about the good news and only hears about the bad news when it is bad enough to become public information.

Sources of Hedge Fund Risk

Many factors contribute to the risk of hedge fund returns. The securities held by the fund, including stocks, bonds, currencies, commodities, and derivatives, contribute substantially to the risk of the portfolio. Hedge funds may choose to apply various hedging techniques to reduce the risk. The presence of leverage may amplify these security risks and introduce other risks. World central bankers are concerned that one of the risks of hedge funds is the collective stress they place on the financial system. Finally, recent history has demonstrated that at least sometimes, hedges fund fail because of outright fraud.

Summary of Hedge Fund Risk and Return Data

Figure 11.1 shows a plot of the risk and return of several hedge fund strategies from 1998 through January 2004. The hedge fund strategies are a collection of passive hedge fund indexes maintained by the Center for International Securities and Derivatives Markets (CISDM). That is, the passive indexes are built from a group of hedge funds actually open for new investment. The return of each group of funds is associated with a dozen or so economic factors (including stock returns, bond returns, credit spreads, market volatilities, etc.). Then, a performance is calculated from these economic variables for each passive strategy. The result is a representative benchmark of performance that is reasonably free from human errors, fraud, or other factors that are not representative of the hedge fund universe. These series do not benefit from diversification found in hedge fund indexes of many funds (sometimes called active indexes) so should be more representative of hedge fund returns than active indexes.

During this time period, stocks earned less than the long-term expected return of 10 or 11 percent that has been typical. As a result, hedge funds as

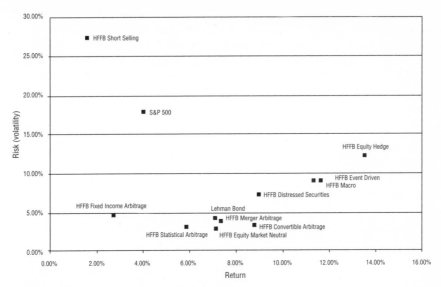

FIGURE 11.1   Performance 1998 to January 2004
Source: CISDM Newsletter, February 2004.
HFFB—Hedge Fund Factor Based index.

a group outperformed the Standard & Poor's 500 index and many other equity benchmarks. The relative performance of hedge funds versus the stock and bond indexes shown may not be representative in the future. When stock performance is good, it is typically higher than hedge fund returns, but the advantage of stock returns over hedge fund returns is determined mostly by how well the more volatile stocks perform.

The relative risk of hedge funds and stock and bond returns is more consistent. All the hedge fund strategies were less risky than the S&P 500 and about half were less risky than the more staid Lehman bond index representing a well-diversified bond portfolio. Perhaps hedge fund returns are less volatile than the securities the hedge funds trade because investors have been quick to pull money out of excessively risky hedge funds.

Table 11.1 shows a variety of risk measurements on the same passive hedge fund indexes. On every measure of risk, all strategies except the short selling index are less risky than the S&P 500.

Hedge funds control the risk of their positions using risk management techniques. The same tools can be used by investors, creditors, and regulators to monitor the risks in a hedge fund, provided that the fund discloses either details about portfolio holdings or the results of its internal risk analyzes.

TABLE 11.1 Performance and Risk of Hedge Fund Styles

	HFFB Convertible Arbitrage	HFFB Equity Hedge	HFFB Event Driven	HFFB Distressed Securities
Annualized Return	8.84%	13.55%	11.43%	9.04%
Annualized Standard Deviation	3.58%	12.37%	9.26%	7.46%
Sharpe Ratio	1.48	0.81	0.85	0.73
Maximum Drawdown	−2.37%	−12.52%	−9.98%	−6.51%
Correlation to S&P 500	31.00%	62.00%	58.00%	46.00%
Correlation to Lehman Bond	2.00%	1.00%	−1.00%	−4.00%
% Winning Months	78.08%	63.01%	63.01%	63.01%
Average Gain	1.11%	3.08%	2.35%	1.88%
% Losing Months	21.92%	36.99%	36.99%	36.99%
Average Loss	−0.71%	−2.20%	−1.45%	−1.18%

	HFFB Merger Arbitrage	HFFB Fixed Income Arbitrage	HFFB Equity Market Neutral	HFFB Short Selling
Annualized Return	7.38%	2.75%	7.21%	1.62%
Annualized Standard Deviation	4.02%	4.77%	3.04%	27.35%
Sharpe Ratio	0.95	−0.17	1.20	−0.07
Maximum Drawdown	−8.85%	−9.66%	−2.34%	−47.12%
Correlation to S&P 500	45.00%	13.00%	−12.00%	−62.00%
Correlation to Lehman Bond	−3.00%	−18.00%	36.00%	7.00%
% Winning Months	78.08%	58.90%	80.82%	49.32%
Average Gain	1.05%	1.09%	0.88%	6.59%
% Losing Months	21.92%	41.10%	19.18%	50.68%
Average Loss	−1.01%	−0.99%	−0.65%	−5.53%

	HFFB Statistical Arbitrage	HFFB Macro	S&P 500	Lehman Bond
Annualized Return	5.92%	11.62%	4.04%	7.18%
Annualized Standard Deviation	3.22%	9.24%	17.90%	4.42%
Sharpe Ratio	0.73	0.87	0.03	0.82
Maximum Drawdown	−7.40%	−9.62%	−44.73%	−4.58%
Correlation to S&P 500	56.00%	48.00%	100.00%	−25.00%
Correlation to Lehman Bond	−10.00%	22.00%	−25.00%	100.00%
% Winning Months	76.71%	71.23%	54.79%	69.86%
Average Gain	0.85%	2.02%	4.26%	1.20%
% Losing Months	23.29%	28.77%	45.21%	30.14%
Average Loss	−0.73%	−1.69%	−4.13%	−0.84%

Source: CISDM Newsletter, February 2004.
HFFB—Hedge Fund Factor Based index.

FIXED INCOME RISK MANAGEMENT

The fixed income markets developed risk management tools earlier than commodity and equity markets because the largest source of risk for most fixed income instruments is interest rates, and interest rates (even for different bonds) move together more closely than either commodity prices or stock prices. Many of the fixed income risk management tools in use today derive from the work attributable to an insurance actuary developed more than a century ago.

Bond Pricing for a Regular Coupon Bond

The mathematics of fixed income risk management begins with fixed income valuation. The price of a bond with annual payments yielding r percent is given by equation (11.1):

$$\text{Dirty Price} = \text{Price} + \text{Accrued Interest}$$
$$= \frac{\text{Coupon}}{1+r} + \frac{\text{Coupon}}{(1+r)^2} + \ldots \frac{\text{Coupon} + \text{Principal}}{(1+r)^{\text{Maturity}}} \quad (11.1)$$

Note the formula provides the present value of the coupon payments. The form of price commonly used by market participants is the value called the net price (or full price minus the value of accrued interest).

Equation (11.1) can be generalized for bonds paying interest monthly or semiannually. Equation (11.2) shows the value of a bond paying semiannual coupon payments for 10 years.

$$\text{Dirty Price} = \sum_{i=1}^{2 \times 10} \frac{\dfrac{\text{Coupon}}{2}}{\left(1+\dfrac{r}{2}\right)^i} + \frac{\text{Principal}}{\left(1+\dfrac{r}{2}\right)^{20}} \quad (11.2)$$

Duration as a Measure of Bond Risk

The risk measure in equation (11.3) is called Macaulay duration. For simplicity, this formula is given for the case of a bond with a coupon paid annually but is otherwise similar to equation (11.2).

$$\text{Duration}_{\text{Macaulay}} = \sum_{i=1}^{\text{Maturity}} \frac{i \times \text{Coupon}}{(1+r)^i} + \frac{\text{Maturity} \times \text{Principal}}{(1+r)^{\text{Maturity}}} \quad (11.3)$$

Notice, however, that the interval of time from the settlement date (now) until each payment is included in the numerator. The denominator is a present value factor, and the remaining term is the particular cash flow. For this reason, duration is sometimes described as the present value weighted time to maturity of the cash flows.

Macaulay duration is usually modified by dividing the entire expression by $(1 + r)$. Equation (11.4) is derived by dividing equation (11.3) by $(1 + r)$:

$$\text{Duration}_{\text{Modified}} = \sum_{i=2}^{\text{Maturity}+1} \frac{i \times \text{Coupon}}{(1+r)^i} + \frac{\text{Maturity} \times \text{Principal}}{(1+r)^{\text{Maturity}+1}} \quad (11.4)$$

The convenient feature of this modified duration is that it equals the percent change in price (in particular, the dirty price) caused by a change in yield of 1 percent (or 100 basis points). For example, a bond with a coupon of 5.5 percent and duration of 5 will decline from 100 to approximately 95 if rates rise from 5.5 percent to 6.5 percent.

Figure 11.2 shows the price sensitivity of a five-year bond. The Excel function MDURATION reports that the modified duration of a bond with a 5.5 percent semiannual coupon is 4.320 at a yield of 5.5 percent. The

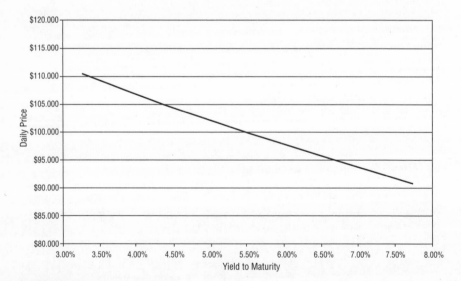

FIGURE 11.2 Price-to-Yield Relationship of a 5.5 Percent Five-Year Bond

bond moves from 100 at 5.5 percent to 104.433 at 4.5 percent, slightly higher than predicted by modified duration, and to 95.789 at 6.5 percent, also slightly higher than predicted by modified duration. This imprecision results from convexity, described later.

A 10-year bond with a 5.5 percent coupon is more sensitive to changes in interest rates. The modified duration of this bond is 7.413. Figure 11.3 shows the price and yield relationships of this bond.

The price at 4.5 percent is 107.983, slightly higher than the price predicted by modified duration, and at 6.5 percent is 92.729, again slightly higher than the price predicted by modified duration. Further, notice that the modified duration of the two bonds correctly predicts that the 10-year bond will be considerably more sensitive to changes in interest rates.

Using Duration to Establish Trade Weightings

A hedge fund may use duration to establish a long position in one bond and short position in another bond so that the combination is hedged from changes in rates. For a particular change in rates equal to Δr, the gain or loss on the long position is the change in rate times the modified duration times the value of the full position. Equation (11.5) permits the trader to

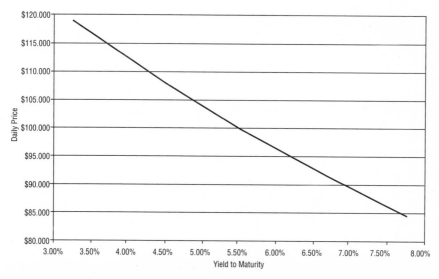

FIGURE 11.3 Price-to-Yield Relationship of a 5.5 Percent 10-Year Bond

calculate a market-neutral weight such that the hedge fund makes the same amount on one position that it loses on the other.

$$\frac{(Price_{Long} + Accrued_{Long})}{100} \times FaceValue_{Long} \times MDur_{Long} \times \Delta r$$
$$= \frac{(Price_{Short} + Accrued_{Short})}{100} \times FaceValue_{Short} \times MDur_{Short} \times \Delta r \qquad (11.5)$$

The dirty price as a percent of face value times the face value is the market value of the position. The modified duration is the percent change in market value for a 1 percent change in yield, and the change in yield scales the gain or loss to the amount of rate change. Each side of the equation represents a dollar amount.

The change in yield appears to be the same on both sides of the equation. If the yields of one bond are more volatile than the other, it is appropriate to include different values for the change in yields. Yields on shorter maturities tend to move more than yields on longer maturities. Yields on bonds with lower ratings may be more volatile than yields on bonds with higher ratings. For equation (11.6), the change in yields was presumed to be the same on both sides (called a parallel yield shift) so the term drops out:

$$FaceValue_{Long} = \frac{DirtyPrice_{Short}}{DirtyPrice_{Long}} \times \frac{MDur_{Short}}{MDur_{Long}} \times FaceValue_{Short} \qquad (11.6)$$

Duration as a Risk Management Tool

Knowing the duration of a bond allows the hedge fund manager to gauge the impact of changing interest rates on individual bonds. Fortunately, it is easy to extrapolate to the impact on a portfolio. See equation (11.7).

$$Duration_{Portfolio} = \sum w_i \times Dur_i \qquad (11.7)$$

where w_i = weight of the ith bond in the portfolio
      Dur_i = modified duration of the $i$the bond

A portfolio with a duration of 5 will gain or lose about 5 percent of value for a change in yield of 1 percent or 100 basis points.

Using Short Positions in Bonds to Control Risk

Hedge funds are not restricted to long-only positions. By carrying long and short positions, hedge funds can set the portfolio duration at any level desired. This doesn't mean that the hedge fund has no risks. However, it is possible to estimate the gains or losses if the yields move the same amount on all bonds in the portfolio.

Convexity and Bond Prices

In the previous example, the price will not rise or fall exactly by the amount predicted by duration because the duration does not remain fixed at the original level. Notice that the yield to maturity (r) appears in equation (11.4). This means that as the bond price moves down from 100, the yield rises and the duration changes. When prices fall (rates rise), the modified duration declines, so the decline in price is smaller than the original forecast over this range of yields. Similarly, when prices rise (rates fall), the modified duration increases, so the rise in price is larger than the original forecast over this range of yields.

Figure 11.4 shows the price of a hypothetical 30-year bond with a 5.5 percent coupon at various yields to maturity. Take care in reviewing

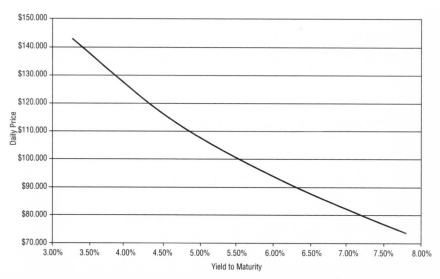

FIGURE 11.4　Price-to-Yield Relationship of a 5.5 Percent 30-Year Bond

Figure 11.4 because the y-axis is expanded to accommodate the even greater price sensitivity of a 30-year bond. Notice, too, that the modified duration of a 30-year bond varies. At higher yields, the price is less sensitive to changes in rate (flatter slope), and at lower yields the price is more sensitive to changes in rate (steeper slope). At 5.5 percent, this bond has a modified duration of 14.223. At 4.5 percent, the bond has a modified duration of 15.363, while at 6.5 percent, the modified duration is only 13.128.

Convexity measures the degree that durations change in response to changes in yield. The traditional formula for convexity is given by equation (11.8) for a bond with an annual coupon:

$$\text{Convexity} = \frac{\sum_{i=1}^{\text{Maturity}} \dfrac{i \times (i+1) \times \text{CashFlow}}{(1+r)^i}}{(1+r)^2 \times \text{DirtyPrice}} \tag{11.8}$$

Note in equation (11.8), cash flow represents both the regular interest payments and the repayment of principal at maturity.

The convexity can be approximated by recalculating duration at yields slightly above and below the initial yield. In equation (11.9), Dur_+ refers to the modified duration at r_+ and Dur_- refers to the modified duration at r_-:

$$\text{Convexity} \cong -2 \times \frac{\text{Dur}_+ - \text{Dur}_-}{r_+ - r_-} \times \frac{100}{\text{DirtyPrice}} \tag{11.9}$$

Convexity provides an adjustment to make to the modified duration (the percent price change). See equation (11.10):

$$\text{Adjustment to } \%\Delta\text{Price} = \text{Convexity} \times (\Delta r)^2 \times 100 \tag{11.10}$$

Convexity Is a Good Thing

In the example, the bond rose more than predicted by modified duration, a good feature for anyone who owns the bond. Also, the price declined less than predicted by modified duration, also a good feature for anyone who owns a bond. Bonds that have convexity benefit from this price behavior.

Some bonds have what is described as negative convexity: Prices rise less than predicted by duration when rates decline but fall further when rates rise. Some types of mortgage-backed bonds have this trait because of the prepayment option owned by the homeowner. Callable bonds may also exhibit negative convexity.

Using Duration and Convexity for Risk Management

It is possible to use duration and convexity to develop scenarios. These scenarios can highlight the risks in a hedge fund portfolio. However, it is simple enough to revalue the positions at different yields without relying on duration and convexity for approximations. The real value of duration and convexity totals on a portfolio is that they provide a very simple indication of interest rate exposure. Because of the simplicity of the two indicators, it is possible to create rules to hold the interest rate risk of the portfolio to a tolerable level.

CURRENCY RISK MANAGEMENT

A simple means to manage currency exposure is to reduce the complexity of currency exposures. At the risk of ignoring real currency risk, some traders have consolidated positions into two or three currencies. For example, Canadian dollar exposure is converted to U.S. dollar and any risk on the exchange relationship between Canada and the United States is ignored. Other currency exposures may be reduced to exposure to the euro and the Japanese yen.

This technique is called proxy hedging and is successful only if the actual currency exposures resemble the proxy currencies. In some cases, where a portfolio has exposure to many currencies, diversification may improve the results but can't guarantee success.

EQUITY RISK MANAGEMENT

Stocks face an even greater risk management problem than currencies. The correlation between most stocks is significantly lower than the correlation of bond returns. It is possible to apply proxy hedging in a way similar to the currency solution but the results are more unpredictable. Under this scheme, stocks are assigned to an index (S&P 500, Nasdaq, or a non-U.S. index, for example).

Ironically, the inability to completely track the indexes is ignored. Generally, these efforts start with the capital asset pricing model that hold that the return on a particular stock (r_i) is driven by the return on a risk-free asset $(r_{RiskFree})$, the return on the market (r_{Market}), and the amount of market risk present in the security (called beta and shown as B_i). See Equation (11.11). Risks particular to an individual stock are called nonsystematic risk and are assumed to vanish through diversification.

$$r_i = r_{RiskFree} + B_i(r_{Market} - r_{RiskFree}) \qquad (11.11)$$

Stocks with betas of 1 are as risky as the market and are included without adjustment. Stocks with betas below 1 are underweighted in determining equity exposure, while stocks with betas above 1 are overweighted.

NEED FOR MORE POWERFUL RISK MANAGEMENT TOOLS

All these techniques have problems as risk management tools for hedge funds. Hedge funds often have exposure to stocks, bonds, and currencies, and a risk measurement tool should accommodate mixed positions. Hedge fund portfolios may not be well-diversified so it may be inappropriate to ignore nonsystematic risk. Funds with currency exposure may want more precise hedging methods than proxy hedging.

The risk management tools described next incorporate uncertainty in the risk calculations. Value at risk, the most popular credit risk models, and option risk management all rely on statistics and don't necessarily require an a priori understanding of the relationships between different assets in the portfolio. As a result, these methods allow the hedge fund to monitor the risk of portfolios containing different types of assets.

Value at Risk (VaR)

Value at risk is an adaptation of classical statistics to risk measurement. The first step is to accumulate the risks of the individual positions. The returns on all the assets held in the portfolio are assumed to be normally distributed. The expected return and risks of the portfolio are reduced to the mean and standard deviation of a familiar bell curve. VaR transforms these values into a loss amount.

Figure 11.5 shows the normal distribution of two assets similar to the bell curves used in Chapter 6. Asset A has a volatility or annualized standard deviation of 20 percent, and asset B has a volatility of 40 percent. No-

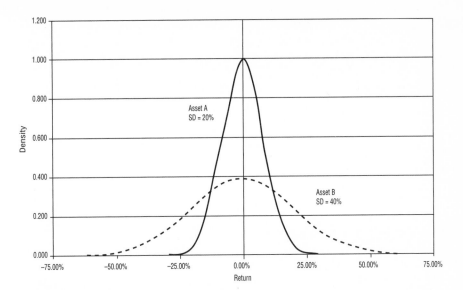

FIGURE 11.5 Normal Distribution

tice that the distribution is actually a probability function. The area under each line corresponds with the probability of that outcome. Half of the outcomes occur to the left of the midpoint of each curve (because it represents half of the area).

The taller bell curve for asset A is actually the less volatile of the two assets. Returns close to the midpoint are likely and either extremely high or extremely low returns are less likely than the asset with the flatter bell curve for asset B. At the same time, both distributions share one characteristic: About 5 percent of the time, return for the year is lower than 1.65 standard deviations below the mean (the one-tailed test in statistics). In other words, 95 percent of the time, asset A with the 20 percent standard deviation will have a return of −39 percent or better (0 percent mean return less 1.65 × 20 percent) and 95 percent of the time, asset B with the 40 percent standard deviation will have a return of −78 percent or better (0 percent mean return less 1.65 × 40 percent).

The 95 percent confidence level is the basis of the VaR calculation. If a hedge fund portfolio holds $2.5 million of asset A, 95 percent of the time the asset will lose less than $975,000 ($2.5 million × 39 percent) over a year. If the hedge fund portfolio holds $5.25 million of asset B, 95 percent of the time, the asset will lose less then $4,095,000 ($5.25 million × 78 percent) over a year.

Adapting the VaR Format into a Risk Model   The one-year horizon is not typical for portfolio managers. Typically, the VaR calculations are based on a one-day holding period. The volatilities of these assets must be adjusted for the shorter time horizon. Equation (11.12) shows the adjustment from annual to daily:

$$\text{Volatility}_{\text{A,Daily}} = \sigma_{\text{A,Daily}} = \frac{\sigma_{\text{A,Annual}}}{\sqrt{250}} \tag{11.12}$$

The adjustment is based on the square root of the difference in time. Equation (11.12) assumes that there are 250 trading days per year (52 weeks × 5 days – 10 market holidays). Most practitioners use a scaling factor around 250 or 251, instead of 365 calendar days.

Revising the VaR calculations for asset A, the daily standard deviation is –2.47 percent. Ninety-five percent of the time, the asset will lose less than $6,166 (–2.47% × 1.65 × $2.5 million). The daily standard deviation for asset B is 4.93 percent. Ninety-five percent of the time, the asset will lose less than $25,899.

Calculating Portfolio VaR   The VaR on a portfolio is not simply the sum of the VaR on each asset held in the portfolio. The portfolio VaR is based on the sum of the squared VaR values of individual assets. However, the portfolio VaR must also account for the effects of diversification. See equation (11.13):

$$\text{VaR}_{1\ldots n} = \sqrt{\sum_{i=1}^{n} (\text{VaR}_i)^2 + 2 \sum_{i=1}^{n} \sum_{j=i+1}^{n} \rho_{i,j} \text{VaR}_i \times \text{VaR}_j} \tag{11.13}$$

CREDIT RISK MEASUREMENT

Several alternative ways to measure credit risk are sponsored by software vendors. The most successful commercial product to evaluate and manage credit risk is the KMV Credit Monitor family of products, now a division of Moody's Investors Service. The KMV suite of programs attaches probably to default and measures the expected liquidation value upon default. The software quantifies the default risk on a wide range of securities and loans and allows traders to compare the expected returns of different types of fixed income assets.

OPTION RISK MEASUREMENT

Many hedge funds trade derivative securities, whose price depends on the price of some underlying asset. This option risk measurement section will not describe the specific options because most of the concepts apply to all derivative instruments.

There are many option models, but most models base the value on the current price of the underlying asset, the volatility of that asset, a short-term borrowing rate, the time to expiration, and the dividend or coupon (if any). Because these factors determine the fair value of an option, changes in any one of these inputs would affect the fair value of the option.

Introduction to the Greeks

The sensitivity of the derivative value to the inputs is described by a series of Greek letters. The formulas of these Greeks differ from model to model but are usually derived along with each valuation model. These sensitivities are a measure of risk in these derivative positions.

Delta—Sensitivity to Changes in the Underlying Asset   When the price of an asset rises, calls gain value and puts lose value. The sensitivity of the option price change to changes in the underlying asset is called delta and is frequently labeled with the Greek letter Δ. For example, a delta of .60 means that a call option rises in value only 60 percent as much as the underlying asset. A hedge fund could buy a call on $10 million in securities or buy $6 million of the security outright. At least with respect to small changes in the price of the asset, the two positions would behave similarly. The risk modeler can treat this $10 million derivative as equivalent to the outright ownership of $6 million of the security for the purposes of determining whether the hedge fund is long or short overall.

Gamma—Sensitivity of Delta to Changes in the Underlying Asset   The delta of an option changes based on changes in the option inputs. The delta of an option is most influenced by the value of the underlying asset. The sensitivity of the hedge ratio delta to changes in the underlying asset is called gamma and is frequently labeled with the Greek letter Γ. Changes in the delta are important to risk measurement because they mean that the risk characteristics of the portfolio can change in rising or falling markets. Often, these changes warrant changes in the composition of the portfolio or of hedges.

Theta—Sensitivity to Time to Expiration   The value of the underlying security moves around randomly. In contrast, the time to expiration trends steadily down over time. Theta measures the impact of passing time on the value of a derivative. Long positions nearly always lose value under the scenario of no change in price or volatility.

QUESTIONS AND PROBLEMS

11.1   What are some of the advantages of using risk control models that do not rely on probability?

11.2   What advantages do probability-based risk control models have over other techniques that do not rely on probability?

11.3   Why is risk management not equivalent to risk elimination or risk minimization?

11.4   What is distinctive about bonds that allows the risk manager to use tools such as duration and convexity that may be of limited value for other types of assets?

11.5   Why is the full price or dirty price as high as or higher than the price conventionally used in securities trading?

11.6   Why is duration a better measure of bond risk than average life?

11.7   For many years, the Argentine peso was pegged to the U.S. dollar. Describe some of the advantages and disadvantages of using the U.S. dollar as a hedge, even if your real exposure is in pesos.

11.8   Why might beta provide an improper hedge for long and short equity positions?

11.9   You are long a call on a futures contract that is correctly delta hedged versus the underlying future. You don't plan to adjust the hedge before expiration. Explain how this position resembles an option straddle.

11.10 Explain why the upper limit for the delta of an option is generally 1.00.

11.11 You calculated the trade weights for a two-year note versus a five-year note. Your calculations suggest that you should sell \$2 million face amount of five-year notes for each $5 million face amount of two-year notes. However, your weightings were based on modified duration and the value of the positions. You are concerned because the yield on the two-year note seems to move 25 percent more than the yield on the five-year note (that is, a 4-basis-point shift in the five-year yield is associated with a 5-basis-point shift in the two-year yield). How should you adjust your hedge ratio, if at all?

11.12 What would happen if you ignored accrued interest in the trade weighting in question 11.11?

CHAPTER 12

Marketing Hedge Funds

Marketing is one of the most important functions of a hedge fund manager. Effective marketing increases the size of the assets under management, which leads to higher fees. Especially for a new fund, the world does not beat a path to the door of a new hedge fund, regardless of the freshness of the investment plan. For certain funds, past performance simplifies the marketing efforts, but the typical hedge fund needs to tell a story about its performance, good and bad.

WHAT IS HEDGE FUND MARKETING?

Marketing is a well-developed discipline. Many consumer goods manufacturers spend considerable effort and expense in marketing their products. Surprisingly, most of the same marketing concepts that are used to analyze beer sales, paper goods, and cosmetics apply to hedge fund marketing. However, very few hedge fund managers start by identifying a need or want and design a product to satisfy that want. Instead, they begin with a particular investment expertise, develop a product, and then set out the sell what they have created. What the manager sells differs from fund to fund. Most managers sell performance. Some managers emphasize the investment process. A small number of fund managers can market the credentials of certain key employees. Many hedge funds market the uniqueness of their investment products.

Types of Hedge Fund Customers

Any attempt to develop a comprehensive marketing plan for a hedge fund must begin from an understanding of the types of hedge fund customers and the needs and wants of each particular group. The major groups of hedge fund investors are described in Chapter 3.

Marketing and Hedge Fund Regulations in the United States

Chapter 8 summarizes the regulations affecting hedge funds and hedge fund investors. To maintain an exemption from registration requirements under the Securities Act of 1933 and the Investment Company Act of 1940, hedge funds may not make general solicitations to sell their investments and may not advertise. This chapter discusses how hedge funds may market within the restrictions imposed on them.

In general, potential investors must approach hedge fund managers about making an investment. The manager may contact potential investors if they have already established a substantial relationship. Hedge funds turn to institutions that have preexisting relationships to introduce potential investors to the hedge fund: independent marketers, prime brokers, fund of funds managers, and high-net-worth divisions of stock brokerage firms.

Many contacts with potential customers that are permitted of a registered company may be prohibited from a hedge fund that relies on exemption from registration. For example, a news release, interview or speech at a conference might be considered a prohibited solicitation or advertisement if the speaker/writer works for an unregistered hedge fund and mentions the fund. Many hedge fund operators restrict web site pages to registered users that could legally invest in the funds.

It is important to emphasize that the restrictions apply to U.S. managers and aren't typical of many other parts of the world. In Canada, where regulation occurs at the province, not the national government, level, advertising is permitted in some provinces and restricted in other areas. In some European markets, it is typical to register the hedge fund shares on a stock exchange, although purchases and sales typically occur away from the trading floor.

Marketing by Providing Services

One way to attract potential hedge fund customers without violating the restrictions on solicitation is to provide hedge-fund-related services to attract potential customers. Some organizations collect and publish performance data. Generally, these organizations don't provide the performance of individual funds. Instead, they publish composite performance, including benchmarks for specific hedge fund strategies. Some hedge fund marketers maintain collections of articles and research papers of interest to hedge fund investors. In the past, hedge fund organizations have distributed due diligence research to facilitate their marketing efforts. In fact, many hedge fund investors seek out fund of funds managers to benefit from the due diligence and portfolio management services these organizations provide.

Hedge Fund Marketing Plan

A hedge fund should have a marketing plan. A marketing plan lays out the key marketing strategies and objectives of the manager. The plan should describe the product positioning of the fund (how the fund compares with other hedge funds and other investment products). The plan should include an analysis of the market for this particular fund, including a measure of the size of the market, growth experience, and expectations for future growth. Several organizations have begun collecting industry data, which is invaluable in developing a marketing plan.

The marketing plan must address the most important marketing challenge for a hedge fund—identifying and marketing to prospective investors. Because of the restrictions on solicitation for U.S. hedge funds, several types of organizations are vital to hedge fund marketing, especially to new or young funds.

MARKETING BUSINESS PARTNERS

Private placement rules place restrictions on the hedge fund that make it difficult to prospect for customers. Several types of marketing services have developed to supplement the efforts of internal marketing staffs.

Third-Party Marketers

Often, a new hedge fund manager has considerable investment expertise and little marketing experience or few contacts. These hedge funds may turn to third-party or independent marketing organizations. A third-party marketer must register with the National Association of Securities Dealers (NASD) as a broker-dealer in the United States because the organization is offering securities to customers (even though the securities are usually unregistered securities). These third-party marketers have already made contact with potential investors and have substantial relationships with these investors. The third-party marketers introduce these potential investors to hedge fund managers and receive compensation if the investors place funds with the manager.

Generally, the third-party marketer operates on the basis of exclusive relationships. The third-party marketer will agree to market no other hedge funds following the same strategy. The hedge fund manager agrees to work with no other third-party marketer. Sometimes, the manager will use a particular marketer exclusively in a single geographical area, so that the fund may work with one marketer in Europe and a second marketer in Japan.

The marketing organization may be paid a retainer to cover out-of-pocket expenses. The marketer will collect a portion of the fees the manager charges the hedge fund. Marketers typically collect 20 percent of fees, although the manager and the third-party marketer may work out a particular agreement to suit their needs. For example, the manager may put a limit on the number of years the marketer will participate in fees or participation rates may trail off over time. The manager may also create "carve-outs," whereby the marketing group will not get paid fees from a designated group of investors (preexisting investors and other investors specifically exempted from the agreement).

Advantages of Third-Party Marketers Third-party marketers can be very helpful to a hedge fund manager. Many hedge funds, especially young funds, do not have the marketing resources to promote the fund themselves. Third-party marketers can be particularly helpful in marketing the hedge fund to international investors. Third-party marketers can pressure a fund to adhere to a stated strategy and can help the manager design an investment plan that has maximum marketing appeal. The marketer should conduct thorough due diligence of the manager, which can help an unknown fund gain credibility.

Disadvantages of Third-Party Marketers The fees charged by third-party markets may seem high to hedge fund managers, even though the fees are paid out of incremental revenues. The efforts of an independent marketer may be unnecessary for a fund that has an attractive performance history. Also, if the manager has already identified many potential investors or if the reputation of the manager is sufficient to attract potential investors, it may prefer to market the fund in-house (discussed later) and avoid sharing fees with a third-party marketer.

Picking a Third-Party Marketer Just as an independent marketer should perform due diligence on the hedge funds it markets, the hedge fund manager should also research the marketer. There are wide differences in the experience and abilities of third-party marketers. The fund manager should inquire to make sure a third-party marketer has no conflicts of interest that could affect the marketer's effectiveness. Finally, there can be considerable difference in fees and the hedge fund manager must decide how these fees correspond with marketing performance. Although many third-party marketers will merely introduce potential investors to a fund manager, other marketers will make significant efforts to motivate a potential investor to put funds in a recommended fund and to keep in touch with the investor and maintain a marketing relationship with the investor.

Using Traditional Brokers to Market Hedge Funds

Most brokerage houses have a group of brokers who concentrate on particularly high-net-worth clients. These brokers have substantial relationships with clients and can market hedge funds without violating U.S. restrictions on general solicitations and general advertising.

Brokers may market a small number of hedge funds to their high-net-worth clients. The list of funds may include funds run internally by another part of the brokerage firm. The brokerage firm may agree to market certain independent hedge funds, much like the third-party marketer already discussed. However, these brokers are more likely than a third-party marketer to have completed due diligence research on the funds they market. The broker will usually make a limited recommendation, by suggesting that the investors should investigate a particular hedge fund but also suggesting that the investors must make their own investment decisions on the basis of their own due diligence and the advice of the investors' own lawyers and accountants.

Prime Brokers and Capital Introductions

Prime brokers began by offering safekeeping and securities lending services to hedge funds. Prime brokers now offer services from all parts of the bank or brokerage firm. Prime brokers have created accounting and risk measurement reports to assist the managers. To compete for business, prime brokers have begun to make capital introductions.

Capital introductions are not full-fledged marketing efforts. Instead, the prime brokers usually sponsor meetings and seminars where potential investors can meet the hedge fund managers who are customers of the prime broker. This limited introduction does serve to inform investors about some of the hedge fund choices they have. Most important, the introductions allow the hedge fund manager to approach interested potential investors without violating U.S. solicitation rules.

Funds of Funds as Marketing Organizations

Fund of funds managers are generally more effective at marketing than are individual hedge funds. By accepting investments from a fund of funds manager, the hedge fund manager is allowing the fund of funds manager to market the hedge fund to investors. Of course, the fund of funds manager may not even disclose the names of the hedge funds it carries, but it is all the same motivating funds from particular investors into particular hedge funds.

Sometimes, a fund of funds manager can develop a relationship with a hedge fund that closely links the fund of funds to individual hedge fund. Many hedge funds grant rights to early fund of funds investors. Some fund of funds investors may have the right to invest in a particular hedge fund, even if the hedge fund is closed to all other new investments. In this case, the fund of funds may market its product as a way to get access to a particular hedge fund.

IN-HOUSE MARKETING

A hedge fund may develop a staff to market directly to existing and potential investors. Hedge funds with established track records may be able to get marketing leads based on word-of-mouth contact with potential investors or from press accounts. These funds save all the fees that would otherwise be paid to third-party marketers or brokers. By keeping control of the marketing, a hedge fund can better determine how the fund is marketed and assure that marketers fairly describe the characteristics of this investment.

In most cases, a hedge fund must register as a broker-dealer if it markets its securities to investors. Securities laws provide an exemption for funds that have employees incidentally involved in marketing as part of a customer relations job or other staff function. To avoid the requirement to register as a broker-dealer, these employees may not be compensated on the basis of their success in marketing. However, even customer relations may create a need for the fund to register if the manager runs several funds.

The Securities and Exchange Commission (SEC) has not been watching for cases of hedge funds that fail to register as broker-dealers. It is possible that the SEC or other enforcement agency will begin to challenge hedge funds to register. It is also likely that disgruntled investors may sue a hedge fund manager to recover losses. The investor may claim that the hedge fund should have been registered as a dealer and violated securities laws in marketing its own shares to the investor. The success of the lawsuit will depend on the facts but funds can reduce this litigation risk by registering as a broker-dealer and requiring marketing and customer relations staff to pass the Series 7 and possibly the Series 3 exams.

OTHER MARKETING ISSUES

Hedge fund management companies face other marketing issues beyond making contact with investors. The most effective hedge funds combine asset management with a successful marketing strategy.

Attracting Seed Capital

In the venture capital industry, the early investments are called seed capital. Often, the investors that provide seed capital are called angel investors, presumably because these investors extract less onerous terms for this early investment than would be expected from an arm's-length investor. A hedge fund also may get seed investments from the manager who creates both the management company and the fund. Sometimes an early investor (often a fund of funds) will make a substantial investment in return for a waiver of fees, preference in making additional investments, or ownership of part of the management company.

The manager must weigh the cost of this seed capital (fee sharing, etc.) against the benefits of an early substantial investment. The seed capital may be necessary to commence operation if a minimum amount of capital is necessary to implement a strategy or get credit lines with trading counterparties. The seed may motivate other investors to commit funds based on the leadership of the early investors. Other investors may refuse to invest more than 10 percent of any fund, so it may be necessary to get to some minimum size to receive consideration.

Early investors have much to gain and lose from an early investment. Early investments in new business ventures are more likely to be unprofitable than investments at a later stage. For hedge funds, this may also be true because the investment strategy is untested. Also, the new fund may not have accounting systems, risk control, depth of management, and other necessities and may not be able to put everything in place quickly enough to succeed. However, early investors often earn high returns, based on evidence that returns on young funds exceed the returns on established hedge funds. Some funds of funds invest in young hedge funds as their investment strategy.

Hedge fund managers can turn to family and friends for seed capital. Often, managers who leave a broker-dealer, mutual fund, or another hedge fund can approach former work partners for early funding. Individuals who managed money for clients in a mutual fund, investment counselor, or trust department may be able to approach investors to move some capital to a new hedge fund if business conditions and employment provisions permit.

Pricing and Terms

The pricing and key terms offered to investors affect the marketing of a hedge fund to potential investors. The traditional marketing literature recognizes pricing as a key marketing variable. Hedge funds must also realize that setting incentive and management fees above prevailing levels will interfere with the growth in assets through marketing. Other provisions, such as lockup periods, hurdle rates, high-water marks, and clawback provisions, affect the desirability of a fund investment. Managers with excellent past performance may demand more restrictive terms, but even successful managers should decide how important these provisions are compared to more assets to manage. Large, successful funds that have little capacity to grow may prefer terms that make their assets more sticky

(sticky money describes investments that tend to stay with the manager longer and despite poor performance).

Large investors may demand more favorable terms. Despite fee schedules listed in a private placement memorandum, investors that can place large investments with a particular hedge fund may be able to negotiate lower fees, shorter lockup periods, or other improved terms. Some large investors have been able to negotiate a waiver of all management fees and incentive fees of 10 percent. Many large investors demand complete transparency. Some investors receive daily detailed position information and can perform daily risk analysis of positions both within the hedge fund and aggregating the hedge fund positions with other assets in the larger portfolio.

Effective Marketing Presentations

The marketing presentation should be clear, but it need not be simple. Hedge fund investors are some of the most sophisticated investors and expect to see thoughtful, analytically sound analysis of the proposed investment.

Marketing presentations are much more effective if they include past performance. For many hedge funds, little past performance exists. Funds can use performance from previous employers if the hedge fund manager was responsible for the performance at the earlier entity and the hedge fund investments are similar to the earlier investments. Past performance is more convincing if it is audited. A hedge fund should seek permission to use past performance from another entity in its marketing material.

QUESTIONS AND PROBLEMS

12.1 The head trader of a XYZ Hedge Fund speaks at a conference and describes the investment characteristics of convertible bond hedge funds without disclosing that XYZ Hedge Fund is a prominent convertible bond hedge fund. After the speech, someone from the audience approaches the speaker and ultimately makes an investment in XYZ Hedge Fund. Has XYZ violated U.S. securities laws prohibiting general solicitation?

12.2 Suppose in question 12.1 the speaker is the director of marketing who gets paid based on the amount of new money raised for the fund and the hedge fund is registered as a broker-dealer. Has XYZ violated U.S. securities laws prohibiting general solicitation?

12.3 Suppose in question 12.1 the speaker is a third-party marketer who uses XYZ performance to demonstrate the desirability of the convertible bond strategy. Has XYZ violated U.S. securities laws prohibiting general solicitation?

12.4 An investor is interested in investing in a long/short equity fund and compiles a list of two dozen candidate funds. She writes to all 24 and inquires about performance and fees. Is she violating securities laws in making a mass mailing? Can the hedge funds legally reply to the request for information?

12.5 You are a potential hedge fund investor and have been talking with an investment professional about Acme Limited Partners, a global macro hedge fund. You learn that your contact does not work for Acme and, in fact, markets several different hedge funds. Should you refuse to invest in Acme because the combined fees will be too high?

12.6 Why do securities laws prevent a hedge fund from advertising?

12.7 A fund with $5 million under management contracts with a third-party marketer to raise additional funds. The agreement calls for the marketer to receive 20 percent of all incentive and management fees collected by the management company for three years. The fund raises an additional $10 million and in the next year earns a 10 percent return before management and incentive fees of 1 and 20. How much does the marketer collect? To simplify the calculations, assume that the management fee is charged at the end of the year, so the entire $15 million earns the return.

12.8 How much of the fee paid to the marketer in question 12.7 represents fees on money not raised by the third-party marketer?

12.9 A hedge fund's prime broker introduces a potential investor to the fund in question 12.7. The investor places $1 million in the hedge fund. How much fee income does the prime broker collect if the gross return is 12 percent the next year?

CHAPTER 13

Derivatives and Hedge Funds

Hedge funds face very few restrictions on their use of derivatives in their portfolios. Hedge funds can use derivatives to create leverage, to more economically carry certain types of positions, and to create patterns of return that cannot be created with the underlying instruments.

Despite the usefulness of derivatives, many hedge funds do not use derivatives to implement their investment strategies. Many hedge funds own only common stocks and use little or no leverage. These types of funds gain little from derivatives and may find it easier to limit their portfolios to cash securities.

This chapter, however, does not describe the use of derivatives by hedge funds. Instead, the text reviews various ways that the returns of hedge funds can be used to create derivative securities that replicate hedge fund performance. These hedge fund derivatives offer several advantages over direct investments in the funds. This chapter discusses the advantages of investing in hedge funds via derivative securities and the means for investing in funds.

WHY USE DERIVATIVES TO INVEST IN HEDGE FUNDS?

Derivative securities act as substitutes for the underlying securities. Frequently, derivatives closely resemble an investment in an underlying instrument paired with financing of the instrument. Other times, the derivatives transform the returns, to create a unique pattern of return. In both situations, hedge fund derivatives can offer advantages over investments in the underlying funds.

One advantage derivatives have over direct investment in the assets is that derivatives allow the investor to create leverage. The amount of leverage differs, depending on the structure of the derivatives. Total return swaps create almost infinite leverage at the start because they are usually designed so that neither party to the swap pays anything at the time the swap is initiated. Calls and puts on hedge fund returns may effectively create leverage because the value of the options may be considerably less than the value of the underlying investment. However, the option prices often move less in response to changes in the underlying assets. (This sensitivity is called the option delta and is discussed in Chapter 11.) The derivative structures based on life insurance products described later may create no leverage.

A second advantage of hedge fund derivatives over direct investment is greater flexibility to adapt the pattern of return. For example, some engineered investments can guarantee an investor's return of principal after a specified period of time. Other derivatives (calls) can create profits when hedge fund returns are positive but limit losses to the purchase price of the option when hedge fund returns are negative. Similarly, puts can create profits when hedge fund returns are negative but limit losses to the purchase price of the option when hedge fund returns are positive.

Derivatives can offer tax advantages over investments directly in hedge funds. In some cases, short-term gains and ordinary income can be taxed at lower capital gains rates. In some cases, returns on hedge funds can avoid taxation altogether. Lowering or eliminating tax on hedge fund returns can substantially increase the effective return on hedge fund investments.

Fourth, it may be possible to provide access to hedge fund returns to investors who might not be able to invest directly in hedge funds. There are many reasons why investors cannot invest directly in hedge funds. In the United States and in many other countries, hedge funds are restricted to the affluent. Other investors may be barred from investing in hedge funds because of investment restrictions placed on the managers. Creating derivatives to sidestep these kinds of restrictions is a dangerous game if such engineering could be seen as aiding and abetting investors to violate securities laws, but there may be situations where such engineering is prudent.

An example of a situation where derivatives trading might be prudent could allow tax-exempt investors to participate in hedge fund strategies that would trigger unrelated business income tax (UBIT—see Chapter 10). Tax-exempt investors avoid problems with UBIT by investing in offshore hedge funds that are organized as corporations and, hence, don't flow interest expenses back to the investors. Tax-exempt investors may also be able to avoid receiving interest expenses by investing in certain hedge fund derivatives, such as structured notes, or bonds that receive a coupon based on the performance of a hedge fund or hedge fund index. Hedge fund derivatives could be used to avoid the restrictions on secondary trading that accompany a private placement partnership because investors would buy or sell derivatives based on the partnership returns instead of buying the partnership interest.

TYPES OF HEDGE FUND DERIVATIVES

Several types of derivatives can be used to replicate a direct investment in a hedge fund.

Total Return Swap

A total return swap can be used to replicate a long or a short position in an asset or portfolio of assets. Suppose an investor bought $1 million of a particular hedge fund and simultaneously borrowed $1 million secured by the hedge fund assets. In practice, a hedge fund is not a marginable asset, so any dealer or bank that falls under the U.S. Federal Reserve System's Regulation T could not count the value of the hedge fund as collateral. Also, the lender would likely lend only a percentage of the total value of the assets. However, for the purposes of the example, assume that the investor can, in fact, borrow the entire purchase price of the hedge fund investment.

Suppose that each quarter, the investor withdraws the gains from the hedge fund investment and makes up any loss. The investor would also pay interest to the lender on the same day. While the investor would have to make the entire interest payment to the lender, the cash flows would net at the investor's bank, as long as the hedge fund pays out the returns on the same schedule as the interest payments. The cash flows for this leveraged transaction appear in Figure 13.1.

In Figure 13.1, the $1 million investment is displayed as a downward arrow representing a cash outflow (truncated in scale). The investor borrows an equal amount, but the time line shows both cash flows, which net to zero. Then, each quarter, the investor receives a payout equal to the hedge fund return and makes an interest payment on the borrowed money. For convenience, the hedge fund returns in Figure 13.1 are all positive, but a hedge fund can have losses. This leveraged transaction would require the hedge fund investor to pay the counterparty the interest payment and make up the loss on the fund.

Figure 13.2 shows the net cash flows in each quarter from Figure 13.1. The total return swap acknowledges the $1 million investment as a notional amount but the investor makes no cash payment at the onset. The swap counterparty pays the investor the cash amount equal to the return on the hedge fund on a $1 million notional amount, reduced by the interest

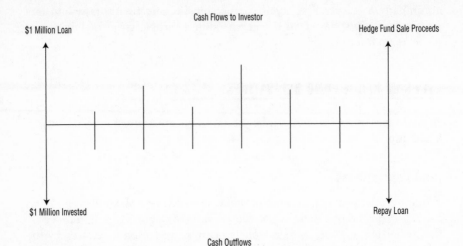

FIGURE 13.1 Cash Flows Depicting a Leveraged Investment in a Hedge Fund

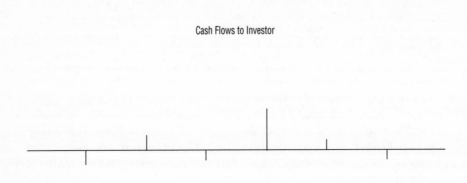

FIGURE 13.2 Swap Replicating a Leveraged Investment in a Hedge Fund

on $1 million. At the end, the investor receives no return of principal and makes no loan repayment because the net return payments keep the value of the hedge fund investment equal to the loan amount.

The counterparties can modify the total return swap in a number of ways. The accumulated return can be deferred, much like the interest on a zero coupon bond. Depending on tax considerations, the investor may be able to defer recognizing the net interest until the cash is paid. The investor may be able to recognize the return as capital gains if the investor and the counterparty close out the swap agreement at a gain before the accumulated return is paid to the investor.

The total return swap may allow certain types of investors to invest in hedge funds that would otherwise not be permitted to do so. First, a fund may be closed to new investment but an investor may be able to find a swap counterparty to pay the return on the fund. A fund manager or marketing partner may participate in hedge fund returns via incentive fees. Hedge fund investors may also be willing to commit to pay out hedge fund returns on a swap if lockup provisions restrict access to previously made investments. Second, the total return swap may permit investors to share an investment in a hedge fund if they qualify to invest but are not able to make the minimum investment alone. Finally, a pension fund may be excluded from a hedge fund because the qualified retirement funds represent nearly 25 percent of the assets in a hedge fund and the hedge fund may not accept additional plan assets (see Chapter 8). The pension fund may be able to participate in the return of a hedge fund closed for pension fund investing.

Calls on Hedge Fund Returns

Alternatively, the investor might have purchased a call option to enter into the swap transaction. Take, for example, the total return swap that pays the net return at the end of the swap period. The value of this agreement rises and falls on the return of the hedge fund. A call would grant the owner the right but not the obligation to replicate an investment in the fund after the returns have been earned and disclosed to investors.

Figure 13.3 depicts the value of a $1 million investment under a range of return scenarios. The swap would gain value when the hedge fund return exceeds the short-term interest rate in the swap agreement and would lose value when the short-term interest rate exceeds the hedge fund return. This call in Figure 13.3 represents the right to buy the swap after some period of time as if the investor made the investment as of the beginning period (that is, a strike price of zero). Clearly, the investor would exercise the call only when the swap agreement gained value, so

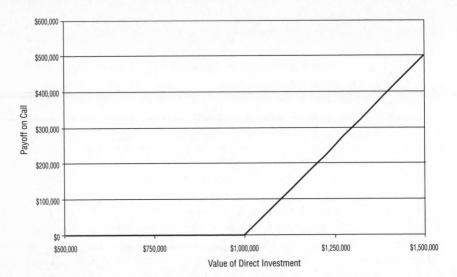

FIGURE 13.3   Payoff from Call on Hedge Fund Returns

the value of the call rises dollar for dollar along with the hedge fund and
cannot go below zero.

Figure 13.3 does not suggest that the call buyer makes money whenever hedge fund returns are positive. Not shown on Figure 13.3 is the fee
paid to purchase the option. Unlike the direct hedge fund investment, the
call buyer makes a profit only if the hedge fund returns exceed the price of
the option.

Investors may buy calls on hedge funds to leverage the hedge fund returns. Hedge fund managers have bought calls on their own performance
as a way of increasing their participation in the returns of their own
funds. Hedge fund investors may buy calls when portfolio considerations
justify the expense to eliminate the chance of hedge fund losses. Investors
may gain some tax advantages from purchasing calls instead of making
direct hedge fund investments. First the calls effectively postpone the timing of hedge fund gains. Second, it might be possible for the investor to
convert the hedge fund returns to capital gains by selling an appreciated
call prior to expiration. Finally, the call can change the characterization
of return for tax-free portfolios because the return on the call does not
flow through the interest expense (both of the underlying hedge fund returns and the interest component of the swap) and may avoid a problem
with UBIT.

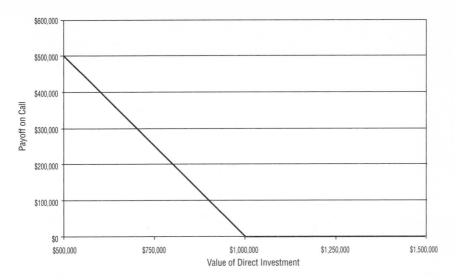

FIGURE 13.4   Payoff from Put on Hedge Fund Returns

Puts on Hedge Fund Returns

Many hedge fund structured products contain some element of protection from losses. Put options offer a way to protect a portfolio for some of the risk of loss. A put gives the owner the right but not the obligation to replicate an investment in the fund after the returns have been earned and disclosed to investors.

The put operates much like the call in that the payoff of the put is based on the difference between the value of the portfolio and the value of the initial investment. However, the put gains value when the value of the portfolio falls below the starting level.

Figure 13.4 shows the payoff profile of a put option. Like the call option, the put can be worth no less than zero. Unlike the call, the put gains value dollar for dollar when the underlying hedge fund *loses* money.

Puts offer many of the same advantages to investors that calls offer. In addition, puts act much like a short position in hedge funds, which is difficult to create without using some form of derivative instrument.

Providing Downside Protection with Zero Coupon Bonds

Hedge funds and commodity pool operators have developed a structure to guarantee return of principal regardless of the returns on the hedge fund or commodity pool. The secret to this strategy is to commit a portion of the hedge fund investment to a zero coupon bond that matures at the full value of the initial investment some years later. Also, the zero coupon bond must be placed in a segregated account, preventing possible creditors of the hedge fund from getting it if the hedge fund loses more than 100 percent of partner capital.

Zero coupon bonds sell at a discount from face value. The amount of that discount can be invested in a hedge fund without regard to risk because, even if the hedge fund loses 100 percent of the money, the zero coupon bonds will still mature at the full value of the initial investment.

Figure 13.5 shows the allocation to zero coupon bonds at a 5 percent rate of return for various maturities. Zero coupon bonds trade near par for short maturities, so little discount is available to invest in the hedge fund strategy. For a commitment period of five years, only 22 percent can be allocated to the hedge fund strategy.

At lower levels of interest rates, nearly all the assets are allocated to the zero coupon bond portion of the strategy. As a result, the blended return on this portfolio is low. However, when rates are higher, the discount on bonds is larger and more of the money can be allocated to the hedge fund strategy. (See Figure 13.6.) As rates rise from 5 percent to 10 percent, the allocation to hedge funds nearly doubles from 22 percent to 39 percent. Higher market returns make it easier to achieve a guaranteed breakeven but the oppor-

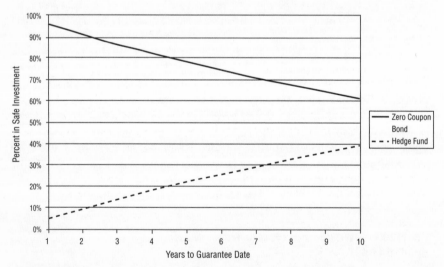

FIGURE 13.5   Impact of Length of Commitment on Hedge Fund Allocation (5 Percent Return)

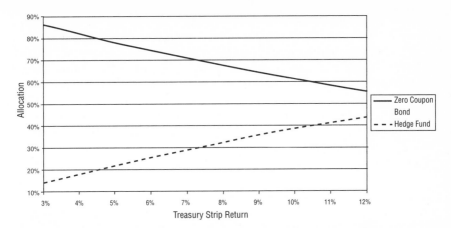

FIGURE 13.6 Impact of Zero Coupon Bond Return on Hedge Fund Allocation (Five-Year Commitment)

tunity cost of merely breaking even rises. For example, at a rate of 14.87 percent, a zero coupon bond could double an investor's return in five years.[1] Few investors should be happy about having the same value when a risk-free alternative could double the value in the same number of years.

Using a Leverage Facility to Limit Downside

Some lending institutions will grant nonrecourse loans to investors in hedge funds. For example, suppose an individual wanted to invest $1 million in a hedge fund. The lender may permit the investor to put up $500,000 and borrow an additional $500,000. The loan is secured by the hedge fund investment and effectively limits the investor's loss to 50 percent of the amount committed to hedge funds.

The downside protection carries costs to the hedge fund investor. The most obvious cost is the interest charge on the money on loan. The lender will also get ultimate control over the hedge fund assets. The lender may not permit investments in particular hedge fund strategies if they put undue risk on the lender. The lender may sell out some or all of the hedge fund assets to protect its security interest.

Principal-Protected Notes

Hedge fund investments can be structured as notes that pay a coupon equal to the return of the underlying hedge fund assets. Unlike the total return swap, it is typical to guarantee the return of principal, regardless of hedge fund returns. As a result, this note resembles a direct investment in the fund bundled with a put designed to guarantee complete return of principal.

The notes are usually issued as privately placed securities. While these notes replicate the effect of investing in a partnership invested in hedge fund assets, some investors may be able to invest in the structured notes but not in the underlying hedge fund. The notes may offer certain tax advantages over a direct investment in either the characterization of returns or the timing of the recognition of returns, as mentioned earlier.

Paying for Downside Protection

Derivative structures that offer downside protection cannot assume the risk without charging for the risk and taking steps to hedge the risk. A structured note that offers a guaranteed return of principal may charge a protection fee that lowers the return below the returns earned by direct investors. It is also possible to give the hedge fund investor some amount of downside protection in return for the hedge fund investor giving the structured products engineer some of the upside on the hedge fund returns. Because at-the-money calls on most non-dividend-paying assets are worth more than at-the-money puts on the same assets, it is possible to engineer securities that allow the buyer to participate in some portion of the upside on a hedge fund investment in return for complete protection against losses.

HEDGE FUND INVESTMENT THROUGH LIFE INSURANCE

The insurance industry offers a variety of instruments that offer significant tax advantages over direct investment in hedge funds. Any whole-life insurance policy combines life insurance with an investment account that is not taxed. In addition, the policies can reduce the estate tax of the insurance buyer because the value of the policy is usually not taxed at the time of death.

Hedge funds are described as being tax inefficient in that most hedge fund investors are wealthy and pay high marginal tax rates. Since hedge funds generate primarily ordinary income and short-term capital gains and little long-term capital gain, they deliver the investment return with the worst tax treatment to the taxpayers with the highest taxes. Incorporating hedge fund returns into insurance policies can offer significant advantages over accumulation outside a tax-favored environment.

Table 13.1 shows how a portfolio grows under three tax situations: taxed, tax-free, and taxed on exit.

The column labeled "Taxed" shows the accumulation of value at 10 percent if taxes are paid at a 40 percent marginal rate each year on the investment return out of a portion of the returns. The column labeled "Tax-Free" shows the accumulation of value at 10 percent if the returns are not taxed. Finally, the column labeled "Tax on Exit" assumes that the value in the account accumulates tax-deferred and the tax (at the same 40 percent marginal rate) applies only when the money is withdrawn. Each value in this column represents the value to the investor if the money is withdrawn in a particular year and the increase in value is taxed at 40 percent.

One goal of insurance structuring is to transform returns that would accumulate to $3,207,135 over 20 years to instead accumulate to $6,727,500 or at least $4,436,500. The hedge fund investor may have

TABLE 13.1 Accumulation After-Tax, Tax-Free, and Deferred

	Tax rate	40%	
	Return	10%	
	Investment	$1,000,000	

Year	Taxed	Tax-Free	Taxed on Exit
1	$1,060,000	$1,100,000	$1,060,000
2	1,123,600	1,210,000	1,126,000
3	1,191,016	1,331,000	1,198,600
4	1,262,477	1,464,100	1,278,460
5	1,338,226	1,610,510	1,366,306
6	1,418,519	1,771,561	1,462,937
7	1,503,630	1,948,717	1,569,230
8	1,593,848	2,143,589	1,686,153
9	1,689,479	2,357,948	1,814,769
10	1,790,848	2,593,742	1,956,245
11	1,898,299	2,853,117	2,111,870
12	2,012,196	3,138,428	2,283,057
13	2,132,928	3,452,271	2,471,363
14	2,260,904	3,797,498	2,678,499
15	2,396,558	4,177,248	2,906,349
16	2,540,352	4,594,973	3,156,984
17	2,692,773	5,054,470	3,432,682
18	2,854,339	5,559,917	3,735,950
19	3,025,600	6,115,909	4,069,545
20	3,207,135	6,727,500	4,436,500

other financial objectives. Estate tax can reduce these ending amounts as much as or more than income tax lowers them.

It isn't particularly hard to modify life insurance products to allow the policyholder to invest in hedge funds. The insurance area is highly regulated and many observers believe that the Internal Revenue Service would like to prevent hedge fund managers from offering their products via life insurance products.

Short Primer on Creating Hedge Fund Insurance Products

Hedge fund policies are developed around a version of whole-life insurance called universal life insurance. Investors buy an insurance policy and pay regular premiums to get a promise of a death benefit from the insurance company. Some part of the premium is invested in a separate account for the policyholder. The investment returns are not taxed if the policyholder maintains the policy until death. Upon death, the separate account and the death benefit are paid to the beneficiary or beneficiaries. The payment usually is not taxed as income for the beneficiary and is excluded from the insured individual's estate.

Hedge funds are generally sold as private placements (see Chapter 8) exempt from registration. Most insurance products are registered with state insurance regulators. The hedge funds can avoid the insurance registration requirements by creating private placement life insurance. These policies could be issued in the United States, but most of the policies tied to hedge funds are offered by offshore insurance companies. The offshore domicile allows the hedge fund investor to avoid paying premium tax or excise tax on the insurance premium that can be 1 to 3 percent of the premium amount.

The Internal Revenue Service will contest certain insurance transactions if the transactions are deemed to be a sham to reduce or avoid taxes. If the investment products tied to the insurance policies can be purchased only via insurance products, the courts have generally held that the insurance policy is not a sham. As a result, hedge funds must create unique products that are not offered to investors except through the separate account of life insurance policies. It appears that a hedge fund manager can create a separate fund and run it substantially the same as a hedge fund offered to investors directly. It also appears that a fund of funds that accepts investments only from insurance investors can invest in hedge funds available to direct hedge fund investors.

Investors who invest through universal life insurance policies must actually buy insurance. If the size of the death benefit is small relative to the premiums paid (that is, too much of the premium is going into the separate account for investment), the policyholder risks being taxed on the investment returns. While the death benefit affects the return calculations, it is important to realize that the death benefit is not a deadweight cost of investing in hedge funds through life insurance. Rather, the impact on return ignores the hybrid nature of the product that offers both tax advantages and insurance benefits.

HEDGE FUND DERIVATIVES TODAY

Nearly all the money invested in the hedge fund industry is invested directly in hedge funds or through funds of hedge funds. The alternative entries into hedge funds offer many advantages over direct investment. In the absence of challenges from government regulators, this indirect investment will likely represent the fastest growing area of hedge fund investment in the future.

QUESTIONS AND PROBLEMS

13.1   Why might an investor be interested in leveraging hedge fund investments by using derivatives tied to hedge fund returns?

13.2   Can an investor use derivatives that are based on hedge fund returns to invest in assets that are not permissible as a direct investment?

13.3   Could a hedge fund derivative be ruled a tax shelter, causing the investor to lose a potential advantage of the derivative over a direct investment?

13.4   Could the IRS look through the hedge fund derivative and argue that a tax-exempt investor must pay unrelated business income tax (UBIT)?

13.5   You enter into a total return swap for $10 million based on the performance of XYZ hedge fund. You receive 80 percent of the gross return before management and incentive fees and you pay London Interbank Offered Rate (LIBOR). After a quarter, XYZ announces a net return of 4 percent. LIBOR was 5 percent on the reset date. The hedge fund charges fees of 1 and 20. What was the net payment to/from your counterparty for the quarter?

13.6   What is the net payment to/from your counterparty in question 13.5 if the gross return on the hedge fund is a loss of 2 percent?

13.7   How much leverage does the example in question 13.5 create?

13.8   You invest $1 million in a hedge fund that is structured to guarantee return of principal over five years. Your investment is allocated 55 percent to a zero coupon bond and 45 percent to the hedge fund. After six months, the hedge fund loses all the fund capital and closes under involuntary liquidation. What is the value of the account at this point?

13.9 Why might someone be willing to write a call on the performance of a particular hedge fund?

13.10 Why might someone be willing to write a put on the performance of a particular hedge fund?

13.11 You are offered a call option on the performance of a particular hedge fund index made up of 10 hedge funds. You learn that you could buy separate calls on the performance of the 10 individual funds for somewhat less than the price of the option on the index of 10 hedge funds. Which alternative is more attractive?

13.12 Can you describe a situation where a call or put could be worth less than zero?

13.13 What are some of the limitations for using insurance policies to improve the after-tax return on hedge funds?

13.14 How does the tax rate structure in the United States affect hedge fund returns compared to other assets?

13.15 You invest $2 million in a hedge fund with a time horizon of 10 years and expect the hedge fund to return 10 percent per year after fees but before taxes of 35 percent per year. How much more value accumulates in a life insurance policy that allows the hedge fund balance to accumulate without being taxed? For simplicity, ignore the costs of providing the death benefit.

NOTE

1. A $1 investment increases to $2 over five years compounded annually at 14.87 percent. In other words, $(1 + 14.87\%)^5 = 2$.

CHAPTER 14

Conclusions

Hedge funds have existed for more than a half century since Alfred Winslow Jones started a revolution in asset management. During those years, the financial markets have grown in many different ways. The average value of daily transactions has risen steadily in most asset categories. The size of most asset groups has risen dramatically. The number of issues has increased significantly. Many new types of securities have been created. Hedge funds have acted as both cause and effect of these many changes.

IMPORTANCE OF HEDGE FUNDS

Chapter 1 documents the growth in the number of hedge funds and the assets under management. These statistics understate the impact of hedge funds on the financial markets. In addition to the assets under management, many hedge funds use leverage to increase the size of trading positions relative to capital. The size of many individual hedge funds has created problems of liquidity. Both dealers and hedge funds have learned to cope with the size of the customers relative to the market makers. Even with a half century of consolidation in the broker-dealer community, many hedge funds are larger than all but the largest dealers.

Hedge funds also trade their positions much more actively than most traditional portfolios. There is, admittedly, some variation in the turnover rates (the percent of the portfolio traded in a year) among traditional asset managers. Nevertheless, while a traditional manager may be comfortable turning over 15 or 20 percent of the portfolio a year, the most active hedge fund traders may sometimes accomplish as much turnover in a day. If turnover is measured as the volume of trading relative to the capital base, turnover rates rise even higher.

The market impact of these hedge funds is greater still because hedge funds may carry similar positions. When groups of hedge funds liquidate certain types of positions, other funds may be pressed to make similar changes. This clustered exposure causes events to sometimes have an exaggerated effect on valuation of different groups of assets. Sometimes, the pressure has been enough to severely strain the capacity of the financial markets.

CHANGES IN THE NATURE OF THE HEDGE FUND MARKET

The hedge fund market has undergone many changes in the past half century. As described earlier, the sheer size of the hedge fund community has doubled and redoubled. As the size of the average fund has risen, as the size of hedge fund assets has grown, and as the funds and assets have clustered into a group of styles that has grown much more slowly, the hedge funds, their customers and their trading counterparties have had to change.

Fashions in Hedge Fund Investing Styles

Hedge fund investors have followed several styles or trends. The original hedge fund started by Jones closely resembled a long/short equity fund. Eventually, a number of these long/short equity funds evolved into a high-risk strategy called global macro hedge funds that involved currencies, stocks, and bonds that, as implied by the name, placed weight on international trading driven by macroeconomic considerations. The next popular strategy was arbitrage strategies, especially fixed income arbitrage, popular as a backlash against the high-risk trading of the global macro funds. Long/short equity strategies then became the best-selling strategy, a strategy that closely resembles the original Jones hedge fund.

New Hedge Fund Delivery Mechanisms

The hedge fund market has evolved several new delivery mechanisms that make hedge fund investing much more accessible to investors and has allowed hedge fund investing to penetrate to investors that might not invest in hedge funds but for the development of these institutions. The first development is the fund of funds. The fund of funds has pressured the hedge fund community to make its investment products more appealing to sophisticated investors, by emphasizing risk as well as return. The fund of funds managers have increased the oversight of the individual hedge fund managers by closely monitoring performance, conducting due diligence, and working together to identify rogue traders early. Fund of funds managers have also been making it easier for smaller investors to experiment with hedge funds by lowering investment minima and offering a diversified hedge fund investment to investors that could not commit enough assets to hedge fund investing to diversify.

The second delivery development is the decision to offer hedge funds as registered securities, rather than as private placements. This movement is just getting started but it promises to make hedge fund investments available to less wealthy investors. The target investors may be less experienced or sophisticated investors and may not qualify to invest in private hedge funds directly. These investors can still benefit from the advantages of hedge fund investing.

The third major change in the delivery mechanism is the advent of engineered financial products that pay off based on hedge fund returns. These products offer potential tax advantages, risk transfer, and potentially greater liquidity. Regulators are watching cautiously to decide if these innovations might increase the risk to the financial system. Tax authorities are motivated to see that these markets are taxed consistently with other financial investments.

Evolution of the Regulatory Environment

The regulatory environment has evolved greatly over the past half century. The hedge fund industry has faced greater oversight from the Commodity Futures Trading Commission, auditors, and investors. Recently, the Securities and Exchange Commission has stepped up efforts to increase disclosure requirements and may impose other regulatory requirements.

Risk Profile of the Typical Hedge Fund

The hedge fund industry grew to a size worth watching with a decade of high-risk trading. Investors looking for high returns with little regard for risk flocked to these high-profile traders. But the market really began to grow when managers began to create funds that offered somewhat lower returns but dramatically lower risks.

Investors in hedge funds were becoming more sophisticated. Investors learned that lowering the risk of a portfolio is as important as increasing the return on the portfolio. Risk-averse investors flocked to a new breed of hedge fund marketed as either low-risk or low-risk relative to the return achieved.

Today, investors measure risk in many ways. These investors reward managers than control risk and pressure managers to control risk. Most of the growth in hedge fund assets has been in strategies have had fairly high returns yet have managed to keep risk exposure to modest levels.

Trading counterparties and regulators have also pressured hedge funds to assume lower risks in their portfolios. Leverage is lower. Managers may be more inclined to look for hedges that can reduce risks without significantly lowering the return to investors.

Growth of the International Hedge Fund Market

Hedge funds have been early to extend trading to securities in foreign markets. Hedge funds have also received investments from international private banks in Switzerland and other locations.

There is an internationalism that is evolving in hedge funds that goes beyond the types of assets in the portfolio. Hedge funds are being created all over the world. Most countries are evolving a regulatory structure to monitor and sometimes control hedge fund activities of their citizens. Investors from many countries are investing in both established and new hedge funds. In addition, there are many more places that have the legal infrastructure and taxation that can act as domiciles for worldwide hedge funds.

FUTURE CONSIDERATIONS

The hedge fund industry has developed rapidly. Recent trends indicate that the industry is still evolving.

Future Growth in Assets under Management

Growth in assets in any investment product reflects the wealth accumulated by investors both from reinvested returns and from net new savings. Hedge fund growth has derived from both compounded returns and new savings, which has made the pie larger. In addition, the hedge fund industry has been accumulating a larger portion of the investment pie.

The growth in assets under management will likely continue. Many industry watchers predict slower growth in the years ahead, in part because the early adopters are already investors. The success in maintaining the nearly double-digit growth rates reflected in Figure 1.2 in Chapter 1 hinges on expanding the group of investors that can invest in hedge funds, getting a higher proportion of investors to invest in hedge funds, and influencing investors to allocate a higher percentage of their portfolios to hedge funds and other alternative assets.

Future of Hedge Fund Strategies

The number of hedge funds seems to increase every year without interruption (see Figure 1.1 in Chapter 1). The funds implement an expanding list of hedge fund strategies. This innovation is important to the future of the industry. Investors will continue to pay hedge fund fees for strategies that are meaningfully different from traditional assets and different from other hedge fund strategies. Investors will continue to pay fees for excellent performance, which may go to the funds that innovatively produce attractive returns for their investors.

Growth in Passive Hedge Fund Management

The traditional asset managers (mutual funds, trust departments, and investment advisers) have developed low-cost investment strategies such as index funds. By keeping management costs and transaction costs low, these passive strategies have produced returns that exceed the average of returns on actively managed portfolios. Early indications suggest that passively managed hedge fund products can produce competitive returns for investors and provide many of the diversification benefits of actively managed hedge funds. Barring performance problems or capacity issues, passive hedge fund portfolios will attract significant funds in the future.

Growth in the Fund of Funds Business

The fund of funds managers have grown rapidly along with the total hedge fund industry—even faster than the hedge fund total has grown because fund of funds managers have been able to convince important institutional investors to become hedge fund investors through investments in their fund of funds portfolios. The market share of fund of funds investments as a percent of total hedge fund assets will continue to rise, reflecting the strong marketing skills of these organizations. The fund of funds managers will also continue to capitalize on the need to perform thorough due diligence beyond the abilities of many hedge fund investors.

Convergence of Financial Institutions Continues

Although the hedge fund industry grew out of an effort to provide an alternative to traditional asset management, the continuing convergence of financial institutions will blur the difference between hedge funds and other financial management alternatives. Mutual funds, insurance companies, and investment counselors can hurdle the barriers to entry easily enough to create hedge fund products reflecting their expertise. Attracted by the higher fees, these traditional managers are creating hedge funds as a way of motivating their star performers to stay with their employers.

Traditional investment managers will also adopt many of the features of hedge funds into their existing products. Insurance companies don't need to tie insurance products to external hedge fund products if the insurance companies can produce nondirectional investment returns or can implement passive hedge fund portfolios. Mutual funds can implement many of the investment strategies commonly used by hedge funds without adopting hedge fund business organizations or fee structures.

Pricing and Profitability of Hedge Fund Management

Hedge fund management and incentive fees have come under pressure for years. Fees are often negotiated below the levels set in the hedge fund disclosure documents. The net fees reflect the size of the hedge fund, the size of the investor, the return history of the fund, the capacity of the manager, the existence of other hedge funds following the same strategy, and many other factors. Innovation allows the hedge fund manager to maintain pricing levels by creating excellent performance or by creating or preserving a uniqueness of value to potential investors.

Hedge fund fees will likely continue to decline. As institutional investors have begun to invest sizable portfolios in hedge funds, managers have found it both necessary and worthwhile to negotiate fees. As fee negotiation becomes more widespread, managers will suffer little by lowering the posted fee levels and should attract additional investment. The profitability of the industry will be sustained by the growth in assets under management, offsetting losses in revenue from downward pressure on fees.

Brave New Hedge Fund World

If trends continue, future generations may make no distinction between the traditional money management business and the hedge fund industry. Instead, business practices reflect the lessons of the traditional managers and the hedge fund managers. Managers in banks, insurance companies, brokers, and other financial institutions will share knowledge of investment management derived from traditional portfolio management and from alternative investment managers. With the help of constructive oversight from governmental regulators, this merger to the mainstream will make for stronger financial markets and better-managed portfolios.

Answers to Questions and Problems

CHAPTER 1   Introduction

1.1   Three reasons often cited for investing in hedge funds are:

1. To increase the return on a portfolio. Some hedge funds are designed to provide very high returns and may accept high degrees of risk to attain those returns.
2. To reduce risk. The average hedge fund is less risky that stocks. Even without the risk-reducing advantage of diversification, an asset allocation out of stocks and into hedge funds can lower portfolio risk.
3. To diversify returns. Diversification can reduce the risk of individual assets or asset categories. Because many hedge funds are not highly correlated with stock and bond returns, hedge funds can be very effective tools for improving portfolio diversification.

1.2   Thousands of hedge funds exist. These funds follow a variety of strategies and assume different levels and types of risks. As a group, hedge funds have provided reasonable returns and have offered investors an attractive supplement to traditional stock and bond investments.

1.3   Relative return strategies are investment strategies designed to provide attractive returns relative to a benchmark. Most stock investing seeks to provide returns attractive relative to one or more equity index. Absolute return strategies are investment strategies designed to provide a pattern of returns that is substantially independent from stock and bond returns. As a consequence, success of the strategy should be evaluated without regard to how well typical benchmarks have performed.

1.4   To get the most risk reduction from diversification, low correlation is desirable. The funds with a correlation closest to zero are more effective diversifiers than funds with either a positive or a negative correlation. However, a high positive correlation to a particular strategy may be desirable. For example, if you want a convertible bond strategy, you would prefer a fund that is highly correlated to other convertible bond funds or an index of convertible bond hedge funds. Likewise, you would prefer a short equity fund with a correlation near −1.00 if the purpose of the investment is to hedge a long equity portfolio.

1.5 The size of the average hedge fund has also been increasing, so the growth in assets has found its way into more hedge funds and allowed the size of hedge funds to rise.

1.6 It is possible that a fund could assess all the listed fees and incorporate the listed fee designs and more. Hedge funds must declare the fees being assessed. Investors must trade off the level of fees against the return and risk of a hedge fund.

1.7 Private equity funds typically invest in investments that may have no objective mark-to-market value. Because of the uncertainty about the monthly valuation, it is typical to assess no incentive fees until the return is actually realized.

1.8 Many hedge funds register with the National Futures Association (NFA) as commodity pools. Such hedge funds could plausibly be called commodity pools. However, the classification "commodity pool" is commonly reserved for funds that use *only* commodities, futures, and options on futures.

1.9 For most hedge funds, the management fee is prorated monthly but does not reflect the number of days in the month.

$$\text{Management Fee} = \frac{\$100 \text{ million} \times 2.25\%}{12} = \$187,500$$

1.10 A 4.5 percent return on a $100 million hedge fund earned $4.5 million. This is a nominal return so no adjustment for the amount of time is used. The gross return would be reduced by the management fee ($187,500). The incentive fee would be 15 percent of that amount:

$$\text{Incentive Fee} = [(100 \text{ million} \times 4.5\%) - \$187,500] \times 15\%$$
$$= \$646,875$$

1.11 The hurdle rate of 5 percent is an annualized rate. The calculation uses a monthly rate of 5%/12. In practice, a hedge fund may adjust the annualized hurdle rate a number of different ways. In the following calculation, the incentive fee is assessed on only the amount that exceeds the hurdle return.

$$\text{Incentive Fee} = \left\{ \left[\$100 \text{ million} \times \left(4.5\% - \frac{5\%}{12} \right) \right] - \$187,500 \right\} \times 15\%$$
$$= \$584,375$$

1.12 There will be no incentive fee until the fund has made back the 7 percent loss from January. If the fund was previously at a high-water mark, a return of 7.53 percent is required to regain that level. For example, if the NAV was $100 in January and fell 7 percent to $93, it is necessary to return 7.53 percent to return the fund NAV to $100. No incentive fee would be paid on returns until the fund attains a new high-water mark.

CHAPTER 2   Types of Hedge Funds

2.1 Perhaps there are so many indexes because hedge fund performance data is not generally published and individual returns are much less available than returns on stocks or bonds. Many index providers use the indexes as a marketing tool. Frequently, the same providers also sponsor funds of funds or collect some kind of sales charge for facilitating a hedge fund investment.

2.2 A long/short equity hedge fund may be long some stocks and short others. However, the size of the long position need not balance the size of the short position. These funds may be net long stocks (benefiting from rising stock prices) or net short stocks (benefiting from declining stock prices).

2.3 Despite the word "hedge," many hedge funds make little or no attempt to hedge the risk of long positions with short positions. Equity arbitrage funds do create such hedges. These funds generally pursue fairly low-risk strategies and have lower returns than many other hedge fund styles.

2.4 Pairs trading involves buying one class of security and selling another class of security from the same issuer.

2.5 This hedge fund invests primarily in common stocks (long and short). The long and short positions are chosen to provide an attractive return and to offset market risk. Unlike a pairs trading strategy (discussed in Chapter 4), there may be no match of specific long positions to specific short positions.

2.6 Merger arbitrage, spin-offs, divestitures, and bankruptcies are some event driven strategies.

2.7 Convertible bond trading strategies are usually arbitrage strategies. Most commonly, the fund buys a convertible bond or convertible preferred stock and hedges the risk to the underlying common stock. The fund may hedge interest rate risk, volatility risk, and financing risk to greater or lesser degrees. This strategy involves more leverage than most other hedge fund strategies.

2.8   A fixed income arbitrage hedge fund may buy bonds and sell fixed income futures or buy bonds denominated in a foreign currency with a currency hedge. Some fixed income arbitrage funds buy mortgages or mortgage derivatives and hedge the optionlike behavior of those instruments.

2.9   Emerging markets hedge funds may buy either stocks or bonds in a particular region or individual country. Generally, the funds have little opportunity to hedge currency exposure or market risk. Although the performance will be directional with respect to the individual securities market, this return may have low correlation to the securities markets of developed countries.

2.10   Distressed securities hedge funds invest in low-rated or unrated bonds or equities of companies in or near bankruptcy. The largest risk involves that credit exposure: default, mark-to-market loss on downgrading, or assets inadequate to support debt repayment.

2.11   A global macro hedge fund primarily seeks a return by making a number of long and short investments in stock markets, bonds, and foreign currencies.

2.12   A fund of funds is an investment company that invests in other investment companies which then invest in securities, futures, and derivatives. The label "fund of funds" is used to refer to funds of mutual funds or funds of hedge funds. The funds that invest in mutual funds are generally registered investment companies but the funds that invest in hedge funds are generally unregistered like the hedge funds they own.

2.13   The weighted average return is given by the formula:

$$\text{Return}_{\text{Portfolio}} = w_A \times \text{Return}_A + (w_B \times \text{Return}_B)$$
$$= (90\% \times 10\%) + (10\% \times 8\%) = 9.80\%$$

The weighted standard deviation or volatility of returns is given by the formula:

$$\sigma_{\text{Portfolio}} = \sqrt{w_A^2 \sigma_A^2 + 2 w_A w_B \sigma_{A,B} + w_B^2 \sigma_B^2}$$
$$= \sqrt{w_A^2 \sigma_A^2 + 2 w_A w_B \sigma_A \sigma_B \rho_{A,B} + w_B^2 \sigma_B^2}$$
$$= \sqrt{90\%^2 \times 17.32\%^2 + 2 \times 90\% \times 10\% \times 17.32\% \times 4.33\% \times 10\% + 10\%^2 \times 4.33\%^2}$$
$$= 15.64\%$$

2.14   The weighted average return is given by the formula:

$$\text{Return}_{\text{Portfolio}} = (w_A \times \text{Return}_A) + (w_B \times \text{Return}_B)$$
$$= (90\% \times 10\%) + (10\% \times 12\%) = 10.20\%$$

The weighted standard deviation or volatility of returns is given by the formula:

$$\sigma_{\text{Portfolio}} = \sqrt{w_A^2 \sigma_A^2 + 2w_A w_B \sigma_{A,B} + w_B^2 \sigma_B^2}$$

$$= \sqrt{w_A^2 \sigma_A^2 + 2w_A w_B \sigma_A \sigma_B \rho_{A,B} + w_B^2 \sigma_B^2}$$

$$= \sqrt{90\%^2 \times 17.32\%^2 + 2 \times 90\% \times 10\% \times 17.32\% \times 12.99\% \times 25\% + 10\%^2 \times 12.99\%^2}$$

$$= 15.64\%$$

2.15 The weighted average return is given by the formula:

$$\text{Return}_{\text{Portfolio}} = (w_A \times \text{Return}_A) + (w_B \times \text{Return}_B)$$
$$= (90\% \times 10\%) + (10\% \times 10\%) = 100\%$$

The weighted standard deviation or volatility of returns is given by the formula:

$$\sigma_{\text{Portfolio}} = \sqrt{w_A^2 \sigma_A^2 + 2w_A w_B \sigma_{A,B} + w_B^2 \sigma_B^2}$$

$$= \sqrt{w_A^2 \sigma_A^2 + 2w_A w_B \sigma_A \sigma_B \rho_{A,B} + w_B^2 \sigma_B^2}$$

$$= \sqrt{90\%^2 \times 17.32\%^2 + 2 \times 90\% \times 10\% \times 17.32\% \times 8.66\% \times 50\% + 10\%^2 \times 8.66\%^2}$$

$$= 16.04\%$$

2.16 Each of the hedge funds would lower the risk of the portfolio as measured by the standard deviation of return. However, a 10 percent investment in the convertible arbitrage strategy would result in lower volatility and lower returns. Probably the lower risk is sufficient to justify the lower expected return for most investors, but in this case, there are two choices that are unambiguously better than an all-stock portfolio. A 10 percent investment in the long/short strategy would provide the same expected return as an all-stock portfolio with less risk. The global macro strategy would raise the expected return and lower the risk. The portfolio containing the global macro strategy has a higher expected return than a portfolio containing the long/short portfolio and has less risk than the long/short portfolio. However, whether the investor prefers the portfolio containing the global macro strategy to the portfolio containing the convertible arbitrage fund would depend on investor preferences. Hedge fund investors measure risk in a variety of ways. The standard deviation of return is a popular choice, but other measures could yield different answers.

2.17 Even though the hedge fund has a lower expected return (8 percent versus expected returns of 10 percent for stocks) and is riskier (volatility of

20 percent versus 17.32 percent for stocks), it still makes sense to invest part of the portfolio in this fund to get the benefits of diversification. Following the logic in questions 2.13 through 2.16, you could analyze progressively higher investments in this fund:

Stocks	Alternative	Expected Return	Standard Deviation
100%	0%	10.00%	17.32%
90%	10%	9.80%	16.68%
80%	20%	9.60%	16.23%
70%	30%	9.40%	15.99%
60%	40%	9.20%	15.97%
50%	50%	9.00%	16.17%
40%	60%	8.80%	16.59%
30%	70%	8.60%	17.20%
20%	80%	8.40%	17.98%
10%	90%	8.20%	18.93%
0%	100%	8.00%	20.00%

Progressively larger investments in the hedge fund lower the risk of the portfolio until somewhere between 30 percent and 40 percent of the money is invested in the alternative (in this case, the portfolio has the lowest risk when 36 percent of the money is invested in the hedge fund strategy and 64 percent is retained in stocks). The expected return is also somewhat lower, so the investor must trade off the lower return versus the lower standard deviation of returns.

Many times, the alternatives are simpler. If the hedge fund can produce returns similar to the stock portfolio but provides good diversification (because it has a low correlation to stock returns), the blend of a hedge fund with stocks can produce the same or higher returns and lower risk.

2.18 The investor likely has risks that could be reduced by improving the diversification in the portfolio. Unless the investor is willing to sell the closely held family company, any investment in a hedge fund would probably have to be funded by selling the market portfolio. The investor should study hedge funds that have weak correlations to the closely held asset, then design a portfolio to best diversify the risks of the rebalanced portfolio.

2.19 The direct investor avoids a layer of fees charged by the fund of funds. The investor can also pick the portfolio of hedge funds that works best with other assets held by the investor. The investor may be able to demand information about positions held in the hedge funds and perhaps reduce some concentration of risks that might occur if the investor relies on others to select the managers.

2.20 A major part of the appeal of hedge funds is the way they perform differently from traditional portfolios. Investors seek out new and different ideas that may have low correlation to stock and bond returns and to other hedge fund returns.

2.21 The short-only hedge fund would act as a very powerful risk-reducing investment. However, if the investor has the ability to sell futures or buy put options, it would likely be possible to construct a cheaper hedge for the stock risk. The short fund manager selects issues likely to do worse than the market overall, so the short hedge fund may perform better in both rising and falling environments.

2.22 Fixed income arbitrage is one of the most leveraged strategies. Even if the position risk can be completely controlled, there are certain risks inherent to highly leveraged strategies including the loss of borrowing capacity and the inability to borrow issues sold short.

CHAPTER 3   Types of Hedge Fund Investors

3.1 Individuals invest in funds for many of the same reasons that institutions invest in hedge funds. Hedge funds can provide higher returns, better risk-adjusted returns, or returns uncorrelated with their existing portfolios. Taxable investors face unattractive tax consequences, so the advantages of hedge fund investing must outweigh this economic disadvantage. There is some effort to make hedge funds more tax efficient by funding them with IRA or 401(k) money or combining hedge fund investments with several insurance products.

3.2 The manager is careful so that none of the administration of the fund is conducted within the United States. Although the fund may invest in U.S. assets, those assets are deemed to be owned outside the taxing jurisdiction of the IRS. However, if the fund pays a management fee to a U.S. manager, that income *is* taxable to the owners of the management company.

3.3 Probably not. Most countries tax their citizens and business units on investment returns regardless of where the returns occurred. Locating the hedge fund in a tax haven prevents the return from being taxed twice. Failure to report offshore income constitutes tax evasion in most countries.

3.4 Most hedge fund investments are motivated by the return and risk of the investment. In the absence of unusual circumstances, the offshore investor believes the U.S.-managed hedge fund will outperform funds created by managers in the investor's home country. Frequently, the U.S. manager will locate the hedge fund outside of the United States so that the offshore investor isn't burdened with both U.S. taxation and tax at home.

3.5   Some hedge funds are riskier than stock investments but many are less risky than traditional assets. In addition, because the returns on many hedge funds do not closely track the returns of stocks and bonds, an institutional investor such as an endowment or foundation may be able to reduce portfolio risk through diversification. These institutions may be attracted to the prospect of very high returns along with high risk on a part of the portfolio. Finally, these institutions generally aren't taxed on their investment returns so are less disadvantaged by the large amount of short-term gains that penalize high-net-worth individuals.

3.6   With a defined contribution plan, the individual workers are completely exposed to the investment returns on the contributions. If returns are large, benefits are larger. For the same reason, the pension beneficiaries are also exposed to the risk of loss. The plan sponsor and trustees should decide whether a hedge fund investment is appropriate for all the beneficiaries. The pension plan sponsor (often the employer) bears all of the investment risk with a defined benefit plan. There may be situations where a hedge fund investment is imprudent or barred by securities laws, but most plan sponsors are considered qualified investors.

3.7   It is generally regarded as acceptable for corporations to invest in hedge funds for short-term cash management, diversification of returns, or improved corporate profits. From the point of view of traditional financial theory, the corporation that invests in a hedge fund offers no advantage to its shareholders if the shareholders could invest parts of their portfolios directly in hedge funds. Management consultants could question why a corporation would invest time, effort, and capital in areas outside the primary expertise of the corporation. Finally, risk managers may question whether it is wise to expose funds devoted to a future capital project to the risk of loss.

3.8   Many investors value the diversification possible only in a fund of funds because they lack the resources to make multiple hedge fund investments. Many investors, including sophisticated institutional investors, are willing to delegate the fund selection to outside managers.

3.9   The language of the partnership agreement defines specifically how the management fee and incentive fees are applied. Because performance is provided monthly, it is reasonable to allocate 1/12 of the annual percent (2 percent divided by 12 or 0.167 percent per month).

This fee is charged whether the individual fund makes or loses money in a particular month or year. Note that the calculations rely on an initial $100 investment in each of the four funds.

Fund A	After Management Fee	After Incentive Fee	High-Water Mark
1.00%	0.83%	0.67%	$100.67
2.50%	2.33%	1.87%	$102.55
3.45%	3.28%	2.63%	$105.24

For fund A, the return is first reduced by the monthly management fee. Then, because the fund never had to recover a loss, the incentive fee was simply 20 percent of the return after management fee.

Fund B	After Management Fee	After Incentive Fee	High-Water Mark
6.25%	6.08%	4.87%	$104.87
−4.24%	−4.41%	−4.41%	$104.87
2.25%	2.08%	2.08%	$104.87

The incentive fee is never negative (that is, the fund does not get paid 20 percent back on the losses), but most hedge funds do not charge incentive fees on the gains that make up prior losses. For example, the manager of fund B would charge no incentive fee in the second month, reflecting the loss. It would take a 4.43 percent return after the second month to offset the 4.24 percent loss, so the fund manager collects no incentive fee in the third month, because the value of the fund is still below the previous high-water mark. If the third-month return were more than 4.43 percent, the manager would charge no fee on the portion of the return in the third month that brings the investor back to the high-water mark achieved after the first month.

Fund C	After Management Fee	After Incentive Fee	High-Water Mark
−2.25%	−2.42%	−2.42%	$100.00
6.15%	5.98%	5.47%	$102.92
−3.22%	−3.39%	−3.39%	$102.92

The fund manager of fund C charges no incentive fee in the first month. The return in the second month after management fee creates a new high-water mark before incentive fees of $103.42. The incentive fee on the $3.42 gain over the previous high-water mark of

$100.00 reduces the second-month return after incentive fee to 5.47 percent. Again, the manager charges no incentive fee in the third month because of the loss.

Fund D	After Management Fee	After Incentive Fee	High-Water Mark
3.12%	2.95%	2.36%	$102.36
2.40%	2.23%	1.79%	$104.19
1.65%	1.48%	1.19%	$105.43

The net return for fund D simply reflects the 2 percent management fee and 20 percent incentive fee.

The returns are equally weighted in a fund of funds, implying that the fund of funds rebalanced at the end of each month. Alternatively, the fund of funds could have been constructed at the beginning of the period and the differences in performance would weight the winning funds (fund A and fund D) higher than the other funds.

Fund of Funds	After Management Fee	After Incentive Fee	High-Water Mark
1.37%	1.33%	1.20%	101.20%
1.18%	1.14%	1.02%	102.23%
0.63%	0.59%	0.53%	102.77%

The arithmetic average return after management fees and incentive fees imposed by the fund of funds manager is 0.91 percent. In Excel, use {= AVERAGE(1.20%, 1.02%, .53%)}. The geometric average return is 0.92 percent. To calculate the geometric average, simplify the following expression:

$$(1.0277)^{1/3} = 0.92\%$$

because $(1 + 0.92\%)^3$ equals the ending value of a $1 investment in the fund of funds. The monthly return of 0.92 percent compounds to 11.55 percent annual return.

3.10   The return equally weights the four strategies each month.

	Strategy A	Strategy B	Strategy C	Strategy D	Average
	1.00%	6.25%	−2.25%	3.12%	2.03%
	2.50%	−4.24%	6.15%	2.40%	1.70%
	3.45%	2.25%	−3.22%	1.65%	1.03%
Nominal return	7.10%	4.03%	0.42%	7.34%	4.84%

Arithmetic average	2.32%	1.42%	0.23%	2.39%	1.59%
Geometric average	2.31%	1.33%	0.14%	2.39%	1.59%
Annualized return	31.55%	17.14%	1.69%	32.74%	20.80%

3.11 The return calculated in question 3.10 also equals the return on a multistrategy hedge fund that implements the four strategies before fees. The management and incentive fees reduce this gross return, but the investor pays no fees to a fund of funds manager.

Multistrategy	After Management Fee	After Incentive Fee	High-Water Mark
2.03%	1.86%	1.49%	101.49%
1.70%	1.54%	1.23%	102.74%
1.03%	0.87%	0.69%	103.45%

The multistrategy hedge fund produces a nominal return of 3.45 percent after fees. The arithmetic and geometric averages both equal 1.14 percent per month, which compounds to 14.53 percent.

3.12 The average return calculated under question 3.10 reflects no incentive or management fees. The fees on the fund of funds reflect both the management and incentive fees charged by the individual hedge funds plus the additional fees charged by the fund of funds manager. However, in some months, some individual hedge fund managers charged incentive fees while other funds lost money. The incentive fees did not reflect this netting of performance in a particular month. In contrast, the multistrategy hedge fund netted the gains from one strategy and the losses from another before calculating incentive fees. Because fund B and fund C are below their high-water marks, some of the future returns from those individual funds will not be subject to incentive fees.

CHAPTER 4   Hedge Fund Investment Techniques

4.1 Not necessarily. Many technical trading systems are described as a black box, implying that employees do not subjectively override investment or valuation decisions made by the model. However, fundamental models can also be used to construct rules used to build and maintain trading positions.

4.2   This is not a merger arbitrage trade because the hedge fund did not sell the acquiring company. Although the hedge fund will profit if the deal is announced, the position remains exposed to changes in value for stocks generally. If the hedge fund also sold short shares of Company X, then the position is at least roughly insulated from changes in equity prices.

4.3   The answer depends on the particulars of the situation. Many times, the merger doesn't take place according to the first set of terms announced. Another buyer of Company Y may emerge. Company X may be required to raise the bidding price for Company Y, either to entice shareholders to sell or to outbid competing buyers. The merger arbitrage trader should sell Company X only if doing so reduces the risk of carrying shares of Company Y.

4.4   Although a gain of $5 does represent a 5 percent gain on a $100 investment, the return to the merger arbitrage fund may be considerably higher. For example, if the $5 gain could be achieved in four months, this strategy could produce annualized returns of 15 percent (or more if the midyear gains are reinvested). Further, if the manager borrows, the return on the money invested could be considerably higher. Finally, although the best-case gain of $5 does not look attractive if the worst case is a $10 loss, it might be that the gain is very likely and the loss is unlikely.

4.5   It works the other way. XYZ will likely sell short the acquirer and must make substitute payments to the lender of the shares of the acquirer company. Also, XYZ will own shares in the target company, so would prefer to receive higher dividends, all other things being equal. However, the amount of the dividends and the cost of borrowing are usually fairly unimportant factors in the profitability of a deal.

4.6   The hedge fund is a limited liability structure that assures that investors can generally lose no more than their original investment. Buying companies that may risk bankruptcy or are already in bankruptcy creates a situation where hedge fund investors can earn leveraged returns with limited downside. The incentive structure motivates managers to take risks that are likely to offer rewards. The traditional asset management framework, in contrast, often leads to an environment where managers invest in only low-risk assets.

4.7   Pairs trading produces a relatively low-risk and low-return pattern of performance. Because the returns tend not to be highly correlated with stock and bond returns, it is a good strategy to add to a traditional portfolio. Whether it is a good companion to other hedge fund strategies hinges mostly on the nature of the pairs strategy. The definition of pairs trading ranges from very narrowly defined arbitrage trades to relationships based on no more support than the previous behavior of the two stocks. Although the answer depends on the nature of the pairs strategy, it is possible that this strategy is correlated with other types of trades in the multistrategy hedge fund.

4.8 Endowments and foundations pay no income tax on most investment returns. As a result, neither would care whether the trading produced income or capital gains. In general, the strategy is sensible for a tax-exempt account because the tax rate of the marginal trader prices the ex-dividend price change at a level at which tax-exempt investors should make money.

Endowments and foundations must be careful to avoid incurring interest expenses from leveraged trading. Interest expense can trigger a tax called unrelated business income tax (UBIT—see Chapter 10). These tax-exempt organizations must be careful to avoid a hedge fund that regularly uses debt to increase returns to the dividend capture strategy.

4.9 The strategy requires the hedge fund to buy corporate bonds or preferred stocks on smaller, less established companies. Short sales of the common stock only imperfectly hedge changes in credit spreads. In particular, these hedges provide protection from changes in spreads on the individual company securities but may provide no protection from a general widening of spreads.

Depending on how thoroughly the hedge fund lays off risk, a convertible arbitrage position can leave the investor open to the risk that option volatility declines. The investor is also often exposed to the risk that prices trade in a narrow range and the convertible option erodes in value. The investor is at risk as well for default on the bonds the hedge fund owns. Short sales in the equity may provide imperfect protection against losses on the defaulted securities.

4.10 Even if the pattern of returns described is accurate for fixed income arbitrage, hedge fund investors may want to include the strategy in portfolios. Whether to include the strategy hinges on the pattern of return of a portfolio with and without the hedge fund strategy in question. The past performance problems occurred when traditional assets and popular hedge fund strategies were profitable. In fact, fixed income arbitrage strategies are not very correlated to traditional stocks and bonds or to most hedge fund strategies.

4.11 Not necessarily. Problems with mortgage strategies were caused in part by uncertainty when interest rates declined to rates outside the historical experience of most investors. If rates were to rise, the mortgage instruments would be exposed to market loss at an accelerated rate. Market neutral trades involving mortgage-backed securities can become unbalanced when rates decline but also when they rise. The most profitable time to own mortgage-backed assets is when interest rates stay in a narrow range for a considerable period of time.

4.12   The most popular strategies are typically the strategies that have recently been performing the best. A concentration in the strategies that are popular may make it easier to market the fund of funds. It is hard to criticize the fund of funds manager for providing the kind of portfolio that is desired by investors.

However, investing in the strategies and particular funds that have recently performed well might also create a portfolio of hedge funds that provides great returns in the future if the winners of the recent past are the winners of the near future. The fund of funds manager must believe that there is at least some persistence in performance.

Unfortunately, academic researchers have found fairly little persistence in performance of individual managers, although hedge fund styles are more persistent (see S. J. Brown, W. N. Goetzmann, and R. G. Ibbotson, "Offshore Hedge Funds: Survival and Performance, 1989–1995," NBER Working Paper Series, 1997). However, researchers have also found little consistent evidence that last year's stars are more likely to crash than other hedge funds and other hedge fund strategies.

CHAPTER 5   Hedge Fund Business Models

5.1   A C corporation seems like a logical choice for a U.S. hedge fund because it can have unlimited shareholders, there can be more than one class of shares, and the investors have no liability for losses above their committed capital. However, a C corporation must pay corporate income tax on the investment returns. When returns are distributed or the investment in a fund is eliminated, the investor is taxed a second time on this investment return. A partnership or a limited liability corporation would offer the same limitation on loss and the investment return would be taxed only once.

5.2   In locations where the hedge fund would pay no or very little tax, the C corporation is a great business model. The absence of tax at the corporate level means that investors are not taxed twice. Further, in a corporate structure many fewer calculations are necessary to calculate the taxable income of the investors.

5.3   If liabilities exceed assets, the equity shareholders would lose all their equity value. If the equity base is not large enough, the liability holders are exposed to loss.

5.4   Like the equity holders, the partners bear the loss caused by declines in the value of the company's assets. If the value of assets declines below the value of the liabilities, the general partner is liable for the difference, even if it means that the general partner must infuse additional capital into the business.

5.5   A flow-through tax entity is a partnership, an S corporation, a limited liability corporation, or a limited liability partnership. These types of businesses calculate income and expenses and report the net income to the Internal Revenue Service (in the United States). Part of the tax filing is an allocation of the taxable items to each investor as if the investor separately controlled a pro rata part of the business.

5.6   The investor who must invest as a general partner must be a business with limited capital whose owners have no liability beyond their committed investment.

5.7   A general partner has unlimited liability. By putting capital in a business that then serves as general partner, the capital can support the limited partner but the creditors are limited to the capital committed to the business that serves as the general partner. The general partner can be set up as a C corporation, an S corporation, a limited liability partnership, or other structure that relieves the owners from general liability.

5.8   In the event of fraud, the law may ignore liability-limiting structures designed to protect the ultimate owner.

5.9   If a hedge fund sponsors more than one hedge fund, it might set up separate business units for each fund. If one fund lost more than the paid-in capital, the creditors would have no claim on the assets supporting other hedge funds. The business unit that serves as the manager might also act as the general partner of one of the funds, but it probably doesn't make sense to set up multiple managers just because there are multiple funds.

5.10   A mirrored hedge fund structure has a domestic fund for U.S. investors and a fund located in a tax-free or low-tax domicile to accept investments from investors outside the United States. The primary objective of this structure is to avoid backup withholding on the investment returns and to prevent non-U.S. investors from having to pay U.S. taxes.

5.11   The two funds are marketed in tandem. Often, the longer track record of one fund is used to market both funds. Unless the monthly performance of the two funds is similar, it wouldn't be possible to use the earlier performance to market the second fund.

5.12   Partnership accounting and tax reporting are significantly more com-
       plicated than accounting and tax reporting for a corporation. A part-
       nership must maintain the cost basis of each investor in each asset.
       Usually, a partner will have many different costs for each asset. Be-
       cause a corporation is taxed as an entity, it is not necessary to preserve
       details for individual investors.

5.13   With a master-feeder structure, it is possible to maintain one portfolio
       and accept investment from both U.S. and offshore investors. Only
       one track record is created and there is no possibility for the two
       groups of investors to receive significantly different returns.

5.14   Many mirrored funds were created before the master-feeder structure
       was created. Also, it is much easier to create a second, mirrored fund
       if the first fund is already operating and has a number of assets with
       costs already established. Finally, the cost of setting up the master-
       feeder structure is higher than setting up either a U.S. or an offshore
       fund (although probably cheaper than setting up both a domestic and
       an offshore fund).

5.15   Lawyers and accountants have favored Delaware. Most states have
       responded by making their states very competitive as business domi-
       ciles. For many kinds of businesses, the state the business is located in
       would serve as a good domicile. It is important to discuss the location
       question with your lawyer.

5.16   It is important to locate the fund in a domicile with low or no taxes,
       so that investors can avoid unnecessary double taxation. Beyond that,
       some countries have greater protection of privacy, a stronger legal tra-
       dition, conveniences in terms of travel time to the domicile, and time
       zones that are more convenient to the manager and investors. In addi-
       tion, it may be important to pick a domicile that has language skills
       matching the language of the fund's investors. Finally, some domiciles
       are more prepared to deal with special requirements, such as religious
       or cultural rules.

5.17   In order for offshore investors to avoid backup withholding, the U.S.
       Internal Revenue Service must deem the hedge fund to be a non-U.S.
       business. If the fund is administered in the United States, the IRS will
       probably assert that the business is a U.S. entity and require the fund
       to withhold taxes for the offshore investors.

CHAPTER 6   Hedge Fund Leverage

6.1   The stock loan agreements that show up as liabilities include the
       money borrowed to finance the long stock positions. Traders think of

this cash as collateral, but accountants view it as a short-term loan that must be repaid. Note that the accounting records do not document that the stocks held as long positions are actually being held by a dealer because the hedge fund still represents that it owns the common (even though it doesn't currently possess or even have legal title to the shares).

The stock loan agreements that show up as assets include the money posted with other dealers to collateralize shares that the hedge fund has borrowed. Accountants treat this transaction much like a certificate of deposit: The fund has delivered cash to an arm's-length counterparty, who will return the cash with interest.

The $60 million in stock loan assets represent the cash that is collateralizing $50 million of borrowed securities. The $10 million difference represents the haircut or collateral that the securities lender requires.

The $30 million in stock loan liabilities represents the cash that is borrowed by the fund. These loans are secured by some of the $40 million in common stock held as long positions. The $10 million difference represents a haircut or required margin. The fund may also have excess collateral, which gives the fund some room to lose money on its positions without being thrown into liquidation. It is also possible that the fund holds some positions that cannot be financed (restricted stock, small private issues, or other nonmarginable positions).

6.2 It is possible to calculate leverage by adding the long positions to the short positions (treating both as positive values) and dividing by the capital. This result of 2.25:1 ($40 million plus $50 million ÷ $40 million) is reasonable. Frequently, the leverage will be calculated from the assets on the balance sheet and the liabilities will be ignored. Using this methodology, the leverage is 2.5:1 ($40 million + $60 million ÷ $40 million).

The $60 million serves as a proxy for the short positions, because it represents the collateral posted to borrow the stocks held short. The fund has $10 million tied up in haircuts on the short positions.

6.3 A hedge fund probably would not want to buy the asset. It would expect to lose money borrowing at 5 percent to invest in the security expected to earn 3 percent. In fact, the fund probably shouldn't buy the asset at all (without leverage) because any unused capital could earn a higher return as a short-term investment earning 5 percent.

The fund might buy the asset anyway if it is part of a strategy that is expected to make money overall (a basket trade, for example). A manager might buy the asset despite the expected loss if the security improved the characteristics of the portfolio (the risk of loss, favorable cash flow, favorable tax treatment, or other factors).

The fund might want to sell the asset short, however. The fund could expect to lose 3 percent on the security held short but could invest the proceeds of the sale at 5 percent. Whether the trade was profitable would depend on the haircut required and execution costs. The manager should also assess whether a short position in the security would increase or reduce risk to the portfolio.

6.4 The first fund can be described as unlevered. This means the fund has leverage of 1:1. The second fund has leverage of 1:1 only if it can borrow the securities to cover its short without having to put up a haircut. If the fund has to post margin, the leverage of the fund containing the short positions would exceed 1:1 if the leverage ratio is calculated from the asset side of the balance sheet, as is the convention.

6.5 The leverage is 2:1. It doesn't matter that the stock is held in a margin account, but it does imply there might be margin debt (probably less than $25 million) on the liability side of the balance sheet. This margin debt does not enter into the leverage calculation.

It is possible that this hedge fund carries short positions and that some of the $100 million is assets are actually stock loan agreements positions that the fund has borrowed to make delivery on short sales. The leverage calculation does not depend on the size of the liabilities.

6.6 It is sensible to include another $50 million (or $48 million) in assets in the calculation. This fund would resemble a fund that carried only cash positions but had leverage of 3:1. However, investors and trading counterparties would not be given enough information to know what positions exist off the balance sheet. As a result, the leverage would be only 2:1.

6.7 The dealer that executes the trades will limit the size of unsettled positions. The broker is at risk if its customer gets into financial difficulty. A prudent broker will monitor intraday positions real-time. The broker will also monitor intraday realized and unrealized losses. Finally, the broker may watch for exceptions from the pattern of trading typical of the customer (position size, types of assets traded, and other considerations).

6.8 Many futures exchanges have adopted SPAN margining. At the time of this writing, stock exchanges like the New York Stock Exchange and cash options exchanges like the Chicago Board Options Exchange have not adopted SPAN margining. Span margining could apply to currency futures, but much of the trading in foreign exchange takes place over-the-counter (OTC). No regulations govern margin on OTC currency trading, and a creditworthy hedge fund may be required to post only maintenance margin but no initial margin. SPAN margin can reduce the margin required for positions held on a single futures exchange, but the fund will likely get no reduction in margin due to positions held in various futures exchanges, even if the positions are carried by the same broker. Also, the broker is not constrained to collect only the minimum SPAN margin.

6.9   Some hedge funds have registered as broker-dealers to take advantage of 15 percent margin requirements for dealers. A hedge fund can avoid initial and maintenance margin requirements completely by creating a joint back office (JBO) with a dealer. To create a JBO, a hedge fund will appear to structure itself as part of the dealer. The structure may appear to have substance yet create no real economic link between the dealer and the customer. With a JBO, a hedge fund needs to post only enough margin to satisfy the dealer. The fund can use futures and OTC derivatives to create positions subject to lower margin requirements or no margin at all. Finally, the fund may be able to sidestep U.S. margin requirements if the fund is organized offshore and books financing trades with non-U.S. broker-dealers (or offshore subsidiaries of U.S. broker-dealers).

6.10 The haircut equals $300,000, equal to $125,000 on the long position ($50 million × .25%) and $175,000 on the short position ($35 million × .50%).

6.11 The leverage equals 283.92:1 [($50,000,000 + $35,175,000)/$300,000]. Notice that this calculation relies on the asset value of the stock loan on the short position ($35 million plus the haircut of $175,000). Of course, no hedge fund could maintain leverage hundreds of times their capital, but it might be possible to leverage a part of the position to this extent. However, financing counterparties would permit these trades only if the overall leverage of the fund was within guidelines set by the credit departments of the financing desks.

6.12 The question doesn't provide enough information to answer the question precisely. It would be necessary to know the coupons on the bonds long and short. It would be helpful, too, to know the average yield to maturity on the long portfolio versus the average yield to maturity on the short portfolio. Many fixed income funds attribute much of their net return to these factors, which we must assume net to zero.

The financing cost on the long position can be described as $r\%$ × $1 billion (where $r\%$ is the average repo rate on the position). The reverse income on the short position is therefore $(r\% - 0.5\%) \times \$1$ billion (ignoring haircuts). The net cost is therefore:

$$\begin{aligned}
\text{Net Cost} &= \text{Income} - \text{Expense} \\
&= (r\% - 0.5\%) \times \$1 \text{ billion} - r\% \times \$1 \text{ billion} \\
&= (r\% - 0.5\% - r\%) \times \$1 \text{ billion} \\
&= -0.5\% \times \$1 \text{ billion} \\
&= \$5 \text{ million}
\end{aligned}$$

$$\begin{aligned}
\text{Required Return} &= \$5 \text{ million}/\$100 \text{ million} \\
&= 5\%
\end{aligned}$$

6.13 The holder of record on the ex-dividend date gets the dividend. You are not the holder because you delivered the shares to the buyer. Assuming the buyer still owns the shares, the company will pay the dividend to that holder. The company will *not* pay a dividend to the lender of the shares because the lender passed ownership to you. You must, therefore, make a substitute payment of $25,000 to the lender to compensate the lender for the dividend forgone. The payment reduces the dividend income you report on your fund.

6.14 The market value of the 50,000 shares after the split should approximately equal the market value of the 25,000 shares before the split. The cash collateral should therefore remain adequate. You must eventually return 50,000 shares to the lender.

6.15 The lender of the shares loses the right to vote the shares when title is passed to the borrower. Because the proxy vote is announced well before the record date, the lender can recover the right to vote by closing out the financing trade before the record date on the vote. Or, the lender could require a premium (lower rebate rate) to compensate for the lost vote. If the lender had committed to lend the shares for a fixed term prior to the proxy announcement, the borrower pays no compensation to the lender.

6.16 The security lender treats the income the same as if the payment was received from the corporation or Treasury directly. Likewise, a borrower reduces dividend income or Treasury interest by the amount of these substitution payments.

6.17 The counterparty on a futures contract is the clearing corporation, not the entity that actually bought or sold the contract on the floor of the exchange when the hedge fund established the position. The clearing corporation has several advantages in protecting itself from loss compared to a lender in the cash market for the underlying security. First, the clearing corporation has daily margin (both initial and maintenance), which may be more frequently maintained than in other markets. Second, the updated price of the asset is easy to verify because the same standardized asset trades frequently. Third, because the asset trades frequently, it is relatively easy for the clearing corporation to liquidate or buy in a trade if a customer fails to maintain margin.

6.18 The loans affect to total amount of money in the system by restricting the money multiplier. While the Fed has not used the margin regulations to affect economic activity, it is still interested in limiting the chance for shocks to the financial system caused by speculation and bubbles.

6.19 If the hedge fund deposited an additional $1 million and paid down the margin loan to $7 million, the account would be in compliance with the maintenance margin requirement.

6.20 The fund would need to liquidate one-third of its positions:

$$\text{Maintain\%} = \frac{\text{Margin}}{\text{Margin} + \text{Loan}}$$

$$30\% = \frac{\$2 \text{ Million}}{\$2 \text{ Million} + \text{Loan}}$$

$$30\% \times \$2 \text{ Million} + 30\% \times \text{Loan} = \$2 \text{ Million}$$

$$\text{Loan} = \frac{\$2 \text{ Million} - 30\% \times \$2 \text{ Million}}{30\%}$$
$$= \$4,666,667$$

$$\begin{aligned}
\text{Maximum Position} &= \text{Margin} + \text{Loan} \\
&= \$2 \text{ Million} + \$4,666,667 \\
&= \$6,666,667
\end{aligned}$$

$$\begin{aligned}
\text{Liquidation} &= \text{Current Position} - \text{Maximum Position} \\
&= \$10 \text{ Million} - \$6,666,667 \\
&= \$3,333,333
\end{aligned}$$

6.21 The fund must fully pay for the call. The fund must deposit $5. It may not withdraw the $.25 gain in value from the account.

Note: By convention, calls on cash common stocks trade in units of 100 shares. A trade to buy 1 call would actually cost the hedge fund

$500 and control 100 shares of stock. However, options on futures contracts are based on the actual number of futures, not multiple lots.)

6.22 The margin is $23.

> Margin1 = Proceeds + 20% × Share Price − Amount out of the
> Money
> = $5 + 20% × $100 − ($102 − $100)
> = $23
>
> Margin2 = Proceeds + 10% × $100
> = $15
>
> Margin = max(Margin1,Margin2)
> = $23

6.23 The standard deviation of the levered portfolio is 43.98 percent.

$$\sigma_{\text{Portfolio}} = \sqrt{w_A^2 \sigma_A^2 + 2w_A w_B \rho_{AB} \sigma_B \sigma_B + w_B^2 \sigma_B^2}$$
$$= 100\%^2 \times 22\%^2 + 2 \times 100\% \times 100\% \times 75\% \times 22\% \times 25\% + 100\%^2 \times 25\%^2$$
$$= 43.98\%$$

6.24 The expected return on the levered portfolio is 35 percent.

> $$\text{Return}_{\text{Portfolio}} = \text{Return}_A + \text{Return}_B - \text{Rate} \times (w_A + w_B - 1)$$
> $$= 20\% \times 100\% + 20\% \times 100\% - 5\% \times 100\%$$
> $$= 35\%$$

6.25 The probability of loss is 21.3 percent. Using the Excel function:

> NORMDIST(Threshold Return, Expected Return, Standard
> Deviation of Return, TRUE or 1)

NORMDIST(0%, 35%,4 3.98%, 1)=21.3%

Note: The logical variable in the function determines whether the function returns the normal, bell-shaped curve (using 0) or the area under the curve (using 1). As configured, the function returns the probability of a return of zero or less, given a mean return of 35 percent and a standard deviation of 43.98 percent.

6.26 The probability of losing 25 percent or more is 8.6 percent.

> NORMDIST(25%, 35%, 43.98%, 1)=8.6%

CHAPTER 7 Performance Measurement

7.1 Because nominal return ignores the amount of time necessary to produce a return, it fails to distinguish between a return produced over a short period of time and an equal return produced over a longer period of time. Most investors would prefer that a gain occur over a short period of time.

7.2 The process of converting gains to a standard holding period tends to amplify returns, which can be misleading especially when very short time periods are annualized. Also, when comparing nominal returns of many hedge funds over a fixed period of time (a quarter, for example), nominal returns can be fairly compared with no further adjustment.

7.3 The investor has a different investment each time the value of assets change and interest accrues. By not liquidating an investment at the interim value, the investor is implicitly reinvesting. The average of the beginning and ending values approximates a more complete average that includes daily values throughout the period. In using an average, the return acknowledges that the investor should expect a return on the intraperiod returns.

7.4 The compound return incorporates return on return that occurs during the year. This return on return (or interest on interest) is more valuable if the return is received more frequently and is more valuable for higher rates of return.

7.5 The convention goes back to a time before computers were common. Interest was retrieved from tables of interest accruals. To simplify calculations, all months were deemed to have 30 days and all years had 360 days. The tables were much more compact than tables that would be required if actual days were used in the calculations.

7.6 Rates are quoted with knowledge of the day-counting convention. For example, the effective rate of a simple interest quoted on the basis of a 360-day year is about 1.5 percent higher than the stated rate (5 days/360 days). Rates are quoted so that the effective rates are consistent with market levels.

7.7 When payments are made or received at different times, the investor is not indifferent about the timing of the payments. It is better to receive payments early, so that the funds can be invested and earn interest. In calculating present value, delayed payments are adjusted to a level equivalent to an immediate payment, at least with respect to the interest that could have been earned between the present time and the time of the delayed payment.

7.8   The future value represents the amount of a cash flow in the future that is economically equivalent to a cash flow (or multiple cash flows) that occurs earlier. The early cash flows are adjusted as if they were invested at prevailing interest rates and the interest that could be earned is added to the cash flows.

7.9   If a positive return is followed by a loss of the same percentage, the average of these two rates will be zero, but the portfolio will be worth less than the starting value. For example, if a 10 percent loss follows a 10 percent gain, the value of $1 invested in the fund prior to these two periods would be $1 \times (1 + 10\%) \times (1 - 10\%) = \$.99$. The geometric return captures this phenomenon.

7.10   Measures such as the probability of loss ignore the size of loss. Strategies that frequently make small profits and rarely lose, but their infrequent losses are large amounts, would look attractive using these measures.

7.11   The nominal return is ($1,111.55 - $1,010.50)/$1,010.50 = 10%.

$$\text{Nominal Return} = \frac{\text{Ending Value} - \text{Beginning Value}}{\text{Beginning Value}} \quad \text{from (7.2)}$$

$$= \frac{\$1,111.55 - \$1,010.50}{\$1,010.50} = 10\%$$

7.12   There are 31 days in July and 365 days most years (for leap years, it might be necessary to use 366 days for the days in the year depending on the kind of asset the return applies to). Therefore, the annual return is $10\% \times 365/31 = 117.74\%$.

Another major day-counting protocol is the 30/360 day count, whereby each month is assumed to contain 30 days and each year has 360 days. This protocol is not typically used for hedge fund returns, but the calculation would be: $10\% \times 360/30 = 120\%$.

7.13   One dollar invested in the first investment will return $1.10 a year later. A dollar invested at 9.65 percent compounded monthly will pay 9.65%/12 after one month; then apply the same interest rate factor to the principal and interest the next month. The reinvestment continues through the year. At the end of the year, the second dollar would grow to $(1+9.65\%/12)^{12}$ or $1.1009. Although this is fairly close to the annual investment at 10 percent, the return is somewhat higher on the second alternative (i.e., 1.1009 > 1.10). The investment paying 9.65 percent has a higher effective return. If the second investment paid 9.57 percent, the two alternatives would offer identical returns after a year because $(1 + 9.57\%/12)^{12} = 1.10$.

The second investment assumes that the interim interest also accrues at exactly 9.65 percent. From the wording of the question, it is clear that the investment will accrue the interest monthly and will compound at the 9.65 percent rate, to be paid at the end. If the second investment made actual payments each month, it is important to realize that the return indicated would only occur if the payments are reinvested at the same rate as the initial investment.

7.14 The present value is $793,832.24.

$$PV = 1{,}000{,}000 \times (1 + \text{Return})^{-\text{No. of Years}}$$
$$= 1{,}000{,}000 \times (1 + 0.8)^{-3} = \$793{,}832.24$$

Using Excel:

$$PV = 1{,}000{,}000 * 1.08\wedge(-3) = 1{,}000{,}000/1.08\wedge3 = \$793{,}832.24$$

7.15 The present value is $867,997.32.

$$\text{Return}_{\text{AfterTax}} = \text{Return}_{\text{BeforeTax}} \times (1 - \text{Tax Rate})$$
$$= 8\% \times (1 - 39.6\%) = 4.83\%$$

$$PV = 1{,}000{,}000 \times (1 + \text{Return})^{-\text{No. of Years}}$$
$$= 1{,}000{,}000 \times (1 + 0.483)^{-3} = \$867{,}997.32$$

Using Excel:

$$PV = 1{,}000{,}000 * (1 + 8\% * (1 - 39.6\%))\wedge(-3) = \$867{,}997.32$$

7.16 There are five semiannual periods and the semiannual rate is 4.5 percent. Therefore, the future value is $10 \times (1 + 4.5\%)^5 = \$12.46$.

$$FV = 10 \times (1 + \text{Return})^{\text{No. of Years}}$$

Using a semiannual return:

$$FV = 10 \times \left(1 + \frac{\text{Return}}{2}\right)^{\text{No. of Years} \times 2}$$
$$= 10 \times (1 + 4.5\%)^5 = \$12.46$$

Using Excel:

$$FV = 10 * (1.045)^5 = \$12.46$$

7.17 The future value for a continuously compounded rate is given by equation (7.15). The rate (r) is the continuously compounded rate, which is 9 percent or .09. The time T in the formula is 2.50. The future value is \$12.52.

$$FV = 10 \times e^{rT}$$
$$= 10 \times e^{0.09 \times 2.5} = \$12.52$$

Using Excel function for e^x:

$$FV = \exp(9\% * 2.5) = \$12.52$$

7.18 The arithmetic average is 1.73 percent (monthly). The geometric average is 1.64 percent. Note that a dollar invested during that year would have grown to \$1.216. If the arithmetic average is compounded for a year, the future value is \$1.228. However, if the geometric average is compounded for a year, the future value matches the actual experience.

	Rate	1 + Return	Cumulative
	2.25%	1.02	1.022500000
	–1.75%	0.98	1.004606250
	8.15%	1.08	1.086481659
	–4.40%	0.96	1.038676466
	–3.30%	0.97	1.004400143
	3.55%	1.04	1.040056348
	9.15%	1.09	1.135221504
	1.85%	1.02	1.156223102
	3.65%	1.04	1.198425245
	2.25%	1.02	1.225389813
	–3.60%	0.96	1.181275780
	2.95%	1.03	1.216123415
Arithmetic average	1.73%		1.228417070
Geometric average	1.64%		1.216123415
Standard deviation	15.09%		

7.19 The standard deviation of return (also called volatility) is 4.36 percent or 15.09 percent annualized. In this case, the standard deviation was annualized with the scaling factor sqrt(12) to transform from monthly to annual. The standard deviation is usually calculated from continuously compounded returns. Since question 7.18 did not specify the compounding frequency, the data were used as given. It is, of course, fairly likely that such data are nominal returns (implicitly compounded monthly). Had the rates been converted from monthly compounding to continuous, the standard deviation would have been 14.81 percent.

7.20 The 1.64 percent monthly rate is equivalent to an annual rate of 20.56 percent semiannually compounded. Both rates result in a future value of $1.216 one year in the future.

7.21 The 1.64 percent monthly rate is equivalent to an annual rate of 19.57 percent continuously compounded. Both rates result in a future value of $1.216 one year in the future.

7.22 The standard deviation of the return in question 7.19 was easy to calculate using the Excel function {STDEV}. To calculate downside deviation, it is necessary to calculate the deviations one at a time.

Month	Return	Deviation	Squared
January	2.25%	0.00%	0.00%
February	−1.75%	−1.75%	0.03%
March	8.15%	0.00%	0.00%
April	−4.40%	-4.40%	0.19%
May	−3.30%	−3.30%	0.11%
June	3.55%	0.00%	0.00%
July	9.15%	0.00%	0.00%
August	1.85%	0.00%	0.00%
September	3.65%	0.00%	0.00%
October	2.25%	0.00%	0.00%
November	−3.60%	−3.60%	0.13%
December	2.95%	0.00%	0.00%
Sum			0.46%

	Downside Deviation	Downside Semivariance
Monthly	2.05%	0.04%
Annual	7.10%	0.50%

The deviations are calculated as the difference between the threshold (zero) and the monthly return, although positive differences are treated as a deviation of zero. The deviations are squared and summed. The monthly downside semivariance is the sum divided by 11 (12 months less 1). The annualized downside semivariance is 12 times the monthly semivariance. The downside deviation is the square root of the downside semivariance.

7.23   The Sharpe ratio and Sortino ratio can be calculated from the monthly data or annualized values. The arithmetic average is used in the numerator because the arithmetic average is used in the standard deviation calculation.

The monthly Sharpe ratio is:

$$\frac{1.73\% - 5\%/12}{4.36\%} = .301$$

The Sharpe ratio based on annualized performance is:

$$\frac{12 \times 1.73\% - 5\%}{4.36\% \times \sqrt{12}} = 1.044$$

The monthly Sortino ratio is:

$$\frac{1.73\% - 5\%/12}{2.05\%} = 0.640$$

The Sortino ratio based on annualized performance is:

$$\frac{12 \times 1.73\% - 5\%}{2.05 \times \sqrt{12}} = 2.217$$

7.24   The largest drawdown is April–May, equal to 7.55 percent. The drawdown lasted two months.

$$1 - (1 + -4.4\%)(1 + -3.30\%) = 7.55\%$$

7.25   There are four losses in 12 months. A simple measure of the probability of loss is $4/12 = 33.3$ percent.

CHAPTER 8   Hedge Fund Legislation and Regulation

8.1   Registering the hedge fund investment and registering the manager as an investment adviser would increase the reporting requirements and might create problems in collecting incentive fees, unless all the investors are accredited investors, anyway. However, it is possible to register hedge funds, and this is a growing trend. Most commonly, funds of funds register but are permitted to invest in unregistered hedge funds. Although this registration doesn't simplify anything for the individual hedge funds, it has allowed funds of funds to offer their funds to investors with sharply lower minimum investments.

8.2   A Section 3(c)(1) hedge fund is permitted to have not more than 100 investors, so this fund may admit one more investor as a partner. Employees and other key insiders do not count toward the limit, so the hedge fund could admit the trader and an additional outside investor without violating the limitation under Section 3(c)(1).

   Funds subject to a limitation on investors may begin restricting access to the fund before reaching the limit. A fund that has even 95 investors might turn down smaller investments so that it has capacity to accept larger investors. This fund might consider converting to a Section 3(c)(7) fund. This would mean that certain investors who qualify as accredited investors but not as qualified purchasers would be barred from investing in the fund. However, the hedge fund could allow the existing investors to remain in the fund even after adopting the Section 3(c)(7) exemption even if they are not qualified purchasers.

8.3   Yes. In any case, the hedge fund is permitted to admit up to 35 investors who are not accredited, although admitting nonaccredited investors increases the reporting requirement on the fund. However, employees who are partners need not be accredited.

8.4   A person may be a qualified purchaser based on his or her net worth. Investors who do not have enough income or wealth may still be qualified purchasers. An investor with sufficient assets or income but inadequate investment sophistication would still be a qualified purchaser. However, the investor could argue that the hedge fund was an inappropriate investment for someone of his investment experience.

   This type of lawsuit is very fact specific and the success of this suit would depend on a variety of facts not known from the question. In particular, the investor likely signed a document asserting that he had sufficient experience and knowledge to make the decision to invest in this fund. The investor has the resources to have hired accountants, lawyers, tax experts, and investment advisers to review the investment before becoming an investor. If the investor consulted any such experts, it might affect his claim for restitution. Finally, although the hedge fund lost money (presumably 100 percent of its capital), the losses don't automatically mean that the investment would have been considered a risky investment at the time the investor became a partner.

On the other hand, the possibility of such a suit demonstrates why a hedge fund manager should review the background of each investor. In the event of losses, it is very likely that a fund and its managers will be sued for restitution by at least some investors.

8.5   Offshore hedge funds are not subject to the investor limit imposed by Section 3(c)(1) and Section 3(c)(7) because the funds are not governed by U.S. securities laws. These funds are already exempt.

8.6   One easy way to get more investors is to have them invest indirectly through a fund of funds. Generally, a fund that accepts an investment from a fund of funds counts this as one investment and does not need to count the individual fund of funds investors. The fund would need to include the investors in its own total if the fund existed just to consolidate investors. Similarly, a fund that cloned itself would also need to add up the investors in nearly identical funds.

The integration rules and look-through provisions are very complicated. The rules were intended to prevent hedge funds from structuring gimmicks to get around the investor limitations. In fact, Section 3(c)(7) funds that are organized as master-feeder funds generally have enough flexibility to have no capacity problems.

8.7   Tax-exempt investors may have trouble with hedge funds that have substantial interest expenses. Hedge funds that borrow money to carry long positions generate interest expenses. The higher the leverage, the more interest expense is generated.

Hedge funds that do not use leverage will not generate much interest expense. Hedge funds that use leverage may be able to reduce their interest expenses by relying on derivative instruments instead of cash securities and borrowed money.

Hedge funds that borrow securities may receive interest income on collateral (see Chapter 6 describing the techniques of leverage). This interest income probably will not lead to tax problems for a tax-exempt investor.

Hedge funds organized within the United States usually do not incorporate. Instead, these funds set up as partnerships or limited liability corporations taxed as partnerships. Because the domestic funds flow through income and expense items, they avoid being taxed as businesses. Instead, the individual income and expense items flow through to investors. Tax-exempt investors can invest in offshore hedge funds, which do not pass through interest expenses because the corporation does not flow through the income and expenses. Instead, the corporation reports the income and pays tax (if any) on the net income. Tax-exempt investors are not allocated interest expenses.

8.8   The law aims to prevent hedge funds from accepting money from terrorist groups and organized crime. This source of funds probably does not constitute a large amount of assets, so this direct impact will be small.

The considerably larger burden placed on hedge funds is the cost of ensuring compliance. Hedge funds now have a duty to know much more about their customers. A small portion of hedge fund investors may value their privacy so highly that they may elect to invest in hedge funds that are not covered by the Act. Certainly hedge funds operated within the United States must comply regarding both their domestic and their offshore customers. Offshore hedge funds may need to comply as well if they accept money from U.S. residents or conduct business within the United States.

Part of the problem complying is that there is not yet a clear understanding of what constitutes proper compliance. Hedge fund managers could be held to be in violation if the courts require greater effort than is currently being made. Hedge funds risk being held retroactively to a standard once the courts define what constitutes adequate effort to know about their customers.

8.9   Antifraud rules and regulations govern all investment managers, regardless of how or whether a hedge fund is registered.

8.10 One reason why a hedge fund may prefer to avoid registration is to avoid making some of the disclosures required of a public company. For this reason, investors often receive less information about hedge fund investments than they would receive about mutual fund positions or other registered investment portfolios.

Investors may demand more disclosures than the minimum required of an unregistered hedge fund. The investor may receive as much information as would be disclosed if the investment was registered. Hedge funds do not need to make uniform disclosures to all investors, so some investors may be able to demand transparency and daily net asset values and other investors may receive only highly aggregated disclosures and no interim valuations.

CHAPTER 9   Accounting

9.1   Although the question provides no information about the size of the particular positions, it does provide enough information to calculate the leverage. Suppose the hedge fund had $3 in debt and $1 in equity. The fund would have $4 in assets. To calculate leverage, divide the assets by the hedge fund capital. This hedge fund is levered 4:1. The general case is:

$$A = \text{Total assets held by the hedge fund}$$
$$D = \text{Total liabilities of the hedge fund}$$
$$E = \text{Equity or partners' capital}$$
$$A = D + E$$

$$\text{Debt} / \text{Equity Ratio} = \frac{D}{E}$$

$$\text{Leverage} = \frac{A}{E} = \frac{D+E}{E} = \frac{E \times \text{Debt} / \text{Equity Ratio} + E}{E}$$
$$= \text{Debt} / \text{Equity Ratio} + 1$$

This is true for any capital structure!

9.2   The position is carried as an asset worth $25 million regardless of how the position is financed. The financing position creates a $12.5 million liability, not an asset. Because the fund financed half of the position, the cash balance is $12.5 million higher than the cash position would have been if no money was borrowed. Therefore, it might be argued that the position and financing would impact $37.5 million on the hedge fund assets.

9.3   The short position would be carried as a liability, not an asset. The cash collateral of $12 million would appear as a short-term asset.

9.4   The value of the asset depends on what cost was removed from the ledger at the time of the sale. Here are the journal entries of the position as it was acquired:

Buy 10,000 XYZ at $10

XYZ common	$100,000	
Cash		$100,000

Buy 15,000 XYZ at $12.50

XYZ common	$187,500	
Cash		$187,500

Before the sale, the fund carried 25,000 shares at $287,500 or an average cost of $11.50. If the fund uses this average as the cost basis, the accountants will remove $57,500 from the value of XYZ Common (5,000 × $11.50) versus sale proceeds of $75,000.

Remove 5,000 XYZ at $11.50

Cash	$75,000	
XYZ common		$57,500
Gain on sale of XYZ		$17,500

If the hedge fund used the average cost of $11.50, the remaining position in XYZ common would be carried at $230,000 ($287,500 – $57,500 or 20,000 shares × $11.50). However, if the accountants removed the $10 shares:

Remove 5,000 XYZ at $10.00

Cash	$75,000	
XYZ common		$50,000
Gain on sale of XYZ		$25,000

This would leave a position worth $237,000 ($287,500 – $50,000 or 20,000 shares at an average price of $11.88. This method corresponds with the first in, first out (FIFO) method.
    If the accountants removed the $12.50 shares:

Remove 5,000 XYZ at $12.50

Cash	$75,000	
XYZ common		$62,500
Gain on sale of XYZ		$12,500

This would leave a position worth $225,000 ($287,500 – $62,500 or 20,000 shares at an average price of $11.25. This method corresponds with the last in, first out (LIFO) method.

9.5   The hedge fund will likely mark the positions to market regularly and associate the gain or loss to the investors each period. The difference between the two costs will not affect the net income, as long as this unrealized gain or loss is included in the performance. The hedge fund will report a higher realized gain and a lower unrealized gain if the $10 shares are removed instead of the $12.50 lot.

The hedge fund will report the realized gain to investors, who must include their share of the gain in their income. Taxable investors will report higher taxable income if the lower-cost lot is used. However, if the fund sells the remaining shares in the same tax year, the investors will notice no difference in taxable income. For hedge funds that buy and sell frequently, the choice of lots may not matter much.

9.6   Accrual accounting permits the fund to associate revenues and expenses to periods before or after the cash payments. A partner owns a proportional interest in the fund. The accounting records are designed to accumulate results and distribute these to the partners as if each investor owned positions in all the individual assets. Because the fund is legally entitled to accrued income each day, its accounting records must reflect this economic situation in their record keeping.

In addition, the hedge fund may pay certain expenses at times not related to when the benefits of the services were received by the partners. For example, an auditor may bill the fund for the entire year's services in April, after the annual audit is complete. If the fund was unable to accrue this expense throughout the year, the expense would be allocated to investors in April instead of investors who were in the fund during the time of operation being audited.

9.7   Investors demand audited financial statements for a variety of reasons. Managers may refuse to disclose required information and receive a qualified opinion from the auditor. Investors may be satisfied with the statements after talking with the manager but it would be inappropriate for the auditor to represent that statements comply with generally accepted practice when they do not comply.

9.8   It is not true that investors experienced no economic consequence, but the impact would likely be small and relate to minor differences in tax allocation to investors. However, the concept of materiality is defined much more broadly than whether an investor gets hurt. The fund should restate its results if the errors had a material effect on performance.

9.9   The fund manager is wrong but the auditor is probably wrong, too. A fund may value its long positions at a lower price within a fair range of market prices and value its short positions at a higher price within a fair range of market prices. This procedure reduces the net asset value (NAV) by a reasonable estimate of the cost of liquidating positions. As long as the method is consistently employed, it may be used to price hedge fund assets. The auditor is wrong to demand that a hedge fund use a particular methodology in determining ending values of long and short positions. Hedge funds are permitted a range of alternatives, as long as they are consistently applied.

9.10 The auditor is wrong. Hedge fund positions are not valued at the lower of cost or market. For financial reporting/performance calculations, positions are valued at market. For tax reporting (see Chapter 10), positions are valued at historical cost.

9.11 The firm does have assets. First, the fund certainly has cash balances. Second, all of the short positions are collateralized in the stock loan or reverse repo market. These transactions are required because the fund must borrow the securities it has sold short. The cash collateral backing these securities loans are carried as short-term assets. The short-only hedge fund could take substantial short positions in futures or other derivatives. In this case, the leverage calculated from the total assets may understate the effective leverage of the fund substantially. If the leverage calculated using the total assets divided by partner's capital provides a misleading measure of leverage, investors can calculate leverage using the cash market equivalent of the derivatives positions.

9.12 The fund must recognize the dividend in April because the stock has gone ex-dividend in April. On the ex-dividend date, the value of the shares falls by roughly the amount of the dividend. The package of the soon-to-be-received dividend plus the ex-dividend stock approximately equals the price of the stock before the ex-dividend date. To fairly present the NAV at month-end, the accounting records must include the future dividend payment:

On April 29

Dividend receivable	$50,000	
Dividend income		$50,000

In early May, the payment is received but it is of minor economic consequence because the owners of the fund in April are given credit for the income:

On May 5

Cash	$50,000	
Dividend receivable		$50,000

9.13 The equity of the fund is $50 million because the sum of the liabilities and equity must equal the value of the assets. The NAV of a unit is the equity divided by the number of units:

NAV = $50 Million/28,000 Units = $1,786 NAV per Unit

9.14 The financial statements of the hedge fund report the Treasury income and in lieu interest expenses without adjustment for taxes. The fund may subtract the interest expense on short positions from the income received and report the net Treasury interest income. The hedge fund is a flow-through tax entity so it doesn't pay taxes. Other types of businesses, such as C corporations, would make an allowance for the taxes payable on the Treasury income.

A hedge fund investor would exempt the Treasury interest from taxable income on the state income tax form. Similarly, the substitute interest payments would be treated as if the U.S. Treasury made the payments. As a result, the hedge fund investors would not be able to deduct the interest expense on state tax forms.

The hedge fund will likely receive some of the Treasury income on long positions in the form of substitute interest payments. These in lieu payments can be treated as U.S. Treasury income, even though the actual payments were remitted by other parties.

9.15 The hedge fund might accrue the management fee daily. More likely, the fund will book the management fee only once monthly and adjust the NAV during the month for a portion of the fee accrued. The annual management fee on $100 million is 1 percent or $1 million. The partnership agreement defines how this fee is split over 12 months, but often one-twelfth of the amount is assessed each month. If the fund in question follows this simple rule, it will charge a management fee of $83,333 ($1 million/12) for May. Because May has 31 days, the fund may accrue a daily management fee of $2,688 ($83,333/31). On May 5, five days of accrual would total $13,441 ($2,688 × 5). If the general ledger system does not accrue the fee daily, $13,441 should be subtracted from the fund's capital before NAV is calculated.

9.16 If this hedge fund uses cash positions in stocks, bonds, or commodities, it would have leverage of approximately 2:1. Because the futures positions do not appear on the balance sheet, the fund would show only the cash held on deposit at the futures broker plus any excess cash. Unless analysts adjust the futures positions, this fund would appear to be unlevered and not invested in risky positions.

CHAPTER 10   Hedge Fund Taxation

10.1   The manager may prefer to receive the income as a partner distribution if some portion of the return on the fund is long-term capital gain, which is taxed at a lower rate than fee income. If the hedge fund produces only coupon and dividend income and short-term gains and losses, the manager would not gain any advantage from a distribution in lieu of fee income. If the fund does generate long-term capital gains, the manager may receive income taxed at a lower rate if long-term gains are allocated to the manager.

10.2   The investors would prefer to pay the manager with a management fee because any long-term gain distributed to the manager is income taxed at a lower rate that wouldn't be available to distribute to investors. For most hedge funds, the management fee is a deductible expense, so the after-tax cost of the fee is less than the amount paid. Structuring the management fee as a fee may also reduce other taxes. For example, the fee may escape self-employment tax and some state taxes such as the New York unincorporated business tax.

10.3   If a hedge fund is taxed as an investor, not a trader, then investors would prefer to grant a special allocation to the manager instead of paying a fee because the fee would be reported as a miscellaneous expense and would be subject to limitations on deductibility.

10.4   The partnership apparently realized $1 million in taxable gains during the year. This amount may not agree with the total economic profit of the partners during the year. The partnership would have paid corporate income tax of $350,000 if it had instead been organized as a corporation. The $650,000 after-tax profit would not be taxable to the investor until the corporation distributed it as a dividend. The corporation could delay distributing the dividend indefinitely.

   If the corporation paid out the $650,000 and the investor received a 25 percent share ($162,500), the dividend would trigger individual income tax of (162,000 × 35 percent $56,875) and would be left with $ 105,625 ($162,500 – $56,875).

   If the investor sold her investment before the profit was distributed, she would likely be paid more (all other things equal) for her investment stake because of the $650,000 undistributed profit. The gain on sale would be taxed at either the short-term or long-term capital gains rate.

10.5   First, it is necessary to discuss the tax situation of the investor in the mutual fund. Assuming the investor is a taxable individual, the distribution must be included in the investor's taxable income. Suppose the investor had made a $100,000 investment in the mutual fund and was allocated gains of $10,000. Suppose, too, that the investor pays income tax at the marginal rate of 25 percent.

The mutual fund may distribute cash of $10,000 or just report the taxable income. In either case, the investor reports the income and pays tax of $2,500. If the mutual fund distributed no cash, the investment is still worth $100,000 but the investor has an adjusted cost of $110,000. In other words, if the investor subsequently sold the fund for proceeds of $100,000, the sale would create a loss of $10,000 that would reduce taxable income by that amount. Alternatively, if the fund appreciated to $110,000 before the investor liquidated the holding, there would be no gain if the fund was sold for $110,000 because the gain has been already reported as income.

If the mutual fund had distributed $10,000 to the investor along with the taxable gain, the value of the investor's holdings would be only $90,000. But the cost basis for the investor is $100,000. If the investor liquidates the holding for $90,000, the investor would report a $10,000 loss.

In contrast, if the investor had invested in a hedge fund organized as a limited partnership that had realized gains during the tax year, the investor would have been allocated little or no gain in most cases. If the fund uses layered allocation, the investor would be allocated taxable gain for the portion of the appreciation that occurred while the investor was a partner. Since the investor has not been invested in the fund very long, this allocation would be small and would of course be based on the gain enjoyed by the investor on that particular security, not the entire portfolio.

It is possible to create situations where the investor would receive allocations of the gain under aggregate tax allocation. For example, if the investors have generally lost money in the hedge fund but the fund realized a gain on a particular security, the investor might be allocated the gain according to the economic ownership percent for all investors, even though the investor was not invested in the fund when the appreciation occurred.

In most cases, however, the tax allocation in partnerships more closely matches the economic gain of the investors. Subsequent allocations should also tend to correct any overallocation of taxable gain. In contrast, the mutual fund would not base future tax allocations on overallocations that have been made.

It is important to realize that, when the investor liquidates either the mutual fund or the hedge fund, any overallocation of income would net out. If tax rates remain constant for the investor, the impact of the overallocation of income is limited to the timing of tax payments.

10.6 The fund must flow through the income with the same characterization as the type of income received. Because the fund generated a long-term gain, it should report a long-term gain to all investors, including the newest partner, whose holding period is too short to justify receiving long-term income. However, the partners acquire the characterization of the investment activities from the partnership. In this case, more favorable tax treatment results than the new investor would expect based only on the time the investor has carried an investment in the fund.

10.7 Partnerships have considerable leeway to determine the particular rules used to allocate a loss. Hedge funds typically allocate the loss to all the partners based on the percentage of the fund owned by each partner. This will make the negative memo balances still more negative. Similarly, the total of unrecognized losses on the securities still held by the partnership will exceed the net economic loss experienced by the partners. As a result, the partners should gain some tax savings when unrecognized losses are realized.

10.8 Yes. If the cost was described as an annual expense of $360,000 ($30,000 × 12), it would be appropriate to allocate the expense daily, such that individual months are allocated different amounts of expense. But in this case, the fee is described as a monthly expense, so it should be booked as such, in the absence of facts suggesting otherwise.

10.9 It is customary to expense the commissions as they occur, rather than accrue the expense during the holding period of each investment. There is a case for accruing commission expenses based on volume pricing. Some brokers charge sharply discounted commissions or no commissions once a volume of commissions has been paid. In this case, it might be reasonable to accrue the expenses over the later months.

10.10 The allocation of most expenses should be made to the partners on the basis of economic ownership. For certain types of assets (futures, stocks) that charge an explicit commission, the expense should be allocated. Other types of assets (notably bonds and derivative securities), the cost of trading is built into a markup in the price. These trading costs are allocated with the layer or aggregate method as part of the gain or loss on the security.

Since the fee is described as an annual fee, it should be allocated based on the number of days in each break period. For years not containing a leap year, there are 181 days in the first six months of the year. The fund should allocate 49.59 percent (181/365) or $49,589 to the first half of the year. The fund should allocate 10 percent of that amount or $4,959 to the investor. The fund should allocate the balance of the annual expense or $50,411 to the second half of the year. The investor should be allocated 8 percent or $4,033 of this amount. For the year, the investor is allocated $8,992 or roughly 9 percent of the expense.

If the year had contained a leap year, the amount allocated would rise to $8,995 ($100,000 × 49.73% × 10% + $100,000 × 50.27% × 8%).

Exchange memberships are actually paid monthly. If the fund (contrary to the description in question 10.10) paid a monthly amount of $8,333.33, the fund would have paid $50,000 ($8,333.33 × 6) for both the first and second half years. The investor would be allocated 10 percent of $50,000 for the first six months and 8 percent of the $50,000 for the second six months ($4,000) for a total allocation of $9,000.

The three variations differ by only $8 and would likely not be material for any hedge fund. Nevertheless, hedge funds should set up procedures to allocate expenses in a logical and fair way.

10.11 The layered allocations can be observed directly from Table 10.3b in the text of Chapter 10. Investor 1 has gains of $9,750 on position 1. Investor 2 has gains of $14,625, and investor 3 has gains of $5,625. These allocations total to the $30,000 gain realized on the position.

10.12 It would be convenient to allocate the $245 to investor 1 ($98) and investor 2 ($147) because it would allocate taxable gains to positions on the memorandum balance that are no longer being held by the fund. However, the allocation depends on the rules established in advance, which likely aren't mindful of the details in the memorandum accounts. As a result, it is impossible to say which way the gain would be allocated among many acceptable allocations.

CHAPTER 11 Risk Management and Hedge Funds

11.1 Generally, arbitrage-based mathematics requires fewer assumptions about factors that can't be controlled. For example, bond models that rely on duration and convexity require little more than market pricing information. For other types of trades, the inputs may not affect the risk analysis much. For example, a position that is long one option and short another may be fairly insensitive to the level of implied volatility, the price of the underlying instrument, and the financing rate because misspecification of the inputs or changes in the inputs affect both the long positions and the short positions.

11.2 Probabilistic risk models allow the risk manager to measure risk even when there is no arbitrage relationship or other inherent set of mathematical relationships linking positions in a portfolio. Although the probability-based models may not be able to answer exactly the same questions that bond mathematics or option hedging allows, these models can still provide valuable measures of risk. This information can be used by traders and risk managers to influence risk-taking decisions.

11.3 Many investors are not interested in assuming low levels of risk. Generally, higher returns are associated with higher levels of risk in a portfolio. Risk management includes the choice of the level of risk as well as the measurement of risk to manage the match between risk tolerance and the risk in the portfolio. Further, risk management usually includes an analysis of whether the risks assumed in a portfolio provide the best chance for reward in light of those risks.

11.4 The prices of many bonds track key interest rates very closely. Within this large subset of bonds, the specific price sensitivity of a bond can be fairly precisely predicted relative to another bond or other bonds.

11.5 The full price or dirty price is the price of the bond including accrued interest. In the bond pricing formula, the dirty price is the present value of the coupons and final maturity. For the net price or price generally used in trading, quotations, and position reporting, this present value is reduced by the accrued interest.

11.6 The average life is a measure of the time between the settlement date and each of the cash flows. It is a measure of risk because longer bonds generally have more risk than bonds with shorter maturities. Duration, however, adds the additional refinement of valuing each cash flow at its present value, so that payments in the distant future that have little value also have less impact on the duration than the same cash flows have on average life.

11.7 The largest advantage of hedging the currency exposure is the liquidity of the U.S. dollar exchange rates. In addition, the peso exposure might be netted with other dollar or dollar proxy positions, reducing the size of the required hedge. The largest disadvantage comes if the Argentine peso decouples from the U.S. dollar. Such a proxy hedge is an unhedged bet that the Argentine peso remains tied to the dollar.

11.8   Aside from several operational problems like beta not being stable over time, it really isn't the right measure of risk for securities unless the correlation between the assets is very high. In other words, the risk of a stock in a portfolio can be much lower than the risk of the stock as a freestanding investment when diversification offers substantial risk reduction.

11.9   A long straddle consists of a long call plus a long put position. The straddle benefits from substantially higher prices (because the call becomes valuable) *or* substantially lower prices (because the put becomes valuable). The hedged call closely resembles this payoff. In a declining market, the call becomes worthless and the hedge becomes an outright short position similar to the long put position in a straddle. In a rally, the call begins to gain value 1 for 1 with the underlying future and appreciates more than a ratioed short position similar to the call in a straddle.

11.10 The delta of an option is the hedge ratio between an option and the underlying instrument. Because the option confers the right but not the obligation to buy or sell, it can gain or loss money more slowly than an outright position in the underlying instrument. Under most circumstances, an option will move no faster than the underlying instrument from which it derives its value. For deep-in-the-money European options, the maximum hedge ratio is the present value of the delta (hedge ratio) 1.00 because any payoffs on the option are received only in the future.

11.11 You could overweight the five-year by 25 percent. If the relationship between the two-year and five-year follows the past pattern, your positions will not show gain or loss from changes in the yields of the underlying instruments. Alternatively, you could underweight the two-year position by 20 percent because the the unadjusted five-year, at 100 percent of the duration-based weighting, is 125 percent of the two-year that represents only 80 percent of the unadjusted amount.

11.12 Modified duration represents the percent change in value for the position for a change in yield. The formula for modified duration was derived from the present value formula before accrued interest is subtracted. Modified duration will underestimate price changes if applied to the net price instead of the full or dirty price, which includes accrued interest. When applied to trade weightings, the price sensitivity of both the long and short positions will be too low.

Whether that error affects the long position more than the short position depends on the amount of accrued interest on the long position in comparison to the amount of accrued interest on the short position. The error could create a hedge ratio that is not neutral to changes in interest rates.

CHAPTER 12   Marketing Hedge Funds

12.1   Probably not. Conferences frequently feature speakers who discuss particular strategies and those speakers typically list the names of the funds they manage in their credentials. If the presentation resembled a marketing presentation, an unhappy investor might try to argue that the speech was a prohibited solicitation.

12.2   Probably not. The marketing manager must talk about the convertible arbitrage strategy generally, not about XYZ Hedge Fund. The marketing manager is able to discuss XYZ to potential investors who approach the speaker during the conference.

12.3   The speech by the third-party marketer probably would be considered a general advertisement for XYZ Hedge Fund. The marketer would be in violation but the hedge fund would not be in violation unless it could be shown that the hedge fund was involved in preparing the presentation and knew that the third-party marketer would be making a prohibited general solicitation.

12.4   The investor has no restrictions on her ability to contact hedge funds. She can contact as many funds as she wishes with or without having any relationship prior to the contact. Once contacted, the fund managers can reply and solicit her for an investment.

12.5   The manager pays the third-party marketer out of the fees that are paid to the management company. Typically, the investor is charged no more but the manager shares part of the fees with the third-party marketer. Investors should always read the documentation when investing. It is permissible to construct a different fee structure as long as the fees are disclosed to investors.

12.6   The restrictions on advertising were designed to straddle a line between maintaining laws to protect most investors and also allow exceptions for investors that need no protection. The restrictions limit the exempted investments to wealthy investors with a fair degree of investment experience. The advertising ban in particular limits the breadth and scale of a private placement.

Securities laws do not specifically prohibit hedge funds from advertising. The prohibition exists because of an exception built into the laws affecting securities registration. In most cases, hedge funds issue shares in a limited liability corporation or partnership interests in a limited partner as a private placement. That private placement is exempt from registration requirements but the hedge fund manager must not make a general solicitation or a general advertising appeal.

Registered hedge funds and registered funds of hedge funds are being created. These registered investment products can be sold to individuals who would not qualify to invest in a traditional hedge fund. It may be possible to advertise these investments.

Hedge funds in many jurisdictions outside the United States can advertise.

12.7   This fee structure is very simple. The marketer receives 20 percent of all management and incentive fees collected, not just the fees associated with the $10 million raised for the fund. The gross profit of the fund is 10 percent of $15 million or $1.5 million, so the fund is worth $16.5 million before assessing the management fee. A 1 percent management fee is $165,000. The return on the fund after the management fee is $1.5 million less $165,000 or $1,335,000. The management company collects 20 percent of $1,335,000 or $267,000. The third-party marketer collects 20 percent of both the $165,000 fee and the $267,000 incentive fee or $86,400.

12.8   Of the $15 million in assets, $5 million existed before the third-party marketer started to work with the hedge fund. Therefore, one-third of the fees paid to the marketer reflect fees not attributable to the third-party marketer's efforts.

12.9   The prime broker likely will not participate in the fees. However, based on the inclusive provision, the third-party marketer would be paid 20 percent of the fees collected on returns attributed to the $1 million investment.

CHAPTER 13   Derivatives and Hedge Funds

13.1   Many hedge funds provide returns comparable to stock returns but with substantially lower risk. For many hedge funds, a leveraged investment would be no more risky than an investment in the S&P 500 and may provide substantially higher returns.

Investors may be able to improve the diversification of their portfolios by adding leveraged hedge fund returns to traditional portfolios. Suppose a portfolio manager allocated 10 percent of the portfolio to alternative assets. If the 10 percent is invested in a single hedge fund, the portfolio may gain some benefits from diversification but could get even more benefit by investing the money in hedge fund derivatives that would replicate an investment of 20 percent of the portfolio in hedge funds. The additional commitment to the alternatives plus the possibility of including multiple hedge funds means that the total risk of the portfolio might be lower than the portfolio with 10 percent invested directly in hedge funds.

In additional to creating leverage, derivatives that are tied to hedge fund returns can offer downside protection. For example, an investment in calls or swaptions tied to hedge fund returns might have twice the upside potential of a direct investment but no additional downside.

Finally, if hedge fund derivatives can provide tax advantages over direct investment, the derivate alternative may offer higher after-tax returns in a wide range of possible outcomes. This higher after-tax return may justify taking a higher risk profile. Although leverage inherently increases the chance of loss, the higher average return reduces the chance of loss.

13.2   If it is imprudent for an investor to invest directly in a particular hedge fund, it would likely be imprudent for the investor to invest in derivatives based on that hedge fund. If the investor does not have sufficient investment experience or risk tolerance to invest in hedge fund, that investor probably lacks the investment experience or risk tolerance to invest in similar derivatives. However, the derivative may be less risky because of optional characteristics it may have. The derivative may not exactly replicate the return of the hedge fund. Instead, the derivative may be based on an index of hedge fund returns that offers some benefit of diversification over the direct investment in a single fund.

13.3   When there are tax advantages of one investment over another, the taxpayer is permitted to consider the tax treatment as part of an investment decision. However, tax savings cannot be the entire motivation for the derivative trade. It is important to show that there was a business purpose in making the investment and the investor felt there was a reasonable chance to make money with the investment. The results of past court cases have depended on the particular facts, and there have been almost no cases dealing specifically with the tax treatment of hedge fund derivatives.

13.4   The IRS does ask the courts to look through the business structure of sham transactions as if the structures did not exist. It is plausible that the IRS might argue that an investment in a derivative was an artificial way to avoid having to report interest expenses that could require the investor to pay UBIT.

For several reasons, the tax-free investor could argue that a hedge fund derivative was not a sham trade. First, the tax-exempt investor is permitted to consider taxes in making investment decisions and could argue that there was a business purpose and an economic motive for investing in the instrument. Second, the derivative investment could differ materially from a direct investment in terms of downside protection, leverage, or even in the extent that the derivative replicated the direct investment. Third, the tax-free investor can invest in offshore hedge funds that do not pass through interest expense. Tax-free investors can invest in banks that also have large interest expenses. Although the tax code can trigger a UBIT situation, the IRS doesn't view the hedge fund industry and the tax-exempt investors as abusive tax shelters. Finally, tax-exempt investors do invest in a variety of other derivatives and the IRS does not methodically look through these derivatives to see if they can find a way to tax otherwise tax-exempt investors.

13.5   The fund earned 4 percent after a 20 percent incentive fee, which was calculated after a 1 percent management fee (0.25 percent per quarter). A gross return of 5.25 percent reduces to 4 percent net of a quarterly 0.25 percent management fee and 20 percent incentive fee.

$$\left(r - \frac{1\%}{4}\right) \times (100\% - 20\%) = 5\% \times .8$$

$$= 4\%$$

where $r = 5.25\%$

On a notional investment of $10 million, this means you receive 80 percent of 5.25 percent on $10 million or $420,000. You pay LIBOR on $10 million at 5 percent (1.25 percent per quarter) or $125,000. You net the two payments and receive $295,000.

13.6   Because the gross return is given, it is not necessary to make calculations involving the management and incentive fees. The investor receives a payment of 80 percent of –2 percent on a notional balance of $10 million (a loss or negative receipt of $160,000). The investor also pays the $125,000 interest calculated in the answer to question 13.6. Therefore, the investor makes a payment of $285,000.

13.7 The swap agreement would appear to create infinite leverage because the $10 million notional position was created with no out-of-pocket cash commitment. The investor is much more limited in the overall leverage possible. Entering into a total return swap with the counterparty was acceptable to the swap counterparty because the hedge fund investor had sufficient capital to convince the counterparty that it could make the swap payments even if the returns turned significantly negative.

13.8 Apparently, the five-year zero coupon rate is 12.32 percent because that rate is consistent with a zero coupon bond worth 55 percent of face value:

$$\text{Price} = .55 = \frac{1}{\left(1 + \dfrac{r}{2}\right)^{2 \times 5}}$$

$$r = 12.32\%$$

Six months later, if rates are still at 12.32 percent, the zero will be worth $583,883 (58.39 percent of face value). The hedge fund portion of the investment is worthless, so the investor is down about 42 percent.

   If the investment was structured properly, none of the creditors can access the value of the zero coupon bonds to cover obligations of the hedge fund. However, the investor may not be able to withdraw the guaranteed $1 million for four and a half more years. Perhaps the investor may withdraw the $583,883 value of the zero coupon bonds.

13.9 The call seller may own a call option or a payoff that closely resembles a call option. The incentive fee is approximately the same as a call option on a percent of the hedge fund. A manager of a $100 million hedge fund that receives an incentive fee equal to 20 percent of returns has a call option on $20 million of the hedge fund (in fact, 20 percent of the gross return before incentive fees but after management fees).

   Although a hedge fund manager could sell a call on the performance of that fund, it might create conflicts of interest for the manager to sell the incentive fee in advance because this mitigates any motivation the investors are paying for. Other parties that receive part of the incentive fee (third-party marketers, early investors, etc.) might sell calls on the fund that match their incentive payments if they don't make decisions that impact fund performance.

Investors and dealers can sell calls and carry positions in the underlying hedge fund assets as a hedge. For example, an investor might buy into a hedge fund and write calls against the position, much like stock and bond investors write covered calls on traditional assets. Dealers buy and sell options and maintain a tightly hedged position of options and the underlying assets to control risk. The limited liquidity available to hedge fund investors complicates the problem of maintaining a hedge over time, but dealers have been willing to trade options on hedge fund returns despite the challenges.

13.10 Hedge fund operators do not receive fees that resemble a put option. In fact, in most stock, bond, and commodity markets, there are few natural sellers of put options. Similarly, dealers may have a hard time selling and hedging puts on hedge fund performance because the appropriate hedge for a sale of a put option is a short sale of the underlying asset, and selling short the performance of a particular hedge fund is difficult, at least at this stage of development of the hedge fund derivatives market. At least in principal, the seller of a put option on hedge fund performance could hedge the option by selling short assets held in the hedge fund. This hedging alternative is possible only if the hedge fund grants complete transparency. Because the option hedger is likely to be selling all the assets held by the hedge fund whenever fund performance is poor, it is not likely that the hedge fund would continually cooperate with the option market maker.

13.11 The portfolio of individual call options is worth at least as much as a call option on the hedge fund index and is probably worth more than the call option on the index. The difference depends on the extent the hedge funds move together. If hedge fund returns overall are flat to down, the call on the index would be worthless but individual hedge funds might have had profits that make a call option valuable for the individual hedge fund.

13.12 The value of most options should never be less than zero because the owner can simply let the option expire. While it is possible to imagine options that carry costs to abandon them, this is not a common structure.

13.13 Some of the premium payments must go toward providing a death benefit for the insurance policy to gain the tax treatment of insurance. The death benefit has economic value but may not be highly valued by a hedge fund investor.

Also, insurance policy transfers the hedge fund assets to beneficiaries. The purchaser of the policy (i.e., the hedge fund investor) cannot be a beneficiary and the purchaser cannot redeem the cash value of the policy without paying tax on the hedge fund returns. Nevertheless, the policy purchaser can borrow the cash value back if the need arises, but the amount lent reduces the payout to beneficiaries.

13.14 Hedge fund returns are taxed at higher tax rates than long-term investments in common stock because a large part of the stock return is taxed as long-term capital gains. Of course, bond income is a major component of bond returns and this income is also taxed at the higher ordinary income rate.

Assume the following combined state and federal income tax rules:

Ordinary income	40%
Long-term capital gains	20%

Pre-tax Long-Term Gain	After-Tax Return	Pretax Ordinary Breakeven	After-Tax Return
5%	4%	6.67%	4%
10%	8%	13.33%	8%
15%	12%	20.00%	12%
20%	16%	26.67%	16%
25%	20%	33.33%	20%
30%	24%	40.00%	24%

For example, ignoring the additional benefit possible from postponing capital gains tax or the avoidance of capital gains tax altogether at death, the difference in tax rate (here assumed to be 40 percent on ordinary income and short-term gains and 20 percent on long-term capital gains) means that a hedge fund must provide a return of 20 percent before tax to match the after-tax return on stocks making 15 percent if all of the stock return is long-term capital gain and all of the hedge fund return is taxed as ordinary income. Furthermore, if hedge fund returns escape taxation as part of a universal life insurance policy, the hedge fund need earn only 12 percent to match the after-tax return of a taxable investment earning 15 percent subject to capital gains tax or 20 percent subject to ordinary income tax.

13.15 The insurance policy accumulates $2 million $\times (1 + 10\%)^{10} =$ $5,187,485. The after-tax return on the hedge fund is $10\% \times (100\% - 35\%) = 6.5\%$. The hedge fund outside the insurance policy would accumulate $2 million $\times (1 + 6.5\%)^{10} = \$3,754,275$.

Index